Yoga: Sacred and Profane

(Beyond *Hatha yoga*)

ॐ

Dennis Littrell

This is an important message to readers:

I want to thank Amy Burwen for reading an early draft and for her suggestions and proofing, and Lynn for putting up with me while I was learning yoga many years ago.

Table of Contents

Preface

This is not a beginner's yoga book. And it is not strictly speaking a "yoga for health" type of book either. Rather it is a "yoga for liberation" book in which the goal is freedom from the pairs of opposites that dominate our lives, opposites such as pleasure and pain, winning and losing, good and evil, life and death. This is yoga beyond the basics, beyond physical health, beyond religiosity, beyond community. This is the yoga that has come down to us from antiquity, shorn of any pretense or exaggeration, free from political correctness or religious bias. It is yoga as a way of life.

The emphasis is on individual, self-directed practice.

In writing this book I have relied on nearly forty years of experience as both a student and a teacher. My research includes not just the classic and popular yoga texts, but wisdom and practice from other religions and disciplines, in particular Taoism, Buddhism, Christianity, biology and evolutionary psychology. The reader I have in mind is someone who wants to achieve *jnana* yoga, the yoga that allows one to differentiate between what is real and what is not.

Introduction:
Yoga, Religion, and Common Sense

Rationalists believe in common sense, the scientific method of verification, the rule of law and the power of education and technology to improve our lives. For those who follow the rule of reason the current crisis in the world comes about because a significant number of people are still living by the dictates of a fundamentalist religious approach that is not far removed from the tribal ways of our stone age ancestors.

For these unfortunate people it is the power of the war lord (or similar personage) under the banner of an exclusive fiat from a vengeful god that determines individual fates. The use of violence, the subjugation of women and minorities, xenophobia and a fear of change characterize the tribal mentality still extant in many parts of the world, including some places down the block from middle class homes in the West. Mired by a system of education that applies only to the few and otherwise is so narrowly defined that most of human knowledge in literature and the arts, science, philosophy, and government are not taught at all, these places are breeding grounds for human disaster. What is taught is religious fundamentalism. Such a curriculum, which really amounts to indoctrination, produces ignorance, poverty and hopelessness, leading some people to believe in a deity who would appoint them to murder in the name of God.

THE FUNDAMENTALIST MENTALITY

But it is not religion, per se, that is the problem. It is a know-nothing, anti-intellectual, Luddite, fundamentalist mentality, along with a political system that is not separate from the autocratic dictates of the tribal priests and their masses that is at fault. We got a hint of how this might work in the United States when Jerry Falwell and Pat Robertson expressed their view that "God" had brought the events of September 11th on the United States because of "His" displeasure with our way of life. Such a point of view differs little from that of the Taliban and other authoritarian organizations that would have God (interpreted by their ministers) running our lives.

But it is not Christianity or Islam or any other world religion that is at fault. It is a narrow and ignorant interpretation of those religions that is the problem.

WHY HAVE RELIGION AT ALL?

One might ask—and rationalists typically do ask—considering all the harm that religion has done over the millennia, why have religion at all?

But this too is a narrow view, revealing a misunderstanding about the role religion plays in our lives and the function it performs. Rationalists would substitute reason for an obsolete set of beliefs and observe that the world would be the better for it. Whether this is true or not, I do not know, but it is not something that is possible for human beings. We are semi-rational creatures. As Israeli Foreign Minister Abba Eban said on the occasion of the 1967 Arab-Israeli war, "men use reason as a last resort."

Rationalists ask, just what is the role that religion plays? Is it, as Marx said, "the opiate of the masses," a way to keep the life force in check, an instrument of our leaders to control the unruly masses?

THE ROLE OF RELIGION

Clearly religion can and does play such a role. But that is not the primary role of religion or its reason for being. According to the great biologist Edward O. Wilson our tendency to be religious is a mechanism of the evolutionary process that helped our ancestors to survive. He argues that the ability of the individual to conform to the group dynamics of religion is in itself adaptive—that is to say, it has helped humans to survive. As he writes on page 184 of *On Human*

Nature (1978), his highly influential work on evolutionary psychology: "When the gods are served, the Darwinian fitness of the members of the tribe is the ultimate if unrecognized beneficiary."

But religion is more than that. It is in religion that the true psychology of human beings finds its most important and clearest expression. Before the rise of evolutionary psychology, cognitive psychology and brain science, academic psychologies paled in comparison to the psychologies of the great religions. The psychological truths found in Buddhism, Hinduism, Islam, the Judeo-Christian tradition, Taoism, Jainism, etc., are referred to as spiritual truths. The Golden Rule is an example. But the Golden Rule is a psychological truth as well as a spiritual truth because it is wise psychology to do unto others as you would have them do unto you. It is a behavior that is adaptive, a behavior that works. It is a great truth regardless of what we call it. We might even call it a philosophy.

SOMETHING BEYOND MATERIALISM

The one thing that the religious fundamentalists have right is that there is something beyond materialism. What that something is, though, is very far removed from their world view. Most educated people now know that many of the ideas inherent in fundamentalist religions of whatever variety are no longer tenable. Wilson even goes so far as to say that our world will be improved as rationalism (he uses the term "scientific materialism") becomes "the dominate mythology." Note well his secondary point: scientific materialism, like religion and the macabre dance of Marxist-Leninism, is a mythology. (See the final chapter of *On Human Nature* entitled "Hope.") His point is that there is no final or transcending truth that we humans may discover; there is no body of knowledge or suite of disciplines that will lead us to absolute knowledge. There are only better ways of ordering the environment and of understanding our predicament. He believes that toward that end rationalism and a reliance on the scientific method will be a clear improvement over the religious and political mythologies that now dominate most of the world's cultures.

In this regard, one can see in the rise of the "New Age," an embryonic religion in the making, a religion that will ultimately fuse science and religion into a new way of viewing the world and our place in it. True, a lot of New Age thinking is currently fuzzier than a ball of fur in an electrical storm. But give it a couple of hundred years.

YOGA AS A RATIONALIST APPROACH TO LIFE

So what I want to do in this book is to use the way of yoga and its many affinities with Eastern religions, Taoism, Hinduism, Buddhism and especially Zen Buddhism, to demonstrate the ultimate and necessary continuity between religion and rationalism. I want to especially demonstrate that the practice of yoga is a common sense approach to life, and has something to offer even the most firm believer in reason, something that cannot be gotten from a strict reliance on scientific materialism.

Chapter 1:
Yoga Is More than Asana

A REVENGE NOT TAKEN

Let me tell you a story. My wife and I had moved to a new neighborhood and after a few weeks our cat Calico disappeared. I had noticed that our new neighbor, a man I'll call Ralph, chased the cats from his yard, and once I saw him kick a cat who tried to rub his leg.

My wife was heartbroken and we went to the pounds and put ads in the newspapers and chased down leads. But Calico, who was the sweetest cat, was gone and never returned.

Some months later our other cat, Boxer also disappeared. Early that morning I heard Ralph glide his big black car out of the driveway and then return. One day he told me how he had poisoned his German shepherd because the dog had gotten too big for his children to play with. I had found nuggets of dog food in our backyard. I didn't know why. Sometimes I would find rocks. One day I realized that Ralph, unable to sleep some nights, would go into his backyard, stand on a box to see over the fence and throw rocks and/or poisoned dog food nuggets at the cats in our backyard.

Again my wife was heartbroken and put flyers up on telephone poles in the neighborhood offering a reward. Again we went to the pounds (and how sad it was to see the frightened animals in their forlorn cages) and again there were the false leads, and finally there was no hope: Boxer never returned.

Although we could not prove it, we both knew (as did some of the neighbors who had also lost their cats) that Ralph had poisoned them and had disposed of their bodies at night. How angry I was! I wanted revenge. I wanted to do *something* to hurt Ralph the way he had hurt my wife and me and our little kitties. But I did nothing because there is in yoga the practice of *ahimsa*, that is, of non-violence, and I knew from the ethical teachings of yoga that revenge is wrong and can never be right.

We sold our house and moved to another neighborhood. The story might have ended there except that as a high school English teacher I taught Shakespeare's *Hamlet* in which revenge leads to tragedy. While teaching the play I would at some point tell my students the story of Ralph and our cats. And I would tell them all the nasty revenges I had longed to commit, such as cutting down his precious jacaranda tree with a power saw, or burning the word "cat" into his front lawn with something like Agent Orange, or gouging the word "cat" into the hood of his big black car with a steel instrument. And how my students would visualize and identify with these delicious schemes of revenge!

TO ABIDE IN SOFTNESS

But I would tell my students, I did none of these. The "evil" that Ralph had done, the awful little *karmas* he had created, did not go further through me. Because of what I had learned from yoga a terribly sad and negative experience was transformed into a teaching lesson for my students. At the time it was all I could do to keep myself from committing a revenge; but today I am enormously glad I did nothing. Now I have a story and an object lesson to share.

This story illustrates both the power of yoga and its affinity with the watercourse way of the *Tao Te Ching*. While yoga allows us to gain control over our physical selves, it is even more powerful in showing us the way to gain control over our mental and emotional selves, which will lead us the way to freedom.

In Victor Mair's beautifully poetic translation of the *Tao Te Ching* we encounter these words (p. 21):

> *Seeing what is small is called insight,*
> *Abiding in softness is called strength.*

In yoga we abide in softness. We do not grasp and we do not strain. In the close attention we give to ourselves we gain insight into ourselves and into the world around us thereby gaining strength.

There is also in the way of Yoga something of the spirit of Zen. The ideas of modest action, of working at what we have to do every day in a cheerful way without regard for, or in expectation of, any reward are common to Zen, Taoism, and yoga. "Carry water; cook rice" is the sort of Zen wisdom that has a cognate in the yogic admonition to be still. This is not surprising because both Zen and yoga come in part from the Buddha himself, who was a great practitioner of yoga.

Yet in another sense Zen and Taoism are reactions to and criticisms of yoga, arising in India after the time of the Buddha. In yoga we take control of our lives and we actively seek to bring about *samadhi*, while in Zen or according to the watercourse way, such directed activity is anathema. Indeed it is a most amazing paradox because in Zen any attempt at enlightenment is seen as a first step in the wrong direction. Yoga, the yoga of Patanjali and the *Bhagavad Gita*, does not agree with this point of view. Yoga is preeminently a discipline, and yoga is existential. What we make of our lives, the practice of yoga teaches, is exactly proportional to what we put into our lives.

This is not to denigrate or devalue Zen Buddhism or Taoism. Much to the contrary. The ideas of Zen and Taoism serve to correct the yogi who too maniacally strives, the sort of extremism in the pursuit of liberation that one sees in a fakir who holds his arm above his head until it atrophies. This, as the Buddha himself taught after years as an ascetic in the forest, is not the way to liberation. One may whip the body as though it were a stubborn donkey, one may deprive the body until it is skin and bones, but such extremes lead to nothing, spiritually speaking. The eight-limbed yoga of Patanjali is in its essence the very model of reason, moderation and very much in the spirit of the esteemed Middle Way of Buddhism. (Incidentally, I don't think it is an accident that the number eight appears centrally in both methods.)

It has been the fortune of yoga to be associated not only with Buddhism but with Jainism, mystical Christianity, Tibetan Buddhism and other religions, but of course in particular with Hinduism. Indeed often it is impossible to separate the ideas of Hinduism from yogic ideas, which are sometimes one and the same.

Karma for example is both a Hindu idea and a yogic idea. Furthermore, it is a Buddhist idea. In some ways this association has been entirely to the good. Hinduism is a very powerful religion with a multitudinous following and practice. Its lineage is ancient and its wisdom is great. Yet in another way this association has been unfortunate since sometimes the teachers of yoga have not separated that which is purely yogic from that which is distinctly Hindu.

We do not have to be Hindus, nor do we have to believe in the Hindu pantheon of personal gods or in Hindu doctrines to take yoga for our own. Here we have a yoga that is compatible with all religions and yet maintains its own integrity. Indeed I believe that yoga has as much in common with the way of Lao Tzu as it has with Hinduism; as much in common with the instant enlightenment of Zen as it does with Buddhism per se; certainly more in common with the tradition of mystical Christianity than it does with any established church. Yoga, like Taoism, leads to an individual enlightenment, to a mystical union with the Absolute that requires no church or monastic doctrine, no social or public ritual.

A NON-MYSTICAL UNDERSTANDING

Therefore, the way of Yoga that we are seeking is the way shorn of Hindu religiosity and separated from its Indian chaff, made streamlined and rational for the creative mind of the 21st Century. It is the pure kernel that falls after a tossing in the wind. It is the vital essence that remains after a deep distillation.

This is not to say that there is anything wrong with Hinduism or with India. On the contrary, we are indebted to that great religion for helping to maintain yoga, and to the mind and character of the people of India for inventing and developing yoga. But a yoga that was apt for an agrarian people living in a pre-industrialized society needs to be adapted to the circumstances of the modern world. The rationalist approach to yoga presented on these pages is such an adaptation. This is the approach to yoga of Emerson and Thoreau while respecting that of Ramakrishna and Sankara. This is an approach that I hope Einstein and Darwin might admire. This is a yoga of the First Patriarch and the Buddha, as well as the yoga of Patanjali and Iyengar. This is a yoga older than the Vedas and newer than call waiting.

My approach above all else seeks to guide the rational and educated person of the modern world toward a clear and non-mystical understanding of this ancient way of life.

Chapter 2:
What Is Yoga? What Is the Goal of Yoga?

GRACE VERSUS TECHNIQUE

There are those who believe everything spiritual comes by grace. Yogis don't believe this. They believe that technique—the application of skilled effort and discipline—can alter the course of things and bring great well-being to our lives. However grace still plays a role. It is by grace that we are saved, the Bible teaches. Hindus would point to our *karma* from previous lives. Buddhists, who are in many ways the most direct descendants of the ancient yogis, would say it is by right knowledge and right action that we make spiritual progress. But whether by grace or because of inconsistent or faulty technique, we know that some days meditation comes easily and some days it doesn't come at all. Sometimes it really is best to take this simply as a matter of grace. Accept it, but don't stop meditating because of a bad day. Don't give up the practice of asana and *pranayama* just because some days it doesn't go well while other days, seemingly out of the blue when perhaps it is least expected, the bliss and the beauty, the joy and the understanding, are there almost without effort as though manna from heaven.

We should accept that too and continue our practice. The daily ebbs and flows, the highs and lows are best ignored and instead we should concentrate our effort on smoothing out our reaction to them and moving toward a time and place where all is bliss.

We should have a rational approach and a steady practice. We should have faith. It will come.

THE JOY OF THE EXPERIENCE

When you do yoga you will experience a heighten sense of consciousness. You will feel better. The world around you will be clearer, more brilliant. You will think better and life will be more enjoyable. In a way it's like being in love.

The changes will be both subtle and gross. On the one hand you will have to stop and notice the difference. You will have to practice awareness to see and feel the beauty. On the other hand you will suddenly become aware that everything today is very beautiful. You will exclaim, *I feel great and life is wonderful*. This won't happen all the time. Some days in the beginning it won't happen at all. But mostly it will. And as your practice deepens, so will your joy and so will the continuity of your experience. Life really is bliss and any deviation from that bliss (barring accident) is the result of error and ignorance. And even unfortunate accidents can be overcome and one's life made beautiful and full of joy through faith and practice.

Through a firm commitment and a gentle daily discipline, bad habits of mind and body melt away and inert flesh gives way to the effervescence of spirit.

SOME MISCONCEPTIONS

One of the major misconceptions about yoga is that it's an ascetic discipline. It's a discipline in the same sense that science is a discipline, but it's not austere, it's very pleasurable. In fact, pleasure is a constant goal of yoga, although the word "pleasure" is never used. Yogis are not in it for the pain. This misconception comes about because the yogi wants to actually transcend both pleasure and pain and reach bliss, "bliss" being a kind of superior pleasure not subject to the vagaries of the world (which the yogi knows he cannot control).

This is really the crux of the matter. What the yogi wants to do is to control his life so that he is not subject to the terrible ups and downs of triumph and disaster, of winning and losing—and to the extent that it is possible—the vagaries of pleasure and pain.

I remember a cartoon by Charles Schultz, the late artist who did "Peanuts," in which he has Lucy crying "I DON'T WANT any ups and downs! I want to go from up to UPs to...UPPER UPs!"

This is not exactly the way the yogi feels, but it illustrates the predicament so well expressed by Buddhism in the idea of *sukkha*, or the unsatisfactoriness of life.

Another misconception is that yoga is a uniquely Hindu phenomenon. Modern yoga is a synthesis of ideas and practices that come from India of course, but also from Tibet, from Taoist China, and from the far-flung provinces of Buddhism, including Japanese Zen Buddhism. The contemporary phenomenon that is yoga has been further influenced by Western ideas, principally the ideas of modern science. Thus an American yoga instructor would not say that the lotus posture destroys all disease or conquers death (as the classical authors of the *Hathapradipika* or the *Siva-Samhita* do) since that would be unscientific and perhaps misleading. Similarly, Western yogis do not practice, for example, *vahiskriti* (washing the intestines) because this antiquated (and probably only symbolic) practice isn't necessary—or desirable!—in the modern world. The famous seated posture of yoga is the "lotus pose" not *padmasana* (its Sanskrit name). We say the "forward bend" not *paschimottanasana*. We clean our teeth with a toothbrush and toothpaste, not with catechu juice and clay (as prescribed in the *Gheranda-Samhita*).

Furthermore, Western instructors (not "gurus") typically limit themselves to teaching *hatha yoga*, leaving *raja* yoga to either the student himself or to a spiritual teacher (who could be Zen, Taoist, Christian, Hindu, Muslim or anything else).

While yoga's roots are in India, its full-flowering is world-wide.

WHAT YOGA IS NOT

Yoga is not something that can be gotten merely from books or film or from recordings or even ultimately from a guru. Yoga is an experience. It is something learned with mind, body and soul. Although the outlines of yoga can be appreciated, and even its ultimate goal understood through verbal knowledge, the achievement of yoga can only be accomplished by doing yoga.

Yoga then is not the fakir who demonstrates his strength by sleeping on a bed of nails, nor is yoga the Hare Krishnas who used to come shaven-headed into the airports of prosperous countries to beg and intimidate passengers into giving them money (which they in turn gave to a controlling leader). Yoga is just the opposite. Instead of self-mutilation there is the practice of self-harmony. Instead of hustling for a fat and dictatorial "guru" (as sometimes happens in tantra) there is contentment with the self and no hustling at all.

THE APPROACH

It would be best (if it were possible) to come to yoga without preconceptions, to have tossed aside old ideas about what is important in life and to stand ready to begin anew, because to achieve yoga we will have to often embrace that which we previously shunned and to shun that which we previously held in highest esteem.

In this regard there is a symbol from the *Upanishads* of a tree stood upside down with its roots in the sky and its branches in the earth, signifying the diametric change in perception that comes about after one is firmly established in yoga.

A somewhat similar idea is from the Bible: "The meek shall inherit the earth." We have all heard this phrase many times, but have we ever stopped to ask what it really means? What is "meek" and what does it mean "to inherit?" What if I were to say to the CEO of a great international corporation that the meek shall inherit the earth?

The idea would probably annoy her. She would regard me as some kind of kook and/or Green fanatic out to deprive her of her corporate options. (Or maybe she would divine it as a great advertising idea!) If I reminded her that the quote is from the Bible she would probably come up with something like "the devil can quote scripture to his own purposes." At no time would she actually understand what I said nor would she have any idea of what was meant. She would only see that what I said was either in agreement with her world view or opposed to it; either as making her feel comfortable about her way of life or as reminding her that not everybody sees the world the way she does and that she might be wrong.

To achieve success in yoga we have to see as though for the first time, as a child experiences the world. We have to be willing intellectually and emotionally to be "born again."

But to be born again, one must first die to this world. One must allow the old delusive persona to expire so that the new might be born, like a chaparral forest burned to the ground so that an explosive spring of renewal might follow.

By the way, the meek are the modest, the non-violent, the peaceful. They are the wise who will survive after the merchants of war, exploitation, and intolerance are gone.

THE GOAL

The goal of yoga is *moksa*, freedom from pleasure and pain, from that tyrannical pair of opposites that control our lives. Put another way the goal of yoga is to merge with the Supreme Divine Consciousness, to become one with the Ineffable.

This is not exactly a modest undertaking! One might ask, do people actually achieve this? It's a good question and I hope this book provides something close to an answer. For moments, certainly, everyone has achieved *moksa*, everyone has been temporarily liberated. For some very rare persons such as Jesus or Buddha or Sri Ramakrishna or certain saints, the answer is an unqualified yes. For weekend aspirants, the answer is probably not, at least not for a long time to come.

So what's the sense of trying?

The real beauty of yoga is that the benefits that one accrues along the way, even though one may come up far short of the goal, are themselves fabulous achievements: Good health, a serene and confident state of mind, a fuller understanding and appreciation of self, an acceptance of things one cannot control, a greater tolerance of others, an indifference toward evil, but compassion for those who suffer. (Evil, properly understood, is really just a delusion we can't help but believe.)

Contrary to some opinion, yoga is life-affirming. The practice of meditation (which is the core of yoga, as it is of all mystical experience) is not an escape from the world, but a way of ordering oneself into a greater harmony with the world. For the Hindu the goal is the cessation of the endless (and painful) cycle of birth, death and rebirth. For the yogi the expression is more direct. It is pure bliss itself, a heaven on earth.

The first goal, then, is physical health. Toward that end, we practice asana and *pranayama*, we live in harmony with our fellow human beings, we meditate. For the experienced aspirant the goal is *samadhi*, the achievement of the super conscious state that is beyond the power of words to describe. (Although we rationalists might just call it "trance," as it is sometimes translated, and leave it at that.) For the saint it is union with the Supreme Divine Consciousness.

How do we know that Sri Ramakrishna and Jesus, for example, actually achieved this union with God?

We know nothing of course except our own experience, but we can gain trust from the pure veracity of their words. Jesus said, "Seek ye the Kingdom of Heaven within." How did he know that the Kingdom of Heaven was within? He knew because he himself had experienced the Kingdom first hand.

We further have the reports of their disciples to the truth of their experiences. Ramakrishna went into trances of ecstasy sometimes for months on end. His disciples were there with him to share his experience and to experience the wonder (second hand at least). When he spoke during these periods what he said was so charged with truth and the terrific desire to lead others to where he had been that one could hardly doubt that he spoke from personal experience. He was asked how to see God and he said you must cry to him with a yearning heart, and you will see him.

Later he told a story about a guru and his disciple. The disciple too wanted to see God, so the guru took him down to the river and held his head underwater a long time. When he let him up, the guru asked how he felt. The student said, "'Oh, I thought I should die; I was panting for breath!' The teacher said, 'When you feel like that for God, then you will know you haven't long to wait for His vision.'"

But I think the reader should be skeptical. Trust only your own experience and use the experience of others only as a guide. But remember the great psychological truth in the adage, "None are so blind as those who will not see."

IS YOGA A RELIGION?

Surprisingly this is a controversial question—at least in the United States. Most popular yoga books in English are at pains to say that yoga is not a religion and point out that one can practice yoga and still be a Christian or a Buddhist—or an atheist—and it will make no difference. But maybe it would be wiser to see yoga not as a religion per se but as something that aids one in his religious practice. To quote Gopi Krishna from his book, *The Secret of Yoga*, p. 2:

> *Properly speaking, yoga is an adjunct to religion and has always been treated as such in India.... Yoga is not something different or divorced from religion. It is the experimental part of it....*

He adds:

> *Divested of the superstition and myth that surround all religions, Yoga contains absolutely nothing that can be abhorrent to any faith or creed. On the other hand, it uses most of the methods advocated by the founders of great religions, mystics, and sages as a means to God-consciousness and to render the body as a fit vehicle for spiritual illumination.*

WHAT YOGA IS

Yoga is a spiritual practice, an ancient tradition, a science, a religion, a way of life. It is all of these things. Its literature is vast, its lineage ancient, its scope all-encompassing, taking as it does into consideration every aspect of a person's life.

The word yoga itself means "to bind" or "to attach" or "yoke," as to yoke oxen. In a deeper sense it means to yoke the individual soul to God.

It has been called "a poise of the soul" (Mahadev Desai) or "the establishment of perfect harmony between the everyday self and its spiritual source" (Paul Brunton, in Wood's *Practical Yoga*, p. 10).

Patanjali himself defined yoga tersely as "the control of the ideas of the mind."

Dr. Ramurti S. Mishra says that man is "hypnotized by his body" (I like that phrasing) and calls yoga "the process of dehypnotism." He adds that "submission of lower desire to higher desire is called yoga."

In the *Bhagavad Gita* yoga is described as "a deliverance from contact with pain and sorrow."

On a more practical level, the *hatha yoga* teacher Indra Devi called yoga "a method, a system of physical, mental and spiritual development" (*Yoga for Americans*, p. xxii).

Georg Feuerstein in the Preface to *The Shambhala Encyclopedia of Yoga* identifies yoga as "an immensely rich and highly complex spiritual tradition...."

In his *Yoga: Immortality and Freedom*, Mircea Eliade says, "The means of attaining to Being, the effectual techniques for gaining liberation. This...constitutes Yoga properly speaking."

Secularly speaking, then, one might say that yoga is a growing body of knowledge and practice that teaches people to live in harmony with themselves and their environment. Spiritually speaking, some yogis say (as Sachindra Kumar Majumdar did in his *Introduction to Yoga*, p. 20) that "Yoga is the religion of mankind." But this would be going too far.

Yoga is also one of the six orthodox philosophies of Hinduism.

A WAY OF LIFE

As you can surmise, every book on yoga attempts to define what yoga is. All these attempts are fine, but what they usually fail to tell the reader is that to understand what yoga is you have to practice yoga, and I don't mean merely the postures. A definition won't tell you. Reading a book, any book, including this one, won't tell you. You have to live yoga to appreciate what yoga is.

In the beginning of course words help. Yoga is not an exotic herb. That's good to know. Yoga is not an ice cream sundae. Yoga is a practice, of course, as I said above, but more than that yoga is a way of life.

A way of life. These are small words, but their intent is to cover everything. All of life, every experience, every stage, everything we do or say, every experience we have, correctly understood, is covered in yoga.

Sound all-inclusive? That was the intent of the ancient yogis. The science, art and practice of yoga is intended to guide us through everything that life can throw at us, from birth to death. Yoga is a way to meet what life has to offer, yoga is a way of viewing what happens to us, yoga is a theory about what happens to us, yoga is a guide on how to live in this world and how to die.

However words do not suffice. It is only through direct experience that we may know what yoga is.

So let us begin.

Chapter 3:
The Five Yogas

A MEANS TO AN END

The problem of youth is learning how to get what we want. The problem of our middle years is knowing how to live. And the problem of old age is to realize how to die. The Tao suggests an answer, a general answer that is a guide to follow when considering alternatives. That answer is the watercourse way, or the way of least resistance. Follow the watercourse way and you will minimize your pain in this world.

Yoga provides a more detailed, nearly specific answer. The way of yoga is a way toward liberation, "liberation" meaning a solution to the problems of life. The Buddha observed that life is suffering—or at the very least life is unsatisfactory—and then he taught that there is a way out of the suffering. Yoga observes that life as we know it is an illusion and an attachment to things we cannot control. Living an illusion over which we have no control means we have no freedom. But we humans long for freedom and we cry out for deliverance from the forces that control us. Yoga is a means to that end.

THE REAL YOGA IS RATIONAL

But the efficacious yoga is almost always not the yoga found in books or hawked about on the Internet. The yoga that various religious cults espouse and hold as their own is not the complete yoga. The yoga of the Hindus, the yoga of the Muslims, the yoga of the Taoists and the Jainists and the Buddhists, the yoga that goes by

35

many names has been corrupted in its descent to us from the long ago. It has been codified and modified by scribes and various practitioners. The yoga of the *Bhagavad Gita*, the yoga of Patanjali, the yoga of B.K.S. Iyengar, the yoga of the *Hathayogapradipika*, the yoga of the Tibetan tantras, the yoga of Georg Feuerstein, the yoga practiced by my cat—they are the real yoga, but they are incomplete and must be interpreted and practiced, and above all the real yoga must be lived.

I found the real yoga some years ago, and I found that it is not something otherworldly or a touchy-feelie, groupy groping spun out in a New Age cult. It is a rational yoga, a yoga that could be assessed by science, an empirical yoga shorn of any religiosity, a yoga with its feet firmly on the ground, guided by observation, analysis, hypothesis, test and retest. I came to see the world in a different way. I learned that the world as we know it is an illusion, an illusion foisted onto us by the process of evolution so that we might make such limited observations that further the reproduction of our kind. Yoga is a way to dispel these illusions, to remove the veil that the species mechanism and society have pulled over our eyes. It allows us to see—only glimpses at first, almost immediately forgotten, but becoming clearer and longer held as we go along—until at some point we see what and who we are and why, and where we are going, in the stark clarity of the morning light.

ONE GOAL

Everything in yoga works toward one goal and that goal is liberation from the predicament in which we find ourselves on this planet in this world of flesh and blood and rapacious desire. And what is this *liberation* or *nirvana*, or *moksa*, or *samadhi* that is so often mentioned? What is this "peace that passeth understanding"? Is it a trance to escape our woes, or a meeting and yoking with God?

I will give you a quick answer: it is both.

It is precisely because the way to liberation is not easy that yoga exists. Some come to God by means of faith and devotion. That is *bhakti yoga*. Others come by way of good works. That is *karma yoga*, the preeminent yoga of the *Bhagavad Gita*. Still others come by way of knowledge and understanding. That is the way of *jnana yoga* in which one knows the truth and the truth sets one free. For all others, there is the rigorous and methodical path of Patanjali's eight-limbed yoga, the yoga of B. K. S. Iyengar, the yoga of the classic texts of the Middle Ages, a yoga traditionally referred to as *hatha/raja yoga.*

There is also the so-called "left-handed path" of *tantric yoga,* not mentioned in the Gita, a way so unsocial, so unsure, and so dangerous, that it is taken up only by the desperate and the deluded. (We will, however, check it out later on.)

There are therefore five yogas: *bhakti, karma, jnana, hatha/raja* and *tantra.* All other so-called yogas found in coffee table books and personality cults, yogas named after various persons, will be found upon further examination to be parts of, or variations on, these five.

For example, there is Integral Yoga, a yoga begun by or at least credited to the Indian scholar Sri Aurobindo, but it is obviously and frankly a combination of several yogas. It may well be (and I happen to believe it is) true that the best yoga is a combination of all of the five principal yogas, but we'll leave this point for a moment.

Another yoga you often hear about is *kundalini yoga,* which is also called *laya yoga,* the yoga of the latent power of the body, or the yoga of the *chakras* or the yoga of the "serpent power." We'll discuss this yoga in a separate chapter. For now we'll just say *kundalini yoga* comes under the general heading of *hatha yoga,* the yoga of physical health.

Less often we hear about *mantra yoga,* the yoga of sounds and prayers and magical incantations, the yoga of *japa* and the ceaseless repetition of the name of God. This yoga is actually a technique or an efficacious ritual of other yogas, most notably *bhakti* and *tantra.*

BHAKTI YOGA: THE WAY OF FAITH

If you have great faith and you can believe impossible or unlikely things as easily as the report of your senses and the deductions of your mind, then you are favored by the gods, and the path of devotion and faith is open unto you. This is the way of the common people, it is sometimes said, the easiest path, taken up by Christians and Hindus, Muslims and many millions of others throughout the world and in various cultures. Faith is the basis of most religions, and in fact, from the point of view of yoga, Christianity, for example, is a *bhakti* yoga. If your faith is strong enough you will indeed find *nirvana*, and be delivered into the kingdom of heaven.

If your faith is strong enough.

There is the rub, of course. For the person of rationality, the student of science, the practitioner of reason, such a path is not only not easy, it is impossible.

How do you practice *bhakti*? The most important single idea in *bhakti* is unwavering faith in a personal God. Everything else is mere fluff and commentary. If your faith is strong enough, nothing else matters in the slightest. If your faith is strong enough you will be released and find heaven on earth without doubt.

This little "if," as usual, is the bugaboo. Many are called and indeed few, so very few, are chosen.

It is a little thing to believe. It is quite another thing to believe enough and to maintain that belief in the face of all odds, opposition, contrary opinions and the unhappy things that happen to us. To be assured of success in *bhakti* you must have the patience of Job and be prepared to withstand and accept any amount of adversary without having your faith shaken. There is only one thing that can go wrong with the *bhakti* yogini on the road to liberation and that is a loss of faith.

And your love must be strong. You must love God with the most powerful of emotion. You must, as Ramakrishna said, "cry out for Him." Only then will you find Him.

For the average person—or almost anyone actually—it isn't possible to feel that love and find that love for an abstract or impersonal God. So the followers of *bhakti* are taught to love without qualification their guru and their personal God (usually Krishna). In Christianity, one finds God through Christ.

KARMA YOGA: THE WAY OF SELFLESS WORK

It should be mentioned that success in *bhakti* usually goes hand in hand with success in *karma* yoga. In the Gita it is made clear that it is through faith in Krishna and in selfless work that one finds liberation. Most bhaktis would, at any rate, be without something religious to do if they were not able to dedicate their day-to-day work to God. The whole point of the Gita is that one must work (Arjuna must "fight") and to abdicate one's work (or one's dharma) leads to failure.

So, in truth, *bhakti* yoga seldom exists without *karma* yoga. Even Ramakrishna, whose faith was enormous, nonetheless devoted much of his life to not only worship but to showing the way to others. Being a fisher of men (to use a Western phrase) was Ramakrishna's dharma and he knew it and he did it exceptionally well, over and above his great devotional gifts.

So, if you have a selfless nature and a gift for giving of yourself and can expect nothing, truly nothing in return—if you are like Mother Theresa is said to have been and Gandhi, Florence Nightingale and the saints—then you too are favored by the gods and the path of renunciation of the fruits of labor is open unto you. Such is the way of work propounded by Krishna in the *Bhagavad Gita*. It is said to be the second easiest method—if you can achieve a complete and uncompromised non-attachment to the fruits of your labor, and a renunciation of all the things that most people consider valuable. The really hard part is to give up even the slightest expectation of merit, reward, or consideration of any kind. If you can do this, *karma* yoga will work for you.

If you can achieve a complete and uncompromised non-attachment.

This not so easy to do. The mind and the body yearn so for recognition, if nothing else; and if not that, then the sense of being good, of being holy and the doer of good works.

As Eknath Easwaran writes in his translation of *The Bhagavad Gita*: "Philanthropic activity can benefit others and still carry a large measure of ego involvement. Such work is good, but it is not yoga. It may benefit others, but it will not necessarily benefit the doer" (p. xxxix).

We will spend a considerable amount of time on *karma* yoga and the message of the Gita since the central idea of *karma* yoga, that of non-attachment, is basic to all yoga.

THE WAY OF DISCIPLINE: *HATHA* LEADING TO *RAJA*

If you are of a skeptical nature, if your faith isn't strong enough, if you waver between the "truth" of what you see and the "truth" of what happens to you, and you find it difficult to believe in gods that act suspiciously like overwrought human beings, then *bhakti* is probably not for you and you must search elsewhere.

It is in a sense ironic that what I call the yoga of technique—*hatha/raja*—is a yoga that we of lesser faith must pursue by default. But it is true, and it is wise and modest of us to realize that. If our faith were strong enough there would be no need for the arduous path of *hatha/raja* yoga, the royal way. Nonetheless this path of brute strength eventually leads to success—providing we stay on the path.

Therefore if you do not want to leave liberation to chance or to the variables of genetic gifts, but want to ensure success, then you must embrace *hatha/raja*, the eight-limbed yoga, the "path of force," as it is sometimes called, the path that by incremental steps leads inevitably to *samadhi*.

"The path of force" is at once a particularly apt phrasing and misleading, as we shall see. The "force" that one uses to control the monkey mind or the donkey body is the force of intelligence and practice. To beat the body about to make it behave is not what is meant at all. Indeed, it is said in yoga that one may reach, but one must never strain. In Taoism, of course, one does not even reach. But we shall see that this "not reaching," like the famous "no-mind" of Zen, is a kind of reaching in grace, a kind of working mind that does not think, but knows. And so it is with the yoga of force. One applies oneself to the eight limbs, and one is free.

Although I wrote "inevitably" above, that inevitably one is led to *samadhi*, there are obstacles to be overcome. Patanjali speaks of them, Krishna as well. And of course many travelers fall by the way side. Most do not begin at all. You, dear reader, have taken steps already. You will not be among the myriad who have not begun at all. But tighten your resolve, girt up your loins, clear your head with a single shake like a colt before a clearing, and begin.

Begin.

That is the first key. And I will give you a mantra to guide you through this beginning: Regular practice is the key. Repeat after me: Regular practice is the key. When in meditation, or when just sitting, since you are not yet really meditating, repeat this mantra silently to yourself. Later you may graduate to something more esoteric and traditional (if you like), but for now repeat, *regular practice is the key.*

THE WAY OF KNOWLEDGE AND WISDOM: *JNANA*

But where does the seeker go who has neither faith nor brute strength of character?

If you love the world and everything you see; if you find delight in understanding nature and seeing how things really work; if you can be objective in the face of passion and can add the good with the bad and weigh them fairly; if you have a good mind and the love of using it, and you have the power of discrimination without the fault of prejudice—in short if you are a scholar of works and a judge of men, you may hope someday to find liberation through *jnana* yoga, the yoga of knowledge.

Let me say though, few start out in pursuit of liberation through the method of knowing. Fewer still, who do, find success. It is only after all the other yogas have been tried (and the seeker found wanting) that *jnana* yoga comes to the seeker, at long last as almost an afterthought, like a retirement watch or the gray of your hair.

So don't look to jnana, let it look to you. If you have the skills—like the absent-minded professor—of both seeing more than other men and less, *jnana* may eventually call to you.

If you are learned and have a gift for understanding what you have learned; if you have a sense of scholarship and have read widely, you may qualify as a *jnana* yogi, finding the truth and the light through an understanding of who you are and the nature of your existence.

If you are sufficiently gifted and work very hard.

Few are so chosen. Ramakrishna's disciple Vivekananda comes to mind. Patanjali himself of course, Shankaracharya, Georg Feuerstein, and some others.

A YOGA FOR EVERY STAGE OF LIFE

Where do you go when you can neither believe enough nor practice enough?

It is to tantra you go. You must throw yourself on the altar of desire and give in completely to your nature. This is emphatically NOT a yoga that I recommend.

We'll look at tantra in a later chapter. For now I want to suggest a hierarchy of yogas, not in the sense that one yoga might be better than another, but in the sense that there is a particular yoga that is most appropriate for a particular stage in a person's life.

In the beginning there is faith, faith in the mother and the father. One comes into the world alone, small and afraid. One looks to a greater power and has faith.

Next comes the yoga of youth, tantra. The child has become (horrors!) a teenager and the old gods are quite dead and what is more, beside the point. The point being the powerful pressure put on the young person to fulfill his or her role as an evolutionary being. Glandular and herd needs predominate. The teenager seeks God in a blind, perhaps ruthless, certainly rash, self-expression.

After some time has passed, the young person, no longer a teenager, having gained some insight into herself, suddenly sees that the blind pursuit of *bhoga* (pleasure) leads to a dead end. Now some other things are tried, depending on the individual's constitution or *karma*. Some throw themselves into their work and family, becoming householders practicing without knowing it the beginnings of *karma* yoga. Others seek salvation without and look to a leader or a guru or the church and/or a personal God to deliver them. They are beginning bhakti. Still others begin to better themselves physically and mentally—the beginnings of *raja* yoga. A tiny fraction become wise persons already and step back a bit and look at the world with new eyes and try to understand. These very few are practicing *jnana* yoga. Finally there are those who through sloth and stupidity, through ignorance and whatever disability, through an overabundance of *tamas* (the quality or *guna* of inertia or darkness) continue chasing after the endless objects and ego-fulfillments of this world and progress no further.

Then at middle age, another change typically takes place. Again men and women embrace self-improvement. They take up healthy practices, maybe *hatha yoga*. They meditate. Some will be successful, some will not. Most now move deeper into work and responsibility. They are in their prime. They are the men and women who run the affairs of this world. The ones who were lost, chasing after their endless desires are now greatly underdeveloped spiritually and many of them are broken and pitiful creatures. The lost shall be found, the Bible says, and some of these people will indeed find themselves. For most their becoming is delayed.

For everyone else any manner of thing may have happened. But few, very few are anywhere near liberation. But they are close to something almost as important; that is, they are beginning to see the need for liberation.

A person in the middle years of life knows well that the desires of youth are delusive and lead to pain and unhappiness. This is the source of the old saying that "life begins at forty." When a person lays aside the delusions of youth, life truly does begin anew.

Some are dead now as middle age advances. Others have reached the full flowering of who and what they are. The ones who have followed faithfully the dharma that is theirs, who have pursued the path of their chosen yoga now reach the place where they know the truth and they live it. For the chosen few, life is something close to a heaven on earth, a nearly ceaseless *samadhi*.

Most people, even at this advanced time in their life, are still struggling, some flailing about without direction, rudderless in the waters of life, others embittered and barely afloat, paddling halfheartedly toward they know not where. Many, so very many, are living what Thoreau called "lives of quiet desperation"—knowing that something is desperately, horribly wrong and lacking, but not knowing what it is or having any idea of where to look for it.

Yet one thing is clear, for every person regardless of situation, regardless of how lost they may be, there is hope.

Chapter 4:
The Postmodern Predicament

WHERE HAVE ALL THE FLOWER CHILDREN GONE?

When we or our parents were young, forty-five years ago, there were flower children in the streets and they were all going to have an everlasting love-in. Well, that failed and it's kind of embarrassing to recall, to tell you the truth. Certainly the kids today think it was kind of naive or worse. They snicker. There were gurus on every corner and people practiced Eastern ways and meditated and took LSD and chanted, "Hell no, we won't go!"

Today's child, a member of whatever the latest generation calls itself, works for a corporation making products and schemes and proprietary software to seduce a witless population, sodas and cigarettes, television fantasies and insurance frauds. Everything we touch today is more or less corrupt. If we weren't working for MegaFraud Insurance we might be working for a corporation that sells deodorants by making people afraid they smell bad or for a tobacco company that still sees no link between its product and cancer or for a garment manufacturer that exploits child labor overseas. It's not easy to see where virtue ends and the corruption begins, and since corruption is everywhere maybe it's not corruption at all but the natural scheme of things.

All is relative and all ways of knowing are just social constructions shaped by the ever winding, ever clever river of the zeitgeist.

The average person of today doesn't believe in gurus and can't spare the time to meditate.

But our average person as usual is wrong. And we know it. The tide of pollution, the escalation of dependencies of all kinds, the obesity, the growing number of hungry and homeless persons even in our own very rich society (to say nothing of Africa and India), the rise of a mindless terrorism, the continued addiction by many to a false fundamentalism, all attest mightily to the fact that we are lost and desperately need to be found.

We tried yoga once, actually, when we were younger. We needed to relax, we were so uptight all the time. But we lost confidence in the practice because how much faith can you have in something that claims to cure all disease? And take a look at India would you? If yoga's so good how come life in India is so bad? The question fairly begging for an answer here is why should we have the slightest interest in yoga?

ANCIENT INDIA

There is no way in a few words (or even in many words) that I or anyone else can satisfactory answer that question. It is only through the practice of yoga that the answer can be found. But I think I can hint at the answer here in this chapter. At least I hope that I can offer some compelling rationale for turning to yoga. At the very least I can point.

While many of our postmodern problems are unique to our time and place, our basic predicament has not changed in ten thousand years. In fact, our situation is the same today as it was when we still lived in tribes on the savannas and in the primordial forest. Instinctively we know there can be no escape from the sadness of life until we find ourselves and are reunited with the Ineffable.

In ancient India before recorded history there grew up a civilization along the banks of the inland rivers of the Indus Valley. The land was especially fertile and people had just arrived at agriculture. For numerous centuries, some say perhaps five thousand years, there existed a civilization comprised of millions of people. This was one of the first great societies of the world. And during those many years (far more than during all of the experience of recorded history) people had time to contemplate their existence and had ample opportunity to share their conclusions with others.

During this period there were no ancient texts to advise the people on how to live. There was no medical science or social science or mathematics or any of the vast learning we have today that helps us to shape our lives and guide us. There was only human instinct and the social ways of the tribe. Instead of the church there was the shaman. Instead of the teacher there was the mother and father, grandparents, and perhaps the aunt and uncle or the guru. Knowledge grew slowly, by word of mouth, handed down from parent to child. Basic ideas that we take for granted were actually composed in those days, ideas such as the need for cleanliness, for prayer, what was good to eat, what was not, how to behave, what to do and what not to do. Innumerable practices and ideas were tried and discarded, some to be taken up again and discarded again. Some practices (like fertilizing the fields, for example) were shown after a long trial to be essential and became the conventional wisdom and the standard practice. Science itself was still just sympathetic magic.

Society was mixed and remixed; the gene pool stirred mightily for hundreds of generations. All manner of social and sexual practices were tried. Trade developed. People learned how to live together. They learned how to follow the seasons and avoid the worst of the parasites. Yoga was born.

Many yogas were born, actually. They were all tried and tested. People compared experience and knowledge. Centuries passed. Certain practices, *asanas* (postures), *pranayamas* (breathing exercises), diets, etc., were shown to be efficacious. These practices for harmonious living were polished and re-polished, improved upon and built upon until a vast knowledge was accumulated. This knowledge was honed and committed to memory and finally codified and systematized and at last written down.

THE UNCHANGING NATURE OF THE HUMAN CONDITION

Since then, during the 2,000 or so years that have passed since Patanjali wrote his *Yoga Sutras*, yoga has spread throughout the world. Great religions have taken up many of its ideas. Secular schools based on its practices have sprung up in our great cities.

All of this has taken thousands of years. The yogas that grew out of this vast social and existential, this vast political and physical experience, were directed toward solving essentially the same problems that people face today. Nothing important has changed. We still don't know where we came from or why. We don't know the meaning of life (or whether life has a meaning or whether such a word as "meaning" might apply). We live a little longer but still die after around three score and ten. We still suffer from disease and psychological pain. We still have to get up in the morning and go to sleep at night. We still have sex and see our children grow up. We're still subject to anger and hate, love and the finality of death. Nothing important has changed. Our psychological condition is the same.

So the question is asked: Does the yoga that millions of people have developed over countless billions of hours have any relevance for us today? It would be a foolish person who misses the overwhelmingly clear answer. That answer is yes.

Chapter 5:
The Koan of Yoga

EMOTION

The first detriment is emotion. The big, brawny, swaggering bull of emotion. The immediate goal of yoga is the conquest of emotion.

People are ruled by emotion. We don't realize it. It's hard to see most of the time. But we can see it in others. There it's often clear: the green-eyed monster of jealousy, the red-eyed bull of anger and all of their cousins stand out starkly; but in ourselves emotion is so disguised, so invisible.

Emotion is one of nature's tricks to get us to do what nature in general, or nature in the big picture, or nature as the evolutionary force wants us to do. We get *mad*. We feel *hurt*. We want *revenge*. We want to *kick butt*. We are sad. We are happy. We love. We feel exhilaration. We feel *power*.

All of these and many other feelings are the glandular, the neurochemical imperatives that also society through the evolutionary mechanism uses on us to get us to do what it wants us to do. Wave the flag. Hurrah for our side. Love the leader, hate the enemy.

In general, in the long run, for the general animal good, an emotion serves a useful purpose. Fight or flight to save our lives. But if we see someone else with a member of the opposite sex whom we think is in some sense "ours," oh, what horrors will transpire! We perceive a threat to our security or to the expression of our precious genes. To make sure that we aren't substituted for, the evolutionary mechanism makes us cry out: *Get jealous!* And the more ferociously the better. Never mind that we might kill ourselves in the process. Never mind that our precious genes are not really so precious. Never mind that the "damage" may already be done. We have to get mad and we have to risk life and limb and fill ourselves with hate and revenge.

Because that's what the gross, blind and fairly crude evolutionary mechanism requires we feel. It hasn't yet evolved a better technique for controlling us. Having built us a step at a time, through an incredibly long period of trial and error, it has arrived at this rather drastic way of doing things, and only after countless further horrible, painful and totally catastrophic errors will it arrive at the best, most efficient, most beautiful and most spiritual way of doing things—and then only in the very long run. Maybe.

Thus it is said we are "becoming." We are places along the way to becoming. And the games and the techniques and the little hustles of the evolutionary process that are currently being expressed and tried out in us, guinea pigs that we are, will some day cease. And we will have *become*.

WHO AM I?

Many thousands of years ago before we humans were completely human, before we had civilized ourselves, domesticated the pig and the cow, before we learned farming or how to keep track of the seasons, we became aware of the forces within ourselves and without and we asked why are they there? And the answer was always silence or just the wind that blew across the plain. And even though we had no answer, we asked the more profound question: Who am I?

This is not a question an animal asks itself.

And some thousands of years ago the answer came out of the fertile valley of the Indus River and has echoed down through the millennia in the Vedas to us: Thou art that.

This answer when it came to the West in the 19th century seemed to the rationalist mind to be non-responsive, maybe even flippant.

Thou art that.

Ah, but what is "that"? For the mystic, "that" is everything there is, the entire cosmos and everything in time and space forever forward and backward, eternal and beyond mere being and this illusory existence; in short "that" is *Brahman*.

But the first people who formulated this "answer" and tested it in the fire of their souls and found it true, could only express it by analogy—*thou art that* like a drop of water is the ocean.

And beyond this metaphor, the rational mind could not grasp and cannot grasp. And even though there's been an industrial revolution and political ones by the score, and even though the atom has been split and a computer can (or will soon) do a trillion calculations a second—even though the confidence of modernism has given way to a deeply skeptical postmodernism, the answer hasn't changed.

We are still that.

WHY IS THERE ANYTHING AT ALL?

Or we might ask the profound question: *Why is there anything at all?*

This too is not so much a question as a discovery. Why indeed is there anything at all? Why isn't there nothing? Just asking such a question makes one wide-eyed with wonder and initiates one into the inexpressible.

These are both philosophical and spiritual questions. They are profound inquiries into the psychological nature of people and into our "predicament," as it is sometimes called. What is sought isn't mere knowledge but liberation. We want to know, and we want to be set free.

The Bible says the truth shall set us free, but it can't be any textbook truth, any you-told-me and I-accept-it truth. It's got to be an I-lived-it truth.

Yoga is primarily an attitude, a way of looking at ourselves, at the world we live in, and at that something that is greater than we are. Yoga is a way of seeing, a way of knowing and a way of acting. But yoga is above all else a practice. It is something we do.

The yoga that can be learned from books is only the partial yoga. The yoga that is talked about is only a bit of the whole yoga. The yoga that is practiced by others is their yoga and can never be ours. The yoga that is ours is everything we are, everything we do, everything we believe.

Let us end our beginning with the koan of yoga, this fervent "Who am I?"

THE ZEN KOAN

In the Rinzai school of Zen Buddhism the aspirant is given a koan by the master, typically a paradoxical or cryptic query that defies explanation. What was your face before your parents were born? and What is the sound of one hand clapping? are famous examples. After a while the aspirant is given a more sophisticated koan. One of my favorites has the master point to a girl crossing the street and ask, "Is that the older or the younger sister?" Perhaps the most universal is simply Mu? meaning what is Mu? where the word "Mu" signifies nothing.

The idea is to give the student a question he cannot answer with his logical mind—and let him wrestle with it until he reaches a meditative state of mind, and through that meditation after long and earnest practice achieves an enlightenment. Some of the answers that have been found acceptable typically involve a rejection of the question, a non-verbal response (such as sticking out one's tongue), a seemingly irrelevant response (such as "I draw water; I cook rice") or even Bah! The beginning of wisdom comes when the student realizes he truly doesn't know.

In a similar vein we have the story of Zen master Hui-k'o, who would become the Second Patriarch, asking the First Patriarch Bodhidharma to pacify his mind.

Bodhidharma replied, "Bring your mind here before me, and I will pacify it."

"But when I seek my own mind," said Hui-k'o, "I cannot find it."

"There!" snapped Bodhidharma, "I have pacified your mind!"

(I got this story from *The Way of Zen* (1957), a masterwork of erudition and insight by Alan Watts.)

The point was to get Hui-k'o out of the shallows of his verbal thinking and into the depths of actual experience. Let's not be verbal or pretentious. Let's be modest and, above all, concrete.

"NOT THIS, NOT THIS!"

The famous Vedic answer to "Who am I?"—"Not this, not this!"—evolved into and is the same thing as "Thou art that." But this answer isn't the same thing as saying "I am God" because, for one thing, as the question is asked we and God are separate. The religious tradition that grew out of yoga calls the soul of a human being (the essence of us that is eternal) the *Atman*, and the Supreme Divine Consciousness is named *Brahman*. The goal of yoga is the union of the two.

Thou art that.

Neither the question who am I? nor the answer thou art that can be understood with the ordinary mind To work on our koan, we must nonetheless try some answers.

PEELING THE ONION

We might give our name, Jane Williams. But we are more than our name. We might give our occupation. But we are more than our occupation. We might then try to sum up in words what we are, like a child giving a complete address: "Jane Williams, 123 Main Street, Houston, Texas, U.S.A., Western Hemisphere, Earth, Solar System, Milky Way Galaxy..." We might say that we are the atoms of our body, organized in a particular way. We might say that we are human beings with a certain complexion and body type, with a certain education, living in a certain way. We might even say that we believe certain things and don't believe others. After we have said all these things we have not gotten any closer to answering our koan.

"Who am I?" allows us to peel away the layers of identification like onion rings until we come to the place where there is nothing left—and still we won't know who we are.

Even given the beautiful answer of the Vedas "Thou art that," we still know nothing more than we did before because the answer means nothing to the mind that is not prepared to understand it.

Here the rational mind is at an impasse. Further we cannot proceed. We may yet answer our koan and achieve enlightenment and liberation, but it will only come through the fires of personal experience. Each of us must look within ourselves. This is what yoga is all about, finding the transcendental "that" which is within us, the Buddhist's "jewel in the heart of the lotus."

In another sense this question is seen as a question of consciousness. What is the nature of consciousness? is part of what we are asking when we ask Who am I? The Buddhists say that our sense of self, our sense of an ego that lives and dies is an illusion. The *Bhagavad Gita* says the same thing. Two modern, scientifically-oriented books that address this question and do a marvelous job of coming to the same conclusion, namely that we cannot die because that which we think is us doesn't even exist(!), are *The User Illusion: Cutting Consciousness Down to Size* (1991, 1998) by Tor Norretranders, and *Zen Physics: The Science of Death, the Logic of Reincarnation* (1996) by David Darling.

This idea, which is at the heart of yoga, Buddhism and Vedanta, is not an easy idea to grasp, and even when grasped can be lost and in need of being found again. It is especially difficult for those of us raised in the Greek tradition of rationalism to see clear through to the realization that that which we call ourselves is an illusion! It took me years to see it. I used to teach the idea of Who am I? by having my students write about themselves, but at the time I did not realize that the ultimate lesson was that we do not exist in the mundane sense that we think we exist.

A THOUGHT EXPERIMENT

Let's try a thought experiment in the manner of Albert Einstein. Imagine that every atom in your body right down to the atoms that comprise the very blood that flows through your veins, even the atoms that make up the microbes that live in your intestinal tract and on your skin are reproduced exactly so that a new "you" is miraculous manufactured and now sits right beside you. (Of course it is not possible to do this, but just imagine for the sake of the experiment.) What is the difference between you and the person sitting next to you? Every atom is the same. Every memory, every skill and aptitude. Yet, I'll wager, if you were asked which of you should remain and which should go, you would have a preference. But why? What is the difference between the two of you?

From a rational point of view—aside from the fact that you occupy slightly different points in space, which will inevitably lead to differences in the future—there is no difference. The only difference is one of identity. You identify with one of these you's and not the other. And of course the other you feels the same. Again, what and where is the difference?

LOSING THE FEAR OF DEATH

This is the onion peeled all the way to nothing. There is no difference. The two you's are the same. The fact that you and the other you prefer one to the other is just a matter of *identity*, an identity or "consciousness" (I am using the word in a restricted sense) that you cannot but prefer because such a preference is built into our nature by the evolutionary mechanism. This highlights not only the fact that your consciousness and mine are no different, but reveals what Krisna in the *Bhagavad Gita* meant when he said we do not die.

This also illuminates what is meant by the symbolic idea of reincarnation. What is reincarnated is this sense of identity or this "consciousness" which is identical in each of us. It never dies. It is recycled just as the atoms in our bodies are recycled. Death is an illusion, just as the identification with the ego is an illusion.

If you don't see this as clearly as it appears to me, don't despair. It is the sort of truth that takes a while to sink in. It took me a couple of decades. I suspect most readers can do better than that. It is not an easy concept since it goes not only against the powerful force of the evolutionary mechanism, but for Westerners it goes against much of what we have been taught in school and by our parents and have imbibed from the culture. This is the sort of knowledge that has to be lived to be appreciated. I am pointing in a direction, but that's all I can do. You have to peel away the layers yourself and see and feel and know the truth in very heart of your soul. You have to experience the truth. You have to have an "enlightenment." And if you stay with it with an open mind, you will.

Once we see that we do not exist in the way we think we exist, and that we do not "die"—once this truth is comprehended in its entirety, the fear of death disappears completely. Although I certainly would avoid violence if at all possible, and even though I am in no rush to go into "that good night," I have no fear of death, and will be quite pleased when it comes, as I am quite pleased when it does not come.

That is an element of the freedom that the yogi works toward. To fear death is to be enslaved. To be free of the fear of death is an essential part of the freedom to which we aspire.

Chapter 6:
On the Literature of Yoga

THE GARDEN OF EDEN

We gain most of our knowledge of yoga (beyond *hatha yoga*) through the written word. Books and more recently the Internet have replaced the oral formulaic traditions of the guru system of the preliterate world. Many of these books beyond the asana stage are actually books of religious philosophy written many centuries ago by persons half a world away, while books written in recent years have the older works as a source. Some skill is required in the reading.

The first thing we must understand is that much of what we read cannot be taken literally. All important religious knowledge is symbolic, expressed in metaphor and parable. The Garden of Eden was a symbolic place; i.e., the "place" we were before we achieved self-consciousness. Or put another way, the Garden of Eden represents the state of consciousness we were in while we were still like the other animals in the jungle.

Understanding this, we can see that when we (as Adam and Eve) ate of the fruit of the tree of knowledge of good and evil, this eating represented a fundamental change in the nature of our existence. From the point of view of the Christian pulpit we lost our innocence, looked down, saw that we were naked, and experienced shame. To the rational mind, this may not make much sense. But if we view this as a symbolic expression of the evolutionary process we can interpret the elaborate metaphor of the Garden of Eden as a story about the acquisition of the neocortex that caps our reptilian and mammalian brains, giving us the ability to achieve self-awareness, the latest trick of the evolutionary mechanism.

Some may see the Garden of Eden a little differently and say that it isn't a symbolic place on the evolutionary path of humankind, but a spiritual place on the individual's path to finding God—that is, the "place" we were when we were still babes and did not yet know the meaning of good and evil.

To this it should be said, yes, that is also true. It is particularly the nature of symbolic knowledge that it is multifaceted in its meaning, that a symbol may contain more than one truth, and sometimes may contain even seemingly contradictory truths.

WHY SYMBOLIC LANGUAGE IS USED

It might be asked why metaphorical language is used in these writings and not just the straight-forward words as in a textbook.

There are three main reasons. One, the straight-forward words may not exist. The sages who developed the wisdom and the sages who wrote it down knew that there was a difference between the consciousness of people and that of the other animals, but just what the difference was, how to account for it and where to find it, they didn't know. They couldn't talk about the neocortex because they didn't know we had one; and they couldn't talk about acquiring it because they had no idea that we evolved from beings without one. They couldn't talk in a denotative sense because what they wanted to express was known to them in an emotional and psychological sense. As poets have always been at pains to demonstrate, the strictly linear nature of words is inadequate to some tasks.

A further trouble with a purely denotative expression is that such language is subject to an evaluation of its literal truth. As such it must be true in light of today's knowledge as well as yesterday's otherwise the expression will be supplanted. This will, and has, happened again and again. Consequently, few unambiguous factual spiritual (or psychological) statements stand the test of time and come down to us intact. Symbolic or metaphorical statements, because they are inexact and general, are less easily contradicted or in need of correction (they can just be re-interpreted). Consequently they can stand the test of time.

A second problem with the straight-forward statement is that religious ideas are not factual or strictly moral assertions, although such ideas often form the basis for laws and moral rules. If you say something like "do unto others as you would have them do unto you," setting it forward as a moral imperative, they'll always be somebody who will argue, "but what about the guy who, for example, happens to like practical jokes?" As a philosophic assertion, even the golden rule can be seen to have exceptions. If far less generally accepted assertions are made baldly, such as, "self-indulgence leads to unhappiness," there will be people who disagree.

Such assertions tend to invite contradictions or discussions that lead in circles because the real truth to be conveyed is something that is lived and experienced. Any attempt to frame that experience in words is limiting, or it can be an attempt to say something that really can't be said. There are many things we understand, such as how to use our muscles and senses in tandem while walking, that we cannot put into words. There are moods of great power (one recalls Proust) that affect us in ways we cannot adequately express, even after a thousand pages of trying.

Third, a symbol, in one sense, works like a variable in a mathematical equation in that it can stand for something not yet known, allowing us to proceed even though our knowledge is incomplete. Since our knowledge is almost always incomplete, this is very handy indeed.

Consequently, denotative words are not enough, and we must recognize that as we are reading. They are linear representations of a complex four dimensional reality. As Alan Watts expresses it in *The Way of Zen*, "...our conventional words and thoughts are reconstructions of experience in terms of abstract signs." (p. 7)

PSYCHOLOGICAL TRUTH

Another impediment to understanding is to think of religious ideas as philosophic statements, which is something we often do in the West with our rational minds. They are more akin to psychological statements. In fact, it is in religion that one finds the true psychology of human beings. The psychologies taught in our universities are generally short-sighted and so politically correct that they are often wrong, but where they are right they are derivative. (Neuroscience and the relatively new science of evolutionary psychology are exceptions, but their ideas and discoveries are not yet firmly established.)

Even more to the point, the practice of religion itself is a search for the truth about us and our predicament. And this truth is largely a psychological truth. We as people have a problem and that problem does not stem from not having enough to eat (although it sometimes does, but when it does we are not in a religious mood). The real taxing problems of this world are not physical, they are psychological—or more cosmically put, they are spiritual. The people who are not getting enough to eat would beg to differ, but it is their leaders, themselves and others beyond their control whose behaviors are keeping them hungry. And remember in the final analysis it is a belief system that may insist on more mouths than we can feed.

Almost all the great world religions find people in a quandary and tell us how to get out of it. In Christianity, for example, we are in a state of sin and only through the grace of God can we overcome our sins. In Buddhism we are born into a world in which pain and suffering predominate and the goal is to escape from the endless cycle of birth, death and rebirth. The Buddha is said to have been born into a princely environment and to have lived as a youngster an indulged and sheltered life. One day, tradition has it, he wandered outside the castle and saw suffering and death. He realized that such a fate awaited him as well and he saw no permanence in his happiness and so he lost his happiness. These religious experiences are the experiences of us all psychologically speaking.

CHANGE AND THE LACK OF PERMANENCE

Religion can also be seen as a search for something permanent in a constantly changing world. While some religions find permanence in God, others find that the only permanence lies in change itself.

Some religions also come to the conclusion that the nature of ultimate reality is unknowable by us. One might as well expect the goldfish in the goldfish bowl to imagine that there are billions of galaxies each filled with billions of stars when in fact the goldfish can't even see outside the kitchen window.

We are like that goldfish. The deeper we probe into the atom, the more the ultimate reality retreats from us. The further we fling our imagination back in time the more we run up against impossible things. The atom may be infinitely divisible, composed of ever-smaller, ever more nearly fundamental particles, but our ability to perceive and to assimilate these components can't follow very far. Thus we have the quantum and the Planck limit. And what do we suppose is on the other side of the Big Bang?

Our mental and even imaginational limits (if I may) were known long before recorded history. It didn't take us long, even as forest shamans, to leap from the sensible tree we were leaning against to the realization that there was something beyond this world and that something got a lot further away than we could ever imagine very fast, and that "far away" itself got kind of fuzzy after a while, after one ran out of "very far," and "very, very far." And finally to assuage our savage mind, we tried to sum it all up with a great big GOD, or a little bitty "not this, not this," as in the Vedas.

So everywhere man was, if he stopped to think about it—and since he now had self-awareness, thanks to this huge, convoluted neocortex that he grew, he did when he had the time, stop to think about it—he realized he was up against a psychological problem of enormous magnitude, namely the problem of how to live happily in a constantly changing, sometimes hostile, ultimately unknowable, and frankly painful world. The psychological became the spiritual. And for the hard-headed realists and skeptics among my readers—and I hope there are many of you—whenever the word "spiritual" or its equivalent pops up, plug in instead the word "psychological" and little if anything will be lost. Sometimes "spiritual" really is a pretentious word.

But forget about philosophy. The ancients already knew that philosophy, however ingenious, was only more of the same and didn't allow them to come to any ultimate, permanent conclusion leading to serenity and bliss. What was needed was a guide to living, a way to cope, a proper psychological set. And religion was and is the answer. This is one of the things that religion is all about. This, fellow skeptics, is why otherwise rational people have always tried so hard to believe seemingly irrational things.

I should also point out that religion from the standpoint of evolutionary psychology is ipso facto adaptive. That is, those humans that practiced a religion were more effective in leaving viable offspring than those who did not. To repeat the words of the esteemed biologist Edward O. Wilson, "When the gods are served, the Darwinian fitness of the members of the tribe is the ultimate if unrecognized beneficiary." *(On Human Nature* (1978), p. 184)

Why this should be so is apparent: religion made the tribal members feel important (usually as the chosen ones of God) and lent cohesion to the tribe and, quite frankly, made their struggles against the environment and their enemies that much more significant so that they fought harder and won more battles. Even among nation states today one observes that God can usually be found on the side of the victor.

THE EARLIEST RELIGIONS

The earliest religions are lost to us of course since they left no record (aside from a few petroglyphs and small artifacts). The religions since the rise of agriculture however have come down to us in part. We know that the Incas worshiped the sun and so did the Egyptians. We know that certain religious ideas were found to be more agreeable, more "true" (again psychologically) than others, and therefore appeared in more than one religion. The idea of ritual, for example, is common to all religions. The idea of God, nearly so. The ideas of salvation, or *karma*, to pick a couple, are less extensively known. At this moment in fact there is considerable conflict world-wide on whether we believe in *karma* or not, or whether the concept of "sin" is such a good idea. It stands to reason that we can't have both sin and *karma*—or can we? A thousand years from now people may believe in a new concept, a concept that incorporates the best aspects of the notion of sin with those of *karma* and throws out the unnecessary.

Religious knowledge, then, evolves just as everything else does, and the oldest, most experienced religions have been evolving the longest and are psychologically the most advanced and are often the best by the test of time.

The oldest extant great world religion is not a single religion but a combination of various disciplines, all born in India during the rise of agriculture. Elements of this ancient religion, which predates the Vedas and the Brahmans, have come down to us to form the basis for modern Hinduism, Buddhism, Jainism, and Taoism. Some of the ideas have been incorporated into Muslim and Christian, Jewish and other schools of thought as well. We want to examine briefly these ideas and see what they have in common, and especially what they can do for us in our personal struggle to come to grips with our predicament.

Properly said, yoga is the oldest religious discipline. Yogis claim the Buddha as their own, and it can be seen that much of what is modern religion and modern psychology comes from the unknown *siddhas* who predated the Brahmans. (I will leave out the ancient religious traditions of the Middle East since I know little about them, and since what I do know is irrelevant to this discussion.)

HOLY BOOKS

In the bibliography I have listed most of the important books related to yoga that I have read over the last thirty or thirty-five years. I have reviewed and assessed them—it is an annotated bibliography—although some of these books, the Bible and the *Tao Te Ching*, for example, need no assessment, and I have made no comment.

HOW TO READ A SPIRITUAL WORK

The first thing to say (and I'll repeat it even though I said it above) is don't take anything literally. Look for the real meaning. *Feel* for it. Walk a mile in the other guy's shoes and give the author every benefit of the doubt. What the great spiritual communicators, like Jesus and Lao Tzu, for example, have tried to do, through the use of symbol and story, parable and allusion, through the use of contrast and context, with the aid of poetic wording and rhythmic phrasing, is to break out of the prison of mere words and awaken us to the cosmic truths that they feel they have discovered. And it isn't easy—either the expression or the understanding.

The crux of the problem sometimes is that words mean different things to different people—the same words. When Jesus spoke of his "Father" he meant the word with a fervent and fantastic love and adoration that the rest of us can't even imagine, so that the very word "Father" meant something to Jesus so beyond our usual understanding that it's hard for us to appreciate what he said.

And this is the problem that the mystic always faces when trying to share his experience with us: we have to make a special effort to understand and it's not always there. The great mystic communicators (the authors of the Bible, the *Bhagavad Gita*, etc.) try to help us by talking directly to our "hearts" through the use of poetic, rhetorical and symbolic devices.

ADAM AND EVE

To illustrate what I mean let's return to the Garden of Eden. Let's talk about the serpent and the apple. We know—at least those of us who have advanced beyond the know-nothingness of the fundamentalists—that the story of Adam and Eve was meant to be taken symbolically. It was conceived to explain the situation we are in. But what is the situation we are in? The elaborate metaphor of the Garden is an answer to that question.

This is part of what is meant by being "divinely inspired." Sometimes the reader can get much more out of what was written than the authors ever imagined they put into it! True. The point I want so much to get across is that to understand and appreciate—to have any hope at all of comprehending—what a symbolic (and/or poetic) expression means, we have to set aside for the moment our skepticism and find a way to agree with what is being said—better yet to enter into what is being said. This is an essential requirement for reading a religious book. We must be willing—for the moment, for the time being—to believe.

This is not to say that when we're finished reading we have to accept what we've read. Not at all. But while we are reading we must look diligently for ways to believe what we are reading. Without this effort on our part, little or no progress in understanding can be made. It's hard to write it well and it's hard to read it with true understanding, so both writer and reader have to bring with them not only a positive and receptive attitude, but a creative one as well. The reader must use his or her ability to help the writer. The reader must become the highly receptive audience that inspires a great performance even though the performance has already been given.

Now further into the Garden of Eden. It is said that when man ate of the fruit of the tree of knowledge of good and evil he became naked or at least noticed suddenly that he wasn't wearing any clothes. For those of us used to reading the New York *Times* or Matt Ridley or even Dear Abby, this sounds a little preposterous. But look again. What is really being said here is there was a time when we were "innocent"; that is, when we were like the other animals of the forest. We were without self-consciousness, without self-criticism, it might be said, free of guilt and self-doubt. And then we got self-consciousness and ended up taking a new, self-aware look at ourselves and said, "I'm embarrassed by what I see."

As well Adam should have been. Because he was out there trying to steal from and otherwise take advantage of his environment without concern for the consequences and was in fact just a slave to his so-called lower nature, lusting after sex, food and power, and all the time he didn't even know it. But after he ate that forbidden fruit, heaven ended, the Garden dried up, and what was that stuff the serpent served up?

It wasn't just an apple (or a pomegranate). As mentioned above, it was the development of his neocortex—our big, self-aware brain. In a sense we got too smart for our own good; in another, we became an entirely different sort of being, a demigod in the making.

A dog chases after a bitch in heat and has no sense of anything untoward. A man (our demigod in the making) who chases after women without accepting the responsibility or without regard for the consequences is a "sinner." All have sinned and fall short of the glory of God, the Bible says. From the yogic point of view (and from the Buddhist as well) this sex leads only to birth, death and rebirth—the endless cycle of misery. So we ought to be embarrassed. We're clearly up to no good.

RETURN TO THE GRAVEYARD

Another, little symbolic story comes from the tantras. It's actually a ritual—some Middle Eastern fundamentalists would say a satanic ritual. An aspirant is told to take a willing woman to a graveyard at night and have sex with her among the graves.

We can quickly see the rather heavy-handed symbolism here. The sexual act leads to birth which in turn leads to death. By actually performing the ritual, tantrists believe, the symbolic lesson can be brought home forcefully. "Creating karmas" is how the yogis would succinctly describe the act.

Or take this idea from the *Tao Te Ching*. The question is asked, but what is this Way? The answer comes, "The way that can be spoken of is not the eternal Way." No matter what might be pointed to, no matter what might be thought of, the answer is always "not this."

Oh, so beautiful is this Taoist idea. Actually it comes from the Vedas, if we care about precedence, where the question was asked a little differently: "What is God?"; but the answer was the same, "Not this, not this!" And yet we can point to another very familiar idea that is seemingly a direct contradiction in the pantheistic statement that "everything is God." Wherever one may look, whatever one may see, whatever one may think, that too is God!

Yet both of these ideas are true.

We rationalists must accept this and realize the limitations of the Boolean logic.

THE LIMITS OF OUR APPROACH

One of the problems we encounter as we approach cosmic spirituality is that our minds are just too limited to get there. We have difficulty believing and accepting contradictory ideas as true. But in the mind of God (that is a metaphor) both the reverse and the obverse are one and the same, and there is ample room for the thesis and the antithesis. If our minds were better we could, like the Queen of Hearts in *Alice in Wonderland*, believe "as many as six impossible things before breakfast" and still have plenty of room for some serious believing after lunch. Unfortunately we are like the ant who knows only the scent trails between its nest and the latest food. Our minds are trapped in ruts of thought and perception that leave out so much of the cosmos—undreamed of realms within and without—where we cannot venture because of the limitations of our understanding.

The spiritual writings of the sages and the great prophets and the poets are attempts to help us out of our rut and onto the mountain top.

THREE FAMOUS MONKEYS

Let's take another example. Remember the three monkeys who see no evil and hear no evil and speak no evil? To the unaware these little guys are just Kewpie dolls won at the fair. Actually however these three monkeys are spiritual teachers trying to help us see a great psychological truth.

To see no evil is not to close our eyes to the evil that surrounds us. That "evil" is very real, but only in an anthropomorphic sense. (We think it's evil; the AIDS virus, for example, may not agree.) What the advice to "see no evil" really means is to recognize that, in a larger sense, evil seen is in the eye of the beholder.

This spiritual truth is the first understanding of the injunction to "see no evil" and far and away the most important. But on the psychological level we must see no evil because if we see the evil we gain knowledge of it, and in a sense we become a participant in the evil. We might also gain a responsibility to do something about it.

Seeing evil though really implies that we are looking for it. (This is the third truth.) The virtuous being, the saint, the person who loves his fellow man and believes in him and sees only the good in the world sees no evil.

Of course the first point in hearing no evil is not to gossip. If your neighbor says to you so-and-so did such-and-such an evil thing hear it not.

Also of course hearing evil is the same as seeing it. Again if you hear it, generally speaking you are listening for it.

And then there is speak no evil. This is the most important one to follow. Even if we (imperfect creatures that we are) do hear and see some evil, we can still save the situation by speaking it not.

It's funny and ironic that it is monkeys who speak, hear and see no evil; but it is only the very wise person who can achieve the simple behavior of these monkeys.

To put this lesson into yogic terms, we can say: evil seen is a delusion. We think there is evil in the world when it is only our faulty perception.

OUR LIMITED CONSCIOUSNESS

Remember the axiom, to understand all is to forgive all? You don't hear that much anymore, but you will. It's the terse statement of a profound truth, not easily come by, but once known never forgotten. All the evil in the world is a delusion. "You think that you kill, but you slain not," says the Gita.

For me this truth was difficult. I rejected it time and again. I wanted responsibility. I wanted blame (I suppose) and the old accountability. But these ideas too are delusions. We are beings on the way to becoming. We are creatures whose ability to see and understand the world around us is as limited in comparison to objective reality ("what a concept!") as the consciousness of a virus is to us.

Even more so.

We think we reason, but we reason not. We think we do this and we think we do that, but in reality we do nothing at all. We are done.

It's an amazing universe, an amazing world. Our consciousness is just a trick, a trick to keep us in the game. We are trapped within this "consciousness." We think it is so great. We imagine that we are superior to the lesser animals because our consciousness is so much greater (if it is) and how pitiful are the insects who can't think at all and know so little of themselves and their environment. And think of inert rock and stone. Think of the sun. Dead, lifeless, like Mars and the moon.

Ah, such delusions we follow! Such madness we entertain! We, little us, are superior to the sun? The sun "lives" for ten billion years, gives birth to every living thing on this planet, and we with our pitiful three score and ten are superior to the sun?

Believe it not! The truth, we can be sure, is something entirely different from our little suppositions. The sun is probably "alive" in ways we cannot comprehend. Our limited consciousness is undoubtedly whimsical and fleeting in comparison to the mighty reach of the sun. We are dots. The sun is a great majestic entity beyond our comprehension.

"Beyond our comprehension" is usually just a phrase. We've heard it before. But in the case of the sun and its system, it is no mere phrase. The size and attributes of the solar system are so vast that a real appreciation of them lies beyond the reach of our best understanding, and it will remain that way for a long time to come.

Imagine then, how much more beyond our reach is the majesty of God!

Don't even try to imagine. We can't. That's what God is all about. That's part of what the word "God" means from a yogic point of view, and that's why God is referred to as the Ineffable. God is so beyond our comprehension that anything and everything we say about God is simply "not this."

Most people are used to fooling around with demigods and anthropomorphic gods and gods that bring death and destruction upon the earth, and gods that get angry and jealous—Greek gods or Roman gods, Hindu gods or Middle Eastern gods. But such gods are like we are to our kitty cats. We are mighty, but even so the cat knows we aren't all that much. We have our limitations and foibles.

But God has no limitations and the foibles attributed to God are all in our mind.

Chapter 7:
The Classic Texts

EARLIEST WRITINGS

Historically, yoga begins in the Vedas, the most ancient of the Hindu writings; but properly speaking the Vedas are not yogic texts and the unsophisticated yoga found in them is largely incidental to tales of ritual, sacrifice and the expression of an overall pantheism. It is in the Upanishads, the concluding chapters of the Vedas, that we find the first important expressions of yogic philosophy and practice.

Over a hundred Upanishads remain but only ten or eleven are considered important. They form the core of Vedanta, a venerable way of looking at the world that is all but impossible to separate from yoga.

As students we should familiarize ourselves with these principal Upanishads. We should especially read the Katha Upanishad in which the boy Nachiketas, having been given to Death by his father, learns from Yama the secret of rising above death and desire. A highly readable and elegant translation is *The Ten Principal Upanishads* by Shree Purohit Swami and the English poet W. B. Yeats.

Next the student should study the *Bhagavad Gita*, the "Song of the Lord," which is the most beloved of all Hindu scriptures. There are numerous translations available, some in prose, others in verse, some in combination. The Gita is one of the most beautiful books ever written. All of the various schools of yoga try to claim it as their own which is understandable since it is in the Gita that all of the principal yogas find a poetic expression.

After the Gita comes Patanjali's Yoga Aphorisms. Again numerous books have been written on Patanjali's yoga. Iyengar has an instructive, indeed a very detailed translation with extensive commentary. But there are other translations and commentary as well. The classical commentary by Shankaracharya is also available in a number of editions at university and other large libraries. Make a special effort to acquire your own copy of Patanjali's aphorisms because you will want to refer to them often as you go about your practice.

The aphorisms are terse and often ambiguous, so commentaries have always been thought needed. Indeed, Patanjali's text is little more than an outline of practice and theory, but it is the best we have. Scholars believe that the text was used by initiates and teachers of yoga who interpreted and fleshed out the text for their students. There are few public gurus today capable of doing that. After some real experience in the practice of yoga, however, much of what Patanjali says becomes accessible. Unfortunately, Patanjali doesn't elaborate on the individual practices. The only mention he makes of asana, for example, is that it should be steady and pleasurable (but this tells us a lot). It is from Patanjali that we get the famous definition of yoga: "Yoga is the control of the ideas in the mind."

HATHA YOGA TEXTS FROM THE MIDDLE AGES

"*Hatha yoga*" is actually a yoga of health and purification. Many of the purification practices however have been made obsolete by modern sanitation and medical science—thus most yogis no longer practice *dhauti karm* in which a cloth is swallowed to absorb the bile in the stomach, nor do we attempt to clean our intestines in the river. Considering the polluted state of virtually all the rivers in the world, this is just as well. Most of the ideas of *hatha yoga*, of asana, *pranayama* and *kriya* (the cleansing practices) were presumably known during Patanjali's time, but nothing written down has reached us. Patanjali himself did not go into the details. Information about the practice was passed from guru to disciple by word of mouth. Finally in the Middle Ages we come upon books written specifically on the practices of asana, *pranayama* and kriya. When we look at these works, we get a revealing glimpse of what yoga was like before the modern era and we learn something about the evolution of yogic knowledge.

The three most important works to reach us are the *Hathayogapradipika* of Svatmarama, which dates from about the fifteenth century, and the *Geranda Samhita* and the *Siva-Samhita*, which are later.

These books are, if anything even more cryptic than Patanjali's aphorisms. They are also repetitious, sometimes contradictory and written in an "intentional style" mainly for initiates. To be honest, there's not much yoga the modern student can learn from these texts, which is why we have the books by Iyengar, Saraswati, Vishnu-devananda, Feuerstein, etc. Nonetheless almost all the works on *hatha yoga* in existence today are based either directly or indirectly on these antiquated works. For the serious student of yoga perhaps a brief look at them would be rewarding, at least in a historical sense. (You'll probably need access to a university library.) Recently published, however, is Brian Dana Akers' relatively new translation of *The Hatha yoga Pradipika* by Svatmarama, which I highly recommend.

INTENTIONAL LANGUAGE

Sometimes a writer wants to write something for two audiences simultaneously: first a general audience to whom he is introducing his work, and second a special or "knowing" audience he wants to communicate with directly, but without troubling the first audience. Such a writer tends to write in what historians call an "intentional language." The *hatha yoga* books we have been referring to were written in such a manner. Consequently, much of what was said is not available to us today. We haven't the "keys to scriptures," so to speak. Much is available however if we have a good prior knowledge of the subject and use common sense in interpreting what is being said.

To illustrate some of the difficulties, let's begin with the *Hathayogapradipika* by Svatmarama, where we often find the phrase "destroys all disease." Thus Svatmarama says in describing the lotus posture: "This is called *Padmasana* which destroys all disease."

What are we to make of this—and similar, obviously exaggerated, claims?

Part of the meaning of course is symbolic. "Destroys all disease" means the practitioner is preeminently doing the right thing. But this is only part of the meaning. In general what Svatmarama is saying is that while asana is practiced, all "dis-ease" is destroyed and only pure bliss is felt. This is the central accomplishment of yoga: while one is completely fixed in yoga—that is, has achieved the balance of physical, mental and spiritual health that comes from yoga—then one is in a state of ongoing bliss and free from all the diseases of the flesh. If this state lasts until one dies, then one has achieved eternal bliss. In another sense "destroys all disease" is an advertising slogan from India in the Middle Ages.

Svatmarama doesn't limit himself to "destroys all disease," however. In describing what happens when *kundalini* rises, for example, he claims that "death is evaded." Certainly, we can understand that this is true while *kundalini* rises. But there is more to it than that. What Svatmarama is doing is talking in a sort of code: the highest and the best practices evade death, while a really good practice may only "destroy all disease." He has formed a hierarchical and symbolic way of talking. His intent isn't to exaggerate. His intent is to speak in a way that the serious aspirant can understand, the serious student of his time and culture.

This last point is important because it was and is a proper Hindu style to exaggerate. It's expected. This is similar to the Japanese style of being overly polite.

Unfortunately sometimes even learned commentators leave common sense behind when they read the old books. Thus in response to the "death is evaded" statement we find this typical comment (I am using the translation and text edited by Swami Digambarji and Kokaje): Svatmarama does not mean "death of the present body, but escape from the phenomenon of death forever; i.e., from the cycle of birth and death."

But this is an interpretation, a Hindu interpretation. They have missed the hierarchical code that Svatmarama is using and are anxious to explain away what they see as an obvious exaggeration. The conventional Hindu view is that the goal of any and all yogas is freedom from the endless cycle of birth and death. But Svatmarama isn't really interested in that doctrine. He is above all else in his

Hathayogapradipika being practical and trying to communicate. It is the commentators who are thinking about the endless cycle of birth and death.

To take another example: In discussing the *bandhas*, Svatmarama says that "the Yogi becomes a boy of sixteen and is freed from old age," causing our commentators to add the qualification "like" after "becomes" so that the statement reads, "the Yogi becomes like a boy of sixteen..." However the aspiring yogis reading the text or hearing Svatmarama's words know that you don't become a boy of sixteen again; but they understand that because Svatmarama uses this particular way of describing the effects of the *bandhas* that (1) the *bandhas* make the yogi feel younger (and maybe even look younger although the looking doesn't matter at all) and (2) this practice which frees him from old age is better than just curing all disease, but somewhat less in importance to something that evades death.

THE "SECRET" PRACTICES

Svatmarama also says that certain yogic practices are to be kept "secret." What he means is they're to be done in private in the same sense that our toilet is to be conducted in private. There's also the sense that allowing others to see us practice can only lead to trouble because others (who are non-initiates) won't understand what we're doing or why, and their criticism, implied or actual, can do us no good.

It is also true that when something is called secret it may suggest that the practice is pleasurable. Regardless, pleasurable practices are also properly done in private.

This confusion between "secret" and "private" has led to the idea that there exists a whole group of secret yoga practices, known only to initiates. Trading on this misconception, certain writers have penned books with titles like "Sex Secrets of the Yogis Revealed!" etc. There are practices that are well-known in yoga and practices that are less well-known, but none of them are secret. In truth, Svatmarama refers to all of *hatha yoga* as properly a secret, i.e., a private practice.

EUPHEMISM, EXAGGERATION AND PARODY

Svatmarama also speaks euphemistically. For example, he says that if the yogi while performing the *mahamudra* also holds the *vayu* back (the "vital air") and engages the *jalandhara bandha*, what happens is "the *Kundalini* soon becomes straight just as a snake hit by a rod becomes straight." Yes, he's talking about the possibility of getting an erection. Iyengar also suggests as much when he says, (referring to the *mula bandha*) "Even the correct performance...has its dangers. It increases sexual retentive power, thereby tempting the practitioner to abuse that power... All his dormant desires are aroused and become lethal like a sleeping serpent struck with a stick."

Sometimes the exaggerations slip into parody. This is especially true when the talk turns to the psychic powers promised by Patanjali (levitation, invisibility etc.) which the authors knew to be shamanist-type experiences achieved through hypnosis (self- or otherwise) or sleight of hand. Since they used some of the same tricks themselves and knew their value, they sometimes had a laugh at the expense of the over-eager aspirants (as teachers sometimes must because sometimes the students tend to be oh, so serious).

A good example is from the *Siva-Samhita* (III, 101) where it is claimed: "There is no other asana than this (*Siddhasana*) that is prized more in this world. Even the very thought of it saves the yogi from sins."

(Actually this is, in a sense, true: sometimes the "very thought" of doing asana excites my system since it recalls how pleasurable the practice can be!)

Some practices are said to allow the yogi to evade *karma* or to be forgiven for such transgressions as having carnal knowledge of the guru's wife(!). But the topper perhaps is this from Chapter IV, verse 70 of the *Siva-Samhita* in reference to the headstand:

"The yogi who practices this for one *yama* (three hours), conquers death. He is not destroyed even at the time of the final dissolution of the universe!"

As mentioned above, you're not likely to learn much yoga from the old books. They are really just outlines of yoga compiled for teachers to serve as memory aids. The guru tradition of transmitting knowledge orally discouraged lengthy explanations in writing. Also, the same tradition fervently believed (and believes) it is a mistake to tell the student something the student isn't ready to hear.

We don't know what the student is ready to hear and we don't know anything about the final dissolution of the universe, but we do know that yoga has come a long ways from the Middle Ages, at least as far as the written expression goes. The books by Iyengar, Feuerstein, Hittleman, Saraswati, Vishnu-devananda, and others are as superior to the classic texts of the Middle Ages as today's athletes are to those of the last century and for the same reasons. Today's teachers have built on the knowledge of the past. As long as the free exchange of uncensored knowledge continues, yoga will grow and so will our understanding of ourselves.

Chapter 8:
The Far Side of the Moon

When the best student hears about the way
He practices it assiduously;
When the average student hears about the way
It seems to him one moment there and gone the next;
When the worst student hears about the way
He laughs out loud.
If he did not laugh
It would be unworthy of being the way.

—*Tao Te Ching* XLI, 90 (translation by D.C. Lau)

"REALITY"

The world is not as we think it is. Our view of the world is essentially an illusion, served up to us by the evolutionary process to allow us to function at the surface of our biosphere.

The view we have of reality ("Reality—what a concept!" joked the comedian Robin Williams) is not reality. It is a window into the great elusive "way things are" sufficient for our day-to-day purposes, sufficient for us to get around on this planet and to get enough to eat, to avoid violent death and to return our kind to the earth.

An orange is not orange. An apple is not red. It is only our perception that is orange and red. The colors are an experience.

Ours is not however an arbitrary reality, but properly speaking, a subsistence reality, a reality foisted on us by our needs. We need to see oranges as orange and apples as red—and oranges and apples as part of the same process need for us to see them as orange and red. They need for us to smell them sweet and taste them full of sugar, for that is part of their reality. An especially interesting book that explores this biological truth in depth is *The Botany of Desire: A Plant's-Eye View of the World* (2001) by Michael Pollan.

Green grass and green trees, green plants and especially the new greens of spring appeal wonderfully to our senses. Hold us long in a sterile environment of gray stones and concrete streets and we cry out for a glimpse of blue sky and green grass and the sound and smell of running water. Go to the mountains and feel refreshed. Go to the seashore and be renewed. These are the things that nature does to us.

We are creatures in concert with nature. We are beings inseparable from the universe around us. We could not exist in isolation. We both feed on and are fed on by the world around us.

For an eagle the reality of the world is much like ours. The eagle, despite its great wings and its relatively light weight (allowing it to fly!), cannot go through mountains and must dodge the hard trunks of trees, just as we must. But to the eagle the air is something very substantial. It billows up sometimes (near the sea cliffs or around buffs on the plains). The eagle pushes against the air and soars. The eagle stretches out its wings and glides. And there is so much for the eagle to see and it sees so far. It sees everything we could see but more because its eyes are better. The edges around objects are sharp and crisp. Detail can be seen from a great distance. Colors are bold and contrasts are clear. In the ability to see, the eagle is very much like us, but better. But the eagle does not see the bottom of the ocean, nor the far side of the moon.

WHAT WE SEE IS ONLY A PARTIAL REALITY

Contrast the mole. There are no colors in its world. There are mighty smells and there is the ever present feel of the earth, now moist and soft, now dry and hard. There is only the barest sensation of sky, a nervous sensation no doubt. Clouds do not exist. Oh, but how pungent the odor of radishes and dandelion root! How the mole is surrounded by these beautifully monstrous smells! They are everywhere. Can't you just smell them?

The cat does not see colors. Objects have a fuzzy quality compared to what the eagle sees. But, oh, the urgent reality of the scent markings and the sound of the exciting rustle in the leaves!

Somewhere off in a distant galaxy, or perhaps even on a planet revolving around a nearby star, there may be creatures who see the world primarily as energy and light, or as cosmic waves and gamma rays; but probably not because what is the necessity, the evolutionary necessity, for them to see gamma rays? We see what we need to see. But what we need to see is not reality, or at least it is only a small part of the reality there is to see and experience. And indeed it can be misleading.

Astronomers now look into the distant heavens not through visual telescopes (for the most part) but through radio telescopes and x-ray telescopes and infrared telescopes because they have found there is so much more to see in those wave lengths. Our visual wave lengths, the visual wave lengths through which we see the world, are only a small part of the vast spectrum of vibrations that emanate from the objects of the universe. The reality revealed through these wave lengths is both similar to and different from the reality seen only through the visible spectrum. What is "real" then depends on who is doing the looking and the living and how and why they are looking and living.

Chapter 9:
Physical Health: The Eater and the Eaten

Everything begins with physical health. This was recognized by Patanjali and has been reaffirmed by all the important works on yoga. For our purposes we shall begin with diet and the question of vegetarianism.

VEGETARIANISM?

Most books on yoga recommend a vegetarian diet and some insist on it. One reads for example that meat is full of germs, "millions per square inch." But there are "germs" everywhere, all around us, on everything we touch. The germs on a steak are very good at feeding on dead flesh (which is why they are there—again part of the natural order of things) but they haven't much chance of multiplying in a healthy body. For the most part they are not going to affect us because we are going to digest them along with the steak. (It's true their toxins can affect us, so our food should be fresh.)

Held in high regard is the traditional Hindu diet which consists mainly of vegetables, fruits, grains, milk, clarified butter and sweets. Even this diet can be abused however. One Hindu swami in recommending it smiled through obviously false teeth, which made me wonder: did he lose his teeth because they had become decayed (from the toxins of the bacteria that lived on the foods he ate—not likely) or did he lose his teeth to periodontal disease (from the toxins of the bacteria on his teeth, caused by not brushing and cleaning the teeth and gums properly)? In either case, it wasn't the diet that was at fault, but the way the swami handled the diet.

I should also point out that the Inuit people of the north get by on a diet that is almost exclusively meat and blubber—or they used to before we started shipping pizza, Spam and Pepsi-Cola to the Arctic. If they were to suddenly start eating the "healthy" Hindu diet they might very well lose their teeth as well. But let's begin this argument at the beginning.

We ourselves are food. Yogis in fact call this realm we live in the "food sheath." Whenever we eat we are eating something that was previously alive. Therefore, aside from the nutritional and aesthetic aspects of food, there is the purely moral. For the yogi this is a significant consideration—but not an overriding one. It should never be forgotten that however we may view the process of eating other living things, it is our nature to eat them and in turn to be eaten. We often forget that we are eaten by microorganisms when we die; and if our bodies are cremated we are eaten by the fire, our ashes to return to the earth as food for plants.

The fact that many of us view eating and being eaten as disagreeable or even repulsive is prejudice—a result of socialization. It is something we were taught or picked up from the culture. The yogi sees this as part of the delusion he is striving to overcome, the *maya*, the cosmic dance of illusion that veils the truth from us. To anticipate my argument, put it this way: our morality falls far short of God's morality, so let's not give ourselves airs by presuming to know better than what we see all around us.

COULD WE LIVE ON NECTAR ALONE?

Nonetheless, following the universal moral precept of doing unto other living things as we would want them to do unto us, which includes the idea of *ahimsa*, a Sanskrit word that suggests not merely nonviolence but "the positive and comprehensive love that embraces all creation" (Iyengar, p. 513), perhaps we should eat something that doesn't injure or otherwise harm the plant or animal. Is this possible?

The purest attempt that comes to mind is to live by eating only nectar gotten from flowers. This nearly pure energy food is manufactured by the plant for the sole purpose of feeding insects, bats and birds as an inducement to get them to pollinate its flowers. In no sense does eating the plant's nectar harm the plant.

Unfortunately it would take an enormous number of flowers and an incredible amount of work to harvest them to feed creatures as big as people. In addition, sweet nectar is for us an incomplete food.

Much the same can be said about eating fruit (our next attempt). Although the calories are vastly more accessible, even the most plentiful and well-orchestrated purely fruit diet would, like the nectar diet, be insufficient to sustain human life.

So we have to look further, and I am beginning to suspect we may have to "compromise" our moral view. Fruits and certain vegetables obviously were created by the plants to feed mobile animals so that the animals might more widely distribute their seeds. We must make a distinction, however, between fruits and seeds, the latter being the actual reproductive instruments of the plant and therefore less morally agreeable as food since if we ate all the seeds the plant would not reproduce at all.

DO PLANTS WANT TO BE EATEN?

But of course that is precisely the point. The plant in manufacturing so very many seeds (think of rice and wheat, or the nut meats of trees) has assured itself that some of those seeds, because of the imperfect ability of the animals to fully utilize them, will survive and grow. Some plants (especially nut-bearing trees) typically go through cycles of scarcity and plenty so as to make sure that during the years of sudden plenty there will be more seeds around than all the animals can possibly eat, followed (cleverly and brutally) by years of abrupt scarcity when the tree produces none or few nut meats, leaving the animals dependent on them to die.

So the plant has adjusted to having more than its fruit eaten. It's as if the plant says, "You want to eat my seeds? Fine. I will just produce more of them and so long as you agree to leave some uneaten and carry them away from me, I won't care. However, to insure that I am not taken advantage of, I will occasionally cut your numbers with a dearth."

I would like to note here that the plant "knows" (in an evolutionary sense) what it is doing and can protect itself from animals and in fact has pulled off an amazing accommodation by embracing its "enemies" and getting them (the animals) to help it with its reproduction through pollination and seed dispersal.

After nectar and fruits and seeds and nuts come the leaves, stems and other parts of the plants themselves. When we eat spinach, for example, we eat the entire (immature) plant. The plant did not plan it that way, but of course this was going on long before we humans came upon the planet. The plants had to adjust to the herbivores, many of whom would eat the entire plant. In defense the plant did as it did with its seeds: it made more of itself than could possibly be eaten, or put some of itself under ground or otherwise out of reach. Dandelions are typical of such plants: note their long and tough tap roots and the fact that their seeds are very small so that they may escape the notice of the animals that eat their leaves.

PROTEINS

Next we come to animal products, beginning with milk and then eggs. One of the difficulties of a purely vegetarian diet is to get enough available and easily digested protein. (This is not a problem for most people in the developed world, of course.) Vegetables and fruits are low in protein content. Furthermore some of the proteins available in such (fairly) rich plant protein sources as potatoes, grains, nuts and legumes are incomplete proteins and cannot be properly utilized by the human body unless they are taken in unison with other also incomplete (but complementary) proteins. This is one of the reasons that beans eaten with corn or bacon or cheese taste so much better to our palates than just beans alone. The protein in beans alone is incomplete; the protein in corn is also incomplete, but is complementary with the bean protein so that eaten together the body is able to use the proteins in both plant foods.

Incidentally, some authorities now believe we can live on an incomplete protein source since "the body is clever enough to find missing essential amino acids...from the vast numbers of bacteria that inhabit the lower intestinal tract or from the vast numbers of cells that slough off the lining of the digestive tract every day." I have this from Andrew Weil, *Eating Well for Optimum Health: The Essential Guide to Food, Diet, and Nutrition* (2000), p. 104.

This quibble aside, it is fairly obvious that our taste will tell us that some diets are incomplete as regards not only proteins, but vitamins, fiber, etc. Therefore it is not enough to judge our diet on the basis of moral precepts alone. We must also consider taste because taste is the body's natural way to lead us to proper nutrition. (Setting aside for the moment how modern unnatural foods have "fooled" our tastes and can lead us astray.)

For pre-agricultural peoples the question of vegetarianism did not arise. They didn't have storehouses of rich grains and nut meats to serve them. They couldn't preserve eggs and they didn't yet know how to preserve milk by making it into cheese or yogurt. In fact, they couldn't even preserve a bountiful harvest of nut meats since they had no way of preventing them from getting rancid or being eaten by pests while the tree, using its trick mentioned above, was unproductive the next year.

So early humans ate whatever and whenever they could. They were not vegetarians. They were (and we are) omnivores. They ate plant foods. They ate insects and lizards and woolly mammoths. They ate what was available in their environment and we can guess that the moralizing they did about it was scant. As people became agricultural their food habits changed. They learned how to store seeds over the winter and plant them the next spring. They learned how to domesticate animals, to use them for labor and to provide food in the form of milk, blood and meat. Now they could make some very fine moral distinctions if they so chose—and of course they did and we do.

In India cows are not eaten, and in the Middle East pigs are not eaten. The reasons for this have less to do with morality than is usually supposed. The underlying reason Hindus do not eat cows relates to the unique place that the cow occupies in the socioeconomic culture of traditional India. It should especially be noted that it is better for most Indian farmers to keep their cows during a period of drought than to eat them because when the rains do come again they'll need them to plow the fields. In fact, it has been shown (see Marvin Harris' *Cows, Pigs, Wars and Witches: The Riddles of Culture*) that the economic value of a cow used in this manner (while also using its milk for food and its dung for firewood) is greater for the farmer than if he slaughtered the animal.

In the Middle East, the pig is not generally eaten (it is little husbanded in fact) because in addition to being ill-suited to the climate, feeding the pig would cause people to give up the very foods we ourselves need to eat and the loss in food value through the middle man of the pig's body would be a direct loss to us. In areas where the pig is eaten—especially in Polynesia where there is a very real shortage of available protein and a surplus of plant foods—it is worthwhile for the people to feed their vegetable foods to the pig in exchange for its rare protein and fats.

The lesson here is that we should eat what is pleasing to us as individuals. Our attitude should be one of thankfulness and reverence both to God for the food and to the food itself. When we approach food from this point of view, already we have taken great strides toward eating properly. The question of whether to follow a vegetarian diet or not then becomes one of individual choice. As Iyengar so wisely expresses it in the Introduction to *Light on Yoga*:

> *Food, the supporting yet consuming substance of all life is regarded as a phase of Brahman. It should be eaten with the feeling that with each morsel one can gain strength to serve the Lord...Whether or not to be a vegetarian is a purely personal matter as each person is influenced by the tradition and habits of the country in which he was born and bred.*

But if eating meat is offensive to you, for whatever reason, you shouldn't do it. True, it is a little more difficult to maintain a proper diet when one is a vegetarian, mainly because one has to balance protein-containing vegetable and cereal foods properly in order to get an adequate supply of usable protein, and there is an additional strain on the digestion. But in today's food-rich environment that task should not be difficult.

WHERE WE CAN GO WRONG WITH FOOD

For primitive people there were a number of pitfalls. They could poison themselves. We are not likely to do that (at least not at one setting). They could miss out on an essential nutrient because of a too-narrow diet and get scurvy or beriberi. We are unlikely to do that. They could find themselves in a vast grassland during an extended drought and starve to death. (Tragically this still happens.) They could ingest parasites along with their food (tapeworms, trichinosis, etc.). We, at least in the Western temperate zones, seldom do that. But the one thing they were unlikely to do was to poison themselves through overeating, especially through the long-term systematic overeating of fats and over-refined carbohydrates. This is precisely what we do.

Our Stone Age ancestors couldn't kill themselves the way we do because they were too poor. Without agriculture and the domestication of fat animals, the only overeating primitive people could accomplish was short-term—as for example when the nut meats or fruits ripened or they fell an elephant. We don't kill ourselves with too much gorging at one setting because we have over the millennia developed built-in controls. We lose our appetites long before any harm can set in. But our systems haven't had the opportunity to develop built-in controls for the systematic, long-term overeating that is a major cause of disease in the Western world today because such a rich year-round diet was seldom if ever available to our prehistoric ancestors.

Our bodies are therefore having trouble telling us that that extra helping is wrong. We get a hint because overindulgence makes us dull and lethargic, but we sleep it off with seemingly no ill-effects the next day. It is only after some longer period of time has passed that the fat begins to accumulate and we realize that something is wrong. What yoga does is to make us so aware of our body (and so selfish about our comfort) that we are not satisfied with being overweight and we are not satisfied with feeling bloated after a meal and we are not satisfied with having to carry around so many useless pounds of fat. We become sensitive to even a little overeating.

One of the reasons we eat that extra helping or take that unneeded snack has to do with the world we live in. Everywhere we are inundated with advertisements for food: in magazines, on billboards, on television, on the radio, at public events, on the Web— we live in a veritable sea of ads telling us to eat this, eat that, do it NOW and do it MORE, eat, eat, EAT!

Another reason is that the manufacturers and processors of food have spent untold amounts of money to artificially entice us to eat denatured foods leaving our bodies hungry for the real thing, the complete food, forcing us to eat twice to satisfy ourselves. They do this with chemicals and coloring agents, little enhancers that fool Mother Nature. Most commercial breakfast cereals are little more than starch and sugar. Diet soft drinks are nothing but chemical water. These "foods" have no place in a healthy diet. In the case of the former, we'll have to eat some kind of whole food so that our body can get the protein and other nutrients it needs and we will have to overeat to pay the nutritional debt we incurred by eating the empty calories in the first place. In the case of the diet drinks the body will have to process the chemicals out.

I have noticed that people who drink diet drinks usually eat something along with the drink. I wouldn't be surprised to learn that the soft drink manufactures have added a chemical to induce a false appetite. Or it could be that if a drink tastes like it should contain some sort of energy food and doesn't, it makes the body hungry for that missing food. In any case people who drink diet soft drinks are seldom slim.

FOOD AS A DRUG

Our attitude towards food does not end with the moral and nutritional. We should also ask ourselves why we are eating from an emotional point of view. Or more precisely, how does eating fit in with our life in general? Do we live to eat or eat to live or are we somewhere in-between? It would be foolish to deny the body the great pleasure of eating. Since we have to eat it's wise and healthful to enjoy it. But eating, like so many other things in life, is fraught with danger. If eating becomes too important in our lives then the quality of our life suffers. We may become fat; we may spend an inordinate amount of time and energy in digestion. Food may become a drug. We may become dependent on food and the feelings of satiety like a heroin addict depends on his fix. Food may control our moods and preoccupy our minds. Before dinner we may be grim, short-tempered. After dinner we may become expansive, "high." For the yogi all of this is to be avoided. Steadiness and even-temperedness are to be desired. And so dinner can be, quite frankly, quite a problem.

The gourmand, having overeaten again reclines in his easy chair and wonders sleepily and only half-facetiously, "Is there life after dinner?" But for the yogi the question is how to get around this terrible necessity for dinner. How do we as yogis de-emphasize the importance of eating in our lives?

When you don't do drugs, when you have forsaken lust, when you don't gamble or seek power (and such is the yogic stance), other things in your life tend to take on a greater significance. We tend to look forward to eating. When this happens we are inviting trouble because like drugs and video games, eating can be addictive.

What the yogi would like to do is skip dinner entirely—eat nothing at all. Failing this we as yogis try to eat moderately and not very often. Ideally for some people once a day is enough. Or, depending on our constitution, we might take several small "meals" a day, consisting of only a piece of fruit or a small portion of nuts at any one time. And nothing fancy. Whatever is available, rice and vegetables, some cheese and bread. If thoughts of food come to our minds we gently brush them aside. But all of this still doesn't solve our problem. We still lust after food and we know it.

S. K. Majumdar in his *Introduction to Yoga* (p. 121) tells a story about his days as a wandering ascetic, living day to day on handouts in the Himalayas. Almost always he got by on one bowl of food a day, usually just rice or potatoes or bread and lentil soup. Often he went to sleep hungry. Occasionally however a rich sheth from the plains would come up into the mountains and bring with him some food for the wandering holy men. Majumdar recalls:

> *To be honest we generally looked forward to such visits. One afternoon, I vividly recall, as I was reading, sitting near the door of my hut to get the light, I overheard a conversation among my neighbors who said that a sheth had arrived the day before and was going to give a good feast for us. At its mention, to my surprise and embarrassing self-revelation, my heart jumped and began to pound wildly at my scrawny chest. I could not have dreamed before that food could stir such emotions.*

Make no mistake about it: it is not easy to come to grips with this terrible necessity to eat. Imagine what it would be like for the alcoholic who, in trying to stay on the wagon, nonetheless had to drink alcohol every day! When it comes to food, we are in that situation. What is the solution? The Buddha recognized this problem and his famous solution is one we should follow today: moderation. Moderation in eating. Moderation in the importance that food plays in our lives. Moderation in the time spent eating or planning to eat. Moderation in thoughts about eating.

The problem of eating is very much like the entire problem of existence in a nutshell! As the Buddha found, neither the ascetic approach of austere self-denial works, nor does short-sighted self-indulgence. It is only through right knowledge and the middle path of moderation that we can learn to live in harmony with our bodies.

So when we sit down to eat we should remind ourselves that we are both food and the eater of food, and give a prayer of thanks and ask forgiveness.

WEIGHT CONTROL

More important than what we should eat (provided we follow a balanced diet) is how much. The main thing wrong with the modern diet is not its overemphasis on fats and meat (which is certainly bad enough) but that there is too much of it. We simply eat too much. Almost everyone in the United States of an adult age is overweight. Some of us just a little, most of us ten or twenty pounds or more. We just can't stay away from the table or keep the refrigerator door shut. We just can't drive past that McDonalds. Aside from the fact that it is morally reprehensible to eat more than we need, it is just plain unhealthy. An obese person will encounter difficulty in achieving even the beginnings of yoga. The asanas will be difficult if not impossible. Meditation will be short and fitful at best.

Eating is one of the lusts and that is why the ancient yogis recommended one bowl of food a day and no more. We think of three squares a day as the proper way to eat, but this may be a mistake for some of us. It just makes us have food on the brain and in the body more than is necessary. Eating three full meals a day may not allow our digestive organs enough of a rest from their very demanding work while taking energy away from us for other tasks. Of course three moderate to small meals a day might be ideal for some of us.

But let's not get ahead of ourselves. One of the reasons that we have come to yoga is to help us to control our weight. And to be honest and fair, in today's society that can be a very difficult task indeed. For the *sadhu* of the forest who had to go begging for his meals, it was a lot easier. It was no problem to stay trim under those circumstances. When I used to watch the "reality" show "Survivor" on television, the one thing I was struck with more than anything else was just how easily contestants lost weight, and just how much they yearned for the foods they had temporarily left behind. It is easy to see that for modern people with a Burger King or a supermarket close by and with food ads everywhere to entice us, the problem of maintaining a proper weight is raised to a new level of difficulty.

It is true that once you are firmly established in yoga your weight will probably take care of itself. Until that time comes I want to present a few tips that have helped me over the years. I am a bit of a gourmet. I love to eat and I take a lot of pleasure in cooking and eating and I enjoy wine with my evening meal. And I've enjoyed uncounted hours reading about food and nutrition. One of the reasons I have a good appetite is that I absolutely refuse to eat anything I don't want to eat. I know eating is going to be a pleasurable experience because I plan it that way.

EATING ERRORS

Eating out, for example, is almost always a mistake. Unless you eat at a very fine establishment you're liable to be disappointed, especially if you're a stickler (as I am) for freshness and balance without chemical additives. It's a shame that restaurants, especially fast food restaurants, aren't required to list their ingredients. Until they are (and even when they are!) you can be sure they are adding things you wouldn't add yourself. Falling into the habit of going to the local hamburger joint for lunch is a mistake. Pack your lunch instead. That way you eat exactly what you want to eat and exactly the right amount—without thinking about it. Go to a park or curl up in a chair and listen to some music while you eat lunch. Enjoy pleasant company with someone you have encouraged to bring his or her lunch also. Occasionally you can eat out for lunch or dinner, but only occasionally because there is plenty of danger (nutritionally and gastronomically) when you eat out.

If you don't like to prepare your own food maybe you should rethink whether you have the proper attitude for becoming a yogi. I've noticed that people who only like to eat what someone else has prepared for them and served to them, are many of the same people who have digestive and weight problems. They are confusing the act of eating with the ritual of being served. They are looking for gratification of another kind. That kind of gratification is fine—but don't mistake it for lunch!

And do not take food for granted. Eating should be a spiritual event. Take time to eat—do not hurry! Give yourself a moment to appreciate the fact that you are about to eat. Say a prayer. Admire the food. And when you eat it, eat slowly, savoring every bite. Chew it well. Never eat when you aren't hungry. Never. And don't let a tired old voice tell you that you have to eat "to keep your strength up." If you are working on an empty stomach and it is bothering you, stop what you are doing and take time out to eat something small. If you are in a tremendous hurry to get back to work, make it even smaller. But whatever it is (an apple, a small apple, lovingly eaten is excellent), make sure you eat it slowly. After you are more experienced in yoga you will be able to just do an asana or a *pranayama* and return to your tasks without having to eat at all. Your body, properly tuned, can live very well for many hours on its own stored resources, and it does so serenely in the context of proper diet and exercise.

And measure your food before cooking or eating. That way you lay out the proper amount ahead of time before you are into the pleasure of eating the food (and can easily lose your objectivity). Also you know how much there is left to eat at any given time and you know your relationship with the amount you are going to eat. By the way, when you are measuring out your proper allotment, watch out for the "eyes are bigger than the stomach" phenomenon.

SOME GOOD EATING HABITS

You will want to set aside times when you have agreed with your body not to eat anything at all. I call such times "mini-fasts" and they might consist of skipping lunch so that you have the hours from the time you get up until the evening meal in which you eat nothing at all (or perhaps just some non-sugared, fresh juice). When I skip lunch I am aware that I am living off of my accumulated fat reserves and I get into a blissful feeling with no hunger. Try it yourself. With a positive attitude you'll find that the feeling of "weakness" that you may have often associated with meal skipping is actually just a momentary lull that will be followed (if you allow it) by a mood of serenity and easy endurance. Later on in this book I will describe how you can program yourself with yoga postures to quickly tell your body to "switch over" to internal sources of energy so that the lull can be avoided altogether. (Incidentally, in this regard I am sometimes amused when I read of the sacrifice and suffering of those on a political fast. Actually, fasting can be very pleasurable and quite healthy if not overdone.)

Instead of skipping lunch you might skip breakfast; but instead of gorging yourself at lunch, make an agreement with yourself to eat a little later on and make sure it is a moderate meal orchestrated not with food and lots of it, but with a very beautiful approach. In the French manner I sometimes take a leisurely dinner, eating one course at a time slowly with great appreciation so that my digestion is excellent and I am satisfied without overeating.

Another thing you'll want to do is to stop eating when your stomach is only half or two-thirds full instead of to the brim. It's widely known that our hunger mechanism doesn't shut off until sometime after we are full, but if we stop eating before we are full, the hunger mechanism will shut off in due course although the stomach is only two-thirds full. Also it's good to remember that digestion can be hard work. The more you eat the more of your vital energies must be given over to the digestion of food and the less there is for other things.

LONGER FASTS

I've recommended mini-fasts above, fasts lasting anywhere from six to eighteen or so hours. (Think of Muslims who fast from sunup to sundown during Ramadan.) Fasts of a longer duration are usually unnecessary and fall under the heading of extreme behaviors that are to be avoided for success in yoga. The Buddha himself is our authority here. One of his major discoveries was that asceticism and mortifications do not lead to *nirvana*. However, for some persons longer fasts may be valuable, just as some persons can run marathons without ill effect. The problem with long fasts is that one may come to depend on them for weight regulation, and thereby fall into a pattern of feast and famine leading to disruptions and mood swings not conducive to mental equilibrium. Some people even become "addicted" to fasts and only feel completely serene when they are on one. Fasting can be very pleasurable, but unfortunately sooner or later one must return to eating. If you are the sort of person who can make that transition smoothly and without disruptive or ill effects, then fasting might be for you.

Fasting of course will clean out your system. In ancient Indian where yoga grew up most people harbored parasites, so fasting was a wise practice indeed. In the modern society, where parasites are less of a problem, fasting will not be as valuable.

Fasting in order to clean out your insides and remove toxins from your body is usually unnecessary. True, it is better to fast than to go on overeating, but it is superior yet to eat less often and more wisely.

MAKING A LIST OF FOODS EATEN

It might be a good idea right now to take a break from reading and write down what you have eaten so far today. Try to recall what you ate yesterday and write that down also. Be specific: What kind of cookies—chocolate chip or oatmeal? How many potatoes? Of what size? Start from the moment you got up and see if you can recall everything you ate. Keep the list handy to compare the foods on it with the foods mentioned in the next chapter where we get more specific about what is good and what isn't. And tomorrow start a new list and write down as you eat everything you eat tomorrow. If you're like most people that second list will be longer than the first and will remind you of things you left off the first list. You might want to circle the foods you left off because they are probably the key foods in your diet—foods that cause you to gain weight, foods that you eat out of habit or for emotional reasons. They are foods you forgot. Perhaps there is a good reason you forgot them.

Chapter 10:
Physical Health: Making Food Choices

GOOD FOODS/BAD FOODS?

All naturally occurring foods that can be digested by people are "good" foods. Foods (like grass, for example) that are not readily digestible are "bad," as well as foods that are not fresh, foods that are denatured, adulterated, over processed and/or over cooked (under cooked too; beans and potatoes, for example, are largely indigestible unless the walls of their cells are broken down by heat). Again, it is not so much a question of what to eat but when and how much. Some foods are, nonetheless, more compatible with people than other foods. Or perhaps I should say, some foods can be eaten more often than other foods.

EMPTY CALORIES VERSUS COMPLEX CARBOHYDRATES

Our bodies and our tastes are very much attracted to what nutritionists refer to as empty calories, that is, foods that are sugar or starch and little else: candy, sodas, Twinkies, etc. There is nothing wrong with these foods as such. The problem is they are just calories and little else. We probably do not remember our first taste of sugar. But I heard a story the other day about a family that had raised their two-year-old on whole foods as much as possible. The father described watching his son tasting pure sugar for the first time. He said the expression on his son's face was such an astonishment, the child looking at the father as if to say, "Why have you been keeping this incredibly delicious stuff from me?"

The tastes of children tend to focus in on bland sweet and starchy foods because the evolutionary mechanism knows that such foods contain ready energy and are not likely to be poisonous. Children are very careful about eating anything that tastes different from their family experience (which is generally safe) as well as anything that tastes "strange." This is a mechanism that grows less demanding as we grow older and gain experience and can rely on that experience.

These delicious empty calories served up by the great food conglomerates who have taken pains to refine them ever so finely are easily digested and go into our bloodstreams quickly, producing a rise in blood sugar level, which gives us a pleasant glow. This glow is temporary however and is often followed by a low, making us irritable. Complex carbohydrates—whole wheat flour, brown rice, potatoes, vegetables, fruits, etc.—are digested more slowly and result in less fluctuation in our blood sugar level. Our bodies are used to complex carbohydrate foods because they have had a long evolutionary history with them. Not so with the highly refined empty calories.

But this is only one problem with such foods. The next problem is we have to eat something else in addition so that our bodies might have the proper nutrients. With complex carbohydrate foods the need is much less. Potatoes and whole wheat for example contain oils and proteins, vitamins and minerals. Whether we eat a slice of bleached white bread or not we will have to eat virtually the same amount of other foods to gain the proper nutrition. In doing so it is very easy to take in too many calories (and very hard not to). Those empty calories are a burden on the system.

A third problem is that diets high in processed carbohydrates are low in fiber and lead to constipation and colon troubles. To eat the white bread we have to add fiber to our diet. Wouldn't we be much better off eating whole grain bread (which has the fiber) in the first place?

We would indeed. However it is possible for our bodies, being flexible eating machines, to eat some empty calories every day and be just fine as long as we eat the proper accompanying foods. Undoubtedly, there is an approximate but flexible number of empty calories that we can get away with eating each day with no ill effects. Indeed, properly orchestrated, such foods can be valuable since they are easily digested. Is the proportion of empty calorie foods that we can safely eat one-half, one-third, one-fourth or less of our total intake? The answer depends on the individual and his or her unique digestive and nutritional needs. After some experimentation each of us can arrive at our own level of harmonious intake. As a guide, though, it is good to remember that empty calorie foods should be thought of as dessert and the amount eaten should be small compared to the entire meal.

Another likely problem with highly processed, denatured foods is that they may be lacking in micro nutrients, some of which may not even be known to science. Eating a variety of whole, fresh foods is the safe and sane way to go.

Instead of going through these complexities it's much better to avoid processed carbohydrates as much as possible and instead eat complex carbohydrates. When that is done our tastes and our feeling of being satisfied will be an accurate reflection of reality and a healthful diet will be easier.

I should add that it is now thought that many of us are "carbohydrate intolerant," or "carbohydrate insensitive"—that is, unable to eat carbohydrates in moderate amounts, a state of affairs similar to being an alcoholic except that the drug is not alcohol, but carbs. The idea here is that it is not fats that are the main enemy of health for people in the industrialized world (as we have so long been taught) but carbohydrates, especially highly processed ones.

This is indeed a revolutionary idea, or at least it was when it was first expressed some years ago. Fat people are not fat because they eat too much fat. They are fat because they eat too many carbohydrates. When you think about it, especially from the point of view of evolutionary biology, it suddenly makes enormous sense. What was it in the prehistory that we humans never had enough of to overindulge in? Not meat, and for many cultures, not fat, but carbohydrates. There were no fields of amber grain waiting to be harvested and made into flour and bread. There were no rice patties or acres of potatoes. Humans could fell a mammoth or an elephant seal once in a while and load up on meat and fat until they were sick of it, but there is no way they could have eaten enough wild wheat or barley to get sick of it. The sheer caloric expense of harvesting low-yield natural grains by hand prohibited any overdosing. It wasn't until the rise of agriculture about ten thousand years ago that we ever had enough of a carbohydrate to call it a staple of diet. Consequently, we are to some extent carbohydrate intolerant and some of us very much so.

FATS AND OILS

Fats are our richest source of food energy, although this energy is not as readily available to our bodies as is carbohydrate energy.

Incidentally, one of the reasons for the tradition of dessert is that the readily available sugars in the dessert supply the energy to digest the more complex foods, especially fats and oils, without the body having to dip into its reserves, allowing us to more readily layer fat on top of fat. The desire for dessert (apart from the established habit) is a tip-off that the meal we have eaten probably has too much fat in it. Our body is saying to us: let's have some ready energy now because it's going to be awhile before I can unlock the energy from those fats and oils you just ate. Typically if our body isn't given its "fix" of quick energy it may punish us with a little mood depression or a "weak" feeling, and if it does get its fix it rewards us with the "high" we usually experience with dinner. Again a properly orchestrated meal centered around a complex carbohydrate food like brown rice or potatoes or a whole wheat bread, or better yet a variety of vegetables and fruits, allows us to level out these hills and valleys and avoid the attendant mood swings.

Although fats are rich in calories they are devoid of protein and fiber and are low in other nutrients. Our bodies need fats to function properly though and so some fat must be eaten. The amount in the modern diet unfortunately is too much. Many people in America and Europe get more than half their calories from fats and oils. A proper proportion would be more like one-fifth. Fried foods and fatty meats are the main culprits. If we cut out all fried foods and ate only lean meats, fish and poultry, we would get more than enough fat in our diet from those foods plus grains, nuts, milk and cheeses.

SALT

Too much salt is another difficulty for some people and again this often comes from eating processed foods. Manufacturers habitually add salt to just about everything they process—from breakfast cereals to frozen vegetables, to almost all canned foods, to processed meats and cheeses. They do this because we get used to a certain level of salt intake and our foods taste bland without the salt. (We have conditioned ourselves.) Moreover, salt tends to stimulate us, and manufacturers like to stimulate their customers.

However the stimulation passes and salt is needed next time to trigger the "lift." How much better it would be if we got into the habit of using less salt in the first place. Our bodies would soon adjust to a lesser level of intake and everything would taste just fine without added salt.

Also once we reach a reduced level of salt intake we tend to find that many processed and prepared foods are entirely too salty for our taste and nearly inedible. Pleasantly, we also rediscover nuances of taste in foods lost since childhood, nuances hidden from our taste buds by the distraction of too much salt.

In a sense, salt is a relatively benign drug that we can (mostly) withdraw from without a sense of deprivation. The attendant enrichment of our life is a nice bonus.

ADDITIVES

And then there is the problem of additives, some undoubtedly harmless, some we don't know about, and others that have proven to be carcinogenic. One thing we can be sure of is that additives seldom benefit the consumer. Manufacturers argue that additives do benefit the consumer because without such and such a preservative the food would be more expensive or even not available. What they really mean is that without the cheap preservatives they're using they would be out of business.

Some preservatives actually do represent an overall benefit to humankind when we weigh the sum total of calories made available to a hungry world that would otherwise be lost. However for the yogi who has a choice in the food he eats, they represent no gain at all.

Rather than eat a food that can only get to the dinner table laced with additives, the consumer would be better off eating another type of food. Processors use additives to maintain or enhance the market value of their product, usually by increasing the shelf life. They use the least expensive additives available of course. Their primary purpose is the maintenance of the corporate entity. Product safety is important and consumer satisfaction is essential but only to the extent that the public views the processor as responsible. Unfortunately there is often a time lapse before the public becomes aware of harm done by certain products. Cancers may take years to develop. Further, someone getting salmonella poisoning from an unclean product may not realize where he got it or may even mistake it for the stomach flu.

Food processors are responsible to their profit margins and their corporate positions. Their interest in the public's health varies from company to company but is usually secondary. We must assume the primary responsibility for our health.

Preservatives aside, many of the additives used by food processors have nothing to do with preserving the food. Rather they are there to make the food more enticing. Thus dyes are added to make the food match the ads in the magazine. Other chemicals are thrown in to stabilize the product, to give it long shelf life, to give it a pleasing texture, etc.

Yogis don't need to be enticed. They have a healthy appetite and they know that the way to skirt these additive problems is to choose only natural foods, preferably in season, moderately consumed, and in balance.

THE BEST FOODS

Foods to eat often then are:

Fresh fruits and vegetables. There is little or no danger of overindulging in these foods, which is one of the reasons they are always raved about in nutrition and diet books. It's very difficult to eat too many apples (you'd get sick or stuffed, whichever came first and you'd still be in no danger of gaining weight). Drinking the processed juices of these foods however may sometimes pose a problem with overindulgence. Too much orange juice may make the stomach too acidic. Too much carrot juice might turn you a bit orange. Again, processed foods (and extracted juices are processed foods) are to be viewed with suspicion. For elderly people who have difficulty digesting the whole fruit or vegetable, the fresh juice is a good second option.

Fruits and vegetables also have the virtue of providing vitamins and minerals not available in grains as well as helping to regulate our digestive cycles. They add spice and flavor to what would otherwise be a bland diet.

Ideally fruits and vegetables should be eaten raw. As we get older it becomes more and more difficult to gracefully digest raw foods, especially vegetables, and so the next best way to eat them is steamed or stir-fried or in soups. Soups are especially attractive because they are easily digested and because you can put just about whatever you want in the pot, including a mixture of whole grains, spices, legumes, vegetables, etc. I prepare a dish I call "Kitchen Sink Soup." I begin with lentils or beans or dried peas with spices (by the way almost all the widely used spices have anti-microbial properties which is the reason they are often married with meat dishes) and add everything I have on hand into the pot usually along with a small amount of poultry or fish or meat, adding the fresh vegetables last. Last time I made the soup it had 27 ingredients. Here they are:

water   celery   shiitakes
salt   carrots   olive oil
chicken broth   bok choy   sesame seeds
chicken   yu choy   oat flakes
tomato   cabbage   wheat berries
flax seed   cumin seed   rice
tofu   basil   millet
lentils   oregano   bay leaf
onion   cloves   zucchini

I know, I over did it. But I can't tell you how beautiful this soup was steaming in a white bowl and how delicious! I ate it with some wheat bread I had made.

Complex carbohydrates. Grains, potatoes and other natural "starches." They should be whole-grained and not adulterated or denatured in any way. These foods, which include the "big three," of rice, wheat, and corn, are the most important foods on earth, without which we could not maintain our enormous populations. Until these foods were domesticated people lived in small tribes and made their living by hunting and gathering. It was the cultivation of grains that led to civilization. It was the cultivation of grains that allowed people to amass wealth. In truth, it is the production and storage of grain that is the real wealth in this world, a fact that is temporarily forgotten as we move toward the coming population crunch.

Lean meats, fish, shell fish, and poultry. You don't hear this mentioned much but it's also hard to eat too much lean meat. Note well the word "lean." Fat meats, which are primarily the products of civilization, made possible by agriculture, which allows the surplus of vegetable products to be overindulged in by the animals, were not much eaten in the prehistory. Most animals brought down by the hunter-gatherers were lean creatures. So hungry was prehistoric man for fats that he routinely broke open the bones of the animals he killed to eat the fat-rich marrow. You can eat lean meat (and I mean really lean meat, not the kind you generally buy at the supermarket) until you get sick or stuffed and you won't gain weight.

OKAY FOODS

Foods to eat less often are:

Dairy products. One of the most important inventions in the history of humans (comparable to the domestication of grains) was the domestication of animals, particularly the cow. The cow provides muscle to plow the fields, to move goods and people overland, dung to burn at the campfire and especially milk to drink and to make into cheeses and other products. The concomitant discovery that milk could be preserved by making it into cheese or yogurt further increased humankind's growing wealth.

However dairy products can be overindulged in and easily. So tenuous is our relationship with the milk of another animal that many people cannot digest milk sugar at all and can only eat milk products (like cheese) in which the milk sugars have been altered by the action of microorganisms. For those of us who drink milk we should know that it can make us fat. Ditto for cheeses (which have a relatively high butterfat content) and for butter itself of course. The danger of cholesterol is much remarked upon but uncertain. What is certain is that too much fat from dairy products can be dangerous.

SUSPECT FOODS

Processed foods. Of all kinds. Includes fats and oils, TV dinners, fast foods, "diet" foods, etc. A good rule is, if there's a coupon for it, don't buy it. Another good rule is, if it's advertised on TV, don't buy it. Still another good rule is, if it says "New!" or "Improved!" on the label, run the other way. In addition to making you fat, processed foods can make you sick. They routinely contain too much salt, too much refined sugar and starches, to say nothing of dangerous additives and preservatives. What are the "additives" there for? Ask yourself that. To seduce you into buying and eating a denatured product; or in the case of preservatives to give the product a long shelf life. Ask yourself how preservatives preserve. Only by poisoning the microorganisms that would eat the product. Take those poisons into my system?—no thanks! I like my microorganisms the way they are, ecologically balanced along my alimentary canal, helping my body to digest and process food and waste products.

AN UNCERTAIN FOOD

A food about which we cannot be sure is:

Alcohol. Before the advent of caffeinated beverages in Europe, which didn't happen until the seventeenth century, what did people drink? Mostly they drank beer. Indeed for breakfast it was typical to have beer soup sopped up with bread. There were no stimulant beverages available, and when people drank water they were taking a chance since safe water was not readily available. Such a world it must have been with most people drinking alcoholic beverages from sunup to sundown! (Of course the beer then was mostly three percent alcohol compared with about six percent today.) Then came first cacao, and then coffee and tea, and our world changed. It is interesting to realize that part of the value of cocoa, coffee and tea is the fact that they are consumed in water that has been boiled. The health benefits of drinking safe water made habitual by the mildly addictive force of caffeine turned out to be a boon to humankind. When one considers the usually deleterious nature of addiction, this is a delicious irony.

Today, many people in Germany, for example, get most of their calories from beer alone. Many Frenchmen routinely drink over a liter of wine every day. What is called civilized dining in much of the Western world includes wine with meals. However, nearly every book on yoga that I have read condemns the use of alcohol. Are alcoholic beverages incompatible with yoga?

To answer this question we must look to the individual aspirant and see what he drinks and how much. Clearly distilled liquors are to be avoided. First, they are far from natural, never appearing anywhere in the world until we humans did the distilling. They are typically over forty-percent alcohol and lead to alcohol-dependency states (alcoholism).

Beer and wine on the other hand are naturally-occurring beverages. True, there wasn't much beer around before the rise of agriculture, so our experience with drinking beer is perhaps only about ten thousand years old. This is evident from the fact that overindulgence in the relatively low-alcoholic beer (about six percent) can also lead to alcoholism. People are currently in a far from comfortable symbiosis with the yeast that produces alcohol. The prevalence of alcoholism is evidence of that. In truth some people cannot drink without overindulgence. For those people the question is easily answered: Don't drink alcoholic beverages.

Nonetheless, the progenitors of human beings, small insect and fruit eating mammals like lemurs, bats and others have had several millions of years to experience naturally occurring "wines" and "beers" (although again not in abundance and only at certain times of the year). And so the food that is beer and wine can be said to be a natural food.

So, can a yogi drink?

It depends. Some people cannot drink milk because their bodies can't metabolize the milk sugars. For them the "natural" food that is whole milk would be intolerable and not at all natural. But of course there is another reason that yoga theory condemns the use of alcohol, and until we address that question we can't say whether a yogi can drink or not.

Simply put, alcohol used as a drug is a noisy seed to meditation and can adversely affect the aspirant's progress toward his union with the Ineffable. Just as you can't meditate properly on a full stomach, you can't meditate if you're drunk.

I want to add that doing asana while under the influence of alcohol can lead to trouble. At first it seems that alcohol makes the bending and stretching more pleasurable, more easily done, and there is no pain. However, the danger is that it is easy to go through the asanas without sufficient presence of mind. The alcohol masks the natural warning we would get from pain when going too far. Indeed one can strain a muscle, or stay too long in a pose, or in not realizing that the stance is incorrect because there is only a muted feedback from the body. The result of this, and I can attest to this from painful personal experience, is that you will pull or strain a muscle, and unless you are a spring chicken, you will be unable to perform properly next time, and you may find it painful to lie or sit in some positions until you healed. Believe me, alcohol misleads the practitioner when it comes to asana.

To prove my point, here's a test you can try. Assume *Natarajasana*. (Stand on the left leg, stretch the left arm out in front of you, keeping it parallel to the floor. Lift and bend your right leg behind you, grasping the foot with the right hand.) This is a pose of balance, and is of moderate difficulty. Notice how well you are doing and how long you can hold the pose without losing your balance. The next time you have had even one glass of wine, try the pose. You may think that the alcohol has not affected you at all, but as soon as you try the pose you will find that your ability to balance is noticeably diminished! Try as you might you will not have the same ease and control. Such is the effect of only a little alcohol!

So the real answer to the question of alcohol is, it depends on how the alcohol is used and how much is drunk. If the alcohol is used as a food and taken with meals as an adjunct and not overdone, then for some people (perhaps many) the moderate use of alcohol can be compatible with yoga. If alcohol is taken as a drug with the idea of getting drunk or otherwise overindulged in, then it is incompatible with yoga and to be avoided.

One other point: alcohol must be metabolized by the body. It puts a burden on the body's cleansing organs, particularly the liver and is therefore taxing. Too much alcohol is bad for your health and again without a healthy body there can be no progress in yoga.

FOODS TO AVOID

Foods that should never be eaten are:

Bad-tasting foods. This includes anything that smells "bad." If you don't like the way it smells don't eat it. This also includes any food you don't like. It is stupid and counterproductive to good health to eat something you don't like. If you don't like spinach, it's probably just a food prejudice based on some sort of (accidental, probably) negative conditioning; but it could be that you're allergic to or otherwise incompatible with that food. Everyone has food prejudices and everyone is a little different in their ability to handle particular foods, so don't chide yourself if you don't find broccoli delicious. There's always some other nutritious food you can eat. That's one of the adaptive strengths of humans; we can eat an amazing variety of foods and still stay healthy. Only rats and pigs and sea gulls and some other successful omnivores eat as wide a variety (if even they do). Like these successful animals we are scavengers and can eat pretty much what we like.

ACHIEVING A PROPER BALANCE

In short, it is easy to see and understand what a proper diet is. All of us know what a proper diet is, give or take a few particulars. We've been told that since we were children. What is extremely difficult is to achieve balance and harmony in our eating habits. Yoga can help. As we progress in yoga our eating habits will improve. As our eating habits improve we will move closer to liberation.

Understand however at the outset, that the only permanent solution to the bitter sweet problem of being both food and the eater of food is to make the search for liberation more important, vastly more thrilling and fulfilling than the desire to eat. In Zen there is a formula, "Eat when you're hungry, sleep when you're tired." If we can keep it that simple we are well on our way to the proper balance that leads to yoga.

Chapter 11:
Physical Health: A Specific for Addictions

The practice of yoga is a specific for addictions of any kind and is especially effective against drug addiction. I will try to explain why.

DEPENDENCY STATES

First we have to understand that drug addiction is just a special case of the state of dependency into which people naturally enter. Despite the horrors we rightfully associate with drug addiction, dependency states in general are not necessarily harmful. Most dependencies between species (and drug addiction is a dependency state between man and plant or man and yeast, etc.) are beneficial and in biology are called states of symbiosis. (If the dependency is harmful to one of the species, the relationship is called parasitic). Marriage can be seen as a dependency state; friendship also.

One of the reasons we so readily enter into these states is that we are social beings par excellence. We must become dependent on other people and they on us to make the social system work effectively. Most animals are social only in a limited sense and only during certain situations, but we could not exist as human beings outside our social framework. To make that framework a living reality each of us must have an internal mechanism that makes us reach out to others to form relationships, not merely to procreate but for companionship and trade, for education and the strength that is in numbers.

Additionally we find it easy to form dependency relationships with other species, often to our benefit as with wheat, rice, dogs, cats, cows, pigs, etc.; sometimes to our detriment as with cocaine and heroin. We just naturally love the animals and plants but they may or may not "love" us.

We also form dependency relationships with patterns of behavior (habits). Recognized and easily repeated behaviors give continuity and stability to our lives. They allow us to do what we should be doing and avoid doing something that is harmful.

In biology there are many examples of relationships between diverse species that have become so mutually dependent that neither species could survive without the other. I think immediately of certain ants and aphids, of wasps and yucca, and in general of flowers and bees. In a larger sense most flowering plants could not survive without mobile creatures to pollinate their flowers and disperse their seeds. As noted above, modern civilization could not survive without grains.

THE SYMBIOTIC AND THE PARASITIC

More than this though is the tendency for all living things to work toward a symbiosis. This great tendency of life is the mechanism that shaped the biosphere that we live in today. Note that animals respire carbon dioxide which the plants breathe while plants respire oxygen which we breathe. Many scientists believe that it was this mutually beneficial process that created the biosphere—a biosphere that would never have stabilized had it not been for the tendency of living things to work toward mutually beneficial relationships. This idea has been extended by James E. Lovelock into the well-known "Gaia hypothesis" which, in one of its versions, asserts that the entire planet is alive, an idea that I do not find so far-fetched as some of its critics.

Thus the formation of dependency states is natural and necessary, and usually these states are good for us—usually. Where dependency goes awry and we suffer is when the dependency is not to our benefit. The problem for us is that it usually takes a long time before it becomes clear that a dependency state is harmful. As evolutionary creatures we are the guinea pigs of nature.

Put in biological terms, harmful dependency states are parasitic. A healthy species naturally tries to end a parasitic relationship; that is, in evolutionary terms, "selects" away from the non-adaptive aspect of it. In the long run a parasitic relationship may be harmful even to the parasite since it tends to become dependent on a species that it has made less viable, a species that may very well die out. Or the parasite becomes more and more benign. However such is the nature of the state of dependency that it resists being ended.

Sometimes of course the host-parasite relationship becomes mutually beneficial and there is no pressure for it to be resolved. This is what is believed to have happened hundreds of millions of years ago when some free-living cells were invaded by other cells. The invading cells evolved into the mitochondria that now power the cells of our body.

PAIN AND THE CURE FOR PAIN

The crux of this is that for the individual a harmful dependency state leads inexorably to a condition of pain, not to mention low self-esteem.

This is where yoga comes in. Be it understood that the only thing that can successfully take the place of a dependency state is another dependency state. In the beginning, like any good habit properly installed, yoga performs like a positive dependency state. Ultimately, yoga becomes a technique for going beyond the state of dependency. Ideally it becomes a mechanism for freedom from all worldly dependence (or so the old yogis tell us!).

THAT WHICH TAKES THE PLACE OF

Whatever dependency state might haunt your life, whether it's drug addiction (legal or illegal), whether it's alcohol or cigarettes, whether it's a particular person or a pattern of harmful behavior, the first step toward a cure is to speak the truth about your relationship with the source of your dependency. You have to say, loud and clear, in unmistakable terms, preferably with a witness to hear it, that "I, so-and-so, am addicted to X and I need to break the relationship." If you have no witness, say it aloud to yourself.

Now you need something positive in this world with which to replace the negative addictive state. You are giving up something (the substance, habit, person, etc.) upon which you are dependent, but you are getting nothing in return. Make no mistake about it, the human organism does not willingly give up a dependency state without compensation. A drug addict cannot bear the thought of trying to get through the day without his drug. A person romantically dependent upon someone who has left cannot bear life without the beloved.

While it is said that the cure for lost love is time and the birth of a new love, what we have is not a cure but a new dependency state. We might as well say that the cure for a lost drug is time and a new drug. Indeed there are speed addicts who were "cured" by becoming addicted to heroin!

Such "cures" take place all the time. Marijuana habitués by the millions gave up marijuana, some to meditate, others to snort and smoke cocaine, etc. We even hear of heroin addicts who seem to have grown out of their addiction as they have advanced into middle age. But it is not time alone that will cure addiction because time is an illusion. Time for the workaday world is an agreement between the passing of regular events, like the progress of a hand around the face of a clock, but time for the junkie is between fixes. He is just as addicted whether he waits an hour or a day, a week or a year. It is only as he acquires something to replace the drug with that the effect of time seems to express itself.

Time cures all wounds, it is said, but this is just a metaphor. Wounds are cured by the healing forces of the body expressed over time. What it takes to cure addiction is strength and faith as one becomes habituated to "that which takes the place of."

And what is this "that which takes the place of?"

It can be yoga.

WHAT THE DRUG DOES TO US

Dr. Andrew Weil, mentioned above, wrote a book a number of years ago called *The Natural Mind* in which he presented the argument that people have a natural drive to seek altered states of consciousness. So strong is this drive that we will go to terrible and dangerous ends to get away from ordinary consciousness. Children will spin in dizzying circles; teenagers will drink beer, sniff glue and drive too fast. Some people will snort meth and others shoot drugs into their veins. Why should this be so? What is so wrong with ordinary consciousness that we should try so hard to get away from it?

Of course the human being, the ever inventive animal, is always searching for a new way of looking at things—and rightly so. Our consciousness is different from the consciousness of other beings and in many respects this is all to the good. There is plenty to get away from in the ordinary mind of people. In addition there is the desire for the pleasure that initially comes with taking drugs. Getting high feels good, and as they used to ask in the Sixties, what's wrong with feeling good?

Now that the Twenty-First Century has arrived we know what's "wrong" with feeling good. One problem is it doesn't last and we end up feeling miserable. In other words the drug is a trap. While we started out feeling better than ever, we ended up feeling terrible all the time except when we were able to do the drug in ever increasing amounts until finally no amount was enough.

The mind tends to forget. The drug works its will on us making it hard to remember what the world was like before we did the drug. Life used to have its ups and downs. Maybe (we think dimly) that life was the way it is now (when we so desperately need the drug)—and that's horrible! How did we ever exist before we did the drug?

But the world wasn't horrible. It wasn't so great all the time because we didn't know how to live. We lived like leaves fallen into the stream, rushing up against this and that and wondering why. We had little or no control over our lives. Sometimes things were wonderful. Sometimes things were horrible. Most of the time it was somewhere in-between. That's the way it really was. And then when we started doing the drug...! Oh boy was it great! We felt such power! Such a wonderful feeling of being alive! Everything was so beautiful! It's not like that anymore, but it beats going back to life without the drug. We couldn't live like *that*.

But "that" is not what we would have to live with. It's part of the drug's trick to make us think that life without the drug is horrible. For a while, until we "kick," for a long while—call it two years—life will seem dull and drab, without excitement, without anything worthwhile in it. We are in a sense—a very real and true sense—injured. It's a serious, debilitating, even life-threatening injury. If we had broken a leg, we wouldn't be able to walk normally for quite a while. And even after the leg had healed we would have to treat it gingerly and not run on it and rehabilitate the muscles. So it is with the drug, only we're not faced with just a bone that needs to heal and muscles that need to be renewed, but we must rehabilitate our whole system, especially the most powerful organ in our body, our brain.

The mind-body system, when it is forced, for whatever reason, to give up the drug will of course rebel and try to do anything to get the drug. Even after going without the drug for weeks or months, the mind-body system is still injured but doesn't know it and thinks, you're fine now, just do the drug and you'll be great!

We're not yet well. We're a long way from being well. The drug, like a virus hiding from our immune system, has holed up somewhere in our psyche, protected from the various therapies we may be going through, biding its time and whispering, *Come back to me, come back to me.*

The drug does this because it is the drug's nature to do this. This is how the plant that produced the drug helps to insure its reproduction. "Addict people to this substance I produce and they will take care to insure that my seeds will be planted and nurtured and my offspring taken care of." The plant is taking advantage of our human tendency to form dependencies and habits. Instead of enticing us with carbohydrates, proteins and oils, the drug plant entices us with altered states of consciousness.

In another sense what the plant does is prevent us from being rewarded neuro-chemically when we perform good works (i.e., "adaptive" behaviors), but only when we take the drug. We can't get "high on life" anymore because the drug has taken over the chemistry that leads to the high.

HOW THE PLANT CONTROLS THE ANIMAL

This is nothing new. Plants have always tried to control animals by producing substances that the animals need or think they need. At first, in order to get their flowers pollinated or their seeds more widely distributed, the plants enticed the insects and the birds, the monkeys and the apes with nectar and sugars. Sometimes the plants produced chemicals that the animals decidedly did not want, poisons to make the plant inedible.

For the plant the animals were originally just parasites. It was only after millions and millions of years that the plant in its fantastic wisdom "figured out" how it could use some animals for its benefit. The very substances that the plant used for poisoning its enemies became food for other, better adapted animals. The plant responded by changing the chemistry of its toxins. Some became more and more poisonous to particular animals while others became more and more nutritious. The plant, working "in the blind," so to speak, of the evolutionary process, did not know what the result of its newly concocted chemicals might be. What worked survived, what didn't either changed or died out.

When the first animal with the ability to sow and nurture plants came along (us), a new possibility arose for the plant. Instead of just getting its seeds carried away, or its flowers pollinated, it could actually get the animal to take care of and protect its offspring!

Ah, what a prospect that was, being taken care of by such a powerful animal! And so it is not surprising that some plants were quick to take advantage of the new possibilities. Insignificant grasses, producing an abundance of seed so some would surely survive the appetites of insect, bird and animal now became wheat and barley, corn and rice. The plants that worked well with people, producing an abundant seed, nutritious and easily cared for, flourished. Fruits grew larger and more nourishing. Squashes, nut meats, potatoes and root vegetables all quickly adjusted to take advantage of our great nurturing power, and our fabulous mobility. Darwin called this "artificial selection" and saw it as guided by us, but it works both ways.

But some plants couldn't get on board. They had gone too far in perhaps the opposite direction. They produced toxins that made people sick, the mandrake plant, the plants that produced cyanide, and many others. Some however produced toxins that, under special circumstances, helped people in unusual ways: plants that were diuretic, or induced vomiting, substances that reduced fever, etc. People kept an eye out for them and carried their seeds with them when they traveled far.

These were the medicinal plants. Some produced substances that killed pain. People used them. Some produced substances that not only killed pain but kept us coming back for more. People cultivated them: opium, marijuana, perhaps the unknown plant that was the "soma" of ancient India, etc.

But the marriage was not exactly right. People and plant were not yet in a mutually beneficial symbiosis. People became too dependent on the opium plant. We spent too much of our time and energy on the plant and its subsistence or just doing nothing. We did not spend enough time on the more important businesses of life. The barbarian hoards from across the mountains came into camp and found easy conquest. The opium eaters were slaughtered or made into slaves. The conquerors in their turn discovered the plant and fell into the same trap. But not all of them. Some conquerors didn't use the plant. They made it forbidden or taboo. Meanwhile other attempts at a symbiosis were taking place.

Cannabis was not so debilitating as opium. People could live with it; that is, if they didn't do too much or if large numbers of the tribe didn't use the plant or if they couldn't store enough to last all year around, etc., etc.—in other words, as long as they were protected from a too-heavy dependence on the plant. The same with alcohol. (Alcohol is a waste product of yeast, a yeast that can be said to be working in symbiosis with the plant that produces the fruit or the grain on which it lives). People loved alcohol. They loved especially the wine made from grapes and the beer made from grain. As they became more and more expert on growing and nurturing the grains and vines, they drank more and more. Evolution worked on the people and on the plant. Some persons could not stop drinking. They drank until they dropped and after a rest drank again until they dropped. These persons had a compromised ability to survive and they produced fewer successful offspring. Others drank less and found that it was good. They drank perhaps only with meals or on special occasions. Or only during certain seasons. They were able to pay sufficient attention to the more important things in life, like maintaining their health and producing healthy children and taking care of them. They survived and even flourished.

And so it went and so it goes today. People and plant are still working out their roles, refining their respective systems so that they may work better in symbiosis. But some people-plant relationships do not seem to be working very well at all. Opium is troublesome. Its pain-killing chemical is so powerfully addictive that it seems unlikely that we can alter our nature enough to be able to tolerate it. Still the plant will probably survive (we hope people survive) because opium-based drugs are still useful in medicines and because the plant is so widespread that attempts to eradication it wouldn't work.

The coca plant may survive too again as a medicinal. But cocaine as a readily consumable refined substance it is also far too addictive to be in symbiosis with people. It wouldn't be so bad if modern people, like the Peruvian Indians who have long used the plant, would just chew the leaves. But we postmoderns with our great technology have learned to refine the substance and greatly increase the amount we can take into our system in a given period of time. In other words we are attempting to adjust to the plant, but in the wrong way.

This has happened with other drugs as well. Even with alcohol. Most people can tolerate, even coexist quite well with the unrefined product of the yeast and plant, i.e., beer or wine, but not with the distilled product, so-called hard liquor. It is as though we had learned to live peaceably with beer and wine and then suddenly a new drug came on the scene—new not in content, but in dosage: distilled liquors are typically 40 percent or more alcohol by volume while table wines are about 14 percent and beer six percent or less.

So what has happened quickly with the rise of modern technology is the ability of people to highly refine naturally-occurring substances, and thereby to change our relationship with them.

PLANTS THAT ARE SMOKED

Tobacco and marijuana present a different sort of problem. They are smoked. Smoking a substance introduces it more quickly into the blood stream than is possible through the stomach. Man is the only animal who smokes. Humans learned how to start fires, one of our great accomplishments. We sat at campfires keeping warm against the cold nights for thousands of generations—thousands, not millions, be it noted. Our ability to live in harmony with smoke-induced plant substances is still very much in question. Cigarette smoking causes cancer. Maybe those who are susceptible will eventually die out due to their lesser reproductive ability. (Doubtful: the cancer usually doesn't kick in until after they have had their children.) Or maybe people will learn not to smoke. Again we are the guinea pigs.

With marijuana the situation is similar, although marijuana technically is not addictive as nicotine is.

We don't know the future. For the yogi, wise in the ways of his body, such doubtful substances are to be taken once in a blue moon or never. With cocaine and heroin, or any highly refined drug, certainly never. The yogi would not eat rotten food nor would he drink poison. Hard drugs are poisons. Sucking smoke of any kind into our lungs is also poisonous.

SEEDS TO MEDITATION?

In the sixties it was thought for a while that marijuana for example was a good seed to meditation. Marijuana is in fact a very powerful seed to meditation (that is, initially it helps us to concentrate and focus our attention) but experience has shown that it is (to use the popular terminology of that day) "too noisy" to be worthwhile. It has side-effects. And of course its attention-focusing effects are subject to the law of diminishing returns that characterizes all chemical use—a merciless law you can learn more about up close and personal by using drugs.

The habitual use of marijuana will clog up your lungs and may reduce your ability to function without it. Valium and similar drugs sedate the body at the expense of reducing one's awareness and ability to function. A person doing Valium can never achieve *samadhi* because his mind is not sharp enough.

But man-made drugs, like food additives, are dangerous simply because they are unnatural; that is, they are artificially created and did not naturally occur in the environment and therefore, we haven't had an evolutionary period in which to adjust to their effects. The Food and Drug Administration and Merck may say they're safe because they've tested them, but from the yogic point of view their tests are of a hopelessly short duration, tested on a hopelessly small sampling. I might add that the Food and Drug Administration is full of individuals looking to work in the food and drug industry and the food and drug industry is itself primarily concerned with profits and maximizing the corporate influence. For an especially good read about the failure of the drug companies and the FDA to protect the public from man-made drugs see *Dispensing with the Truth: The Victims, the Drug Companies, and the Dramatic Story Behind the Battle over Fen-Phen* (2001) by Alicia Mundy.

To close this section let me say that using the so-called "designer drugs" that are manufactured in clandestine laboratories is like playing Russian roulette with a full clip.

COFFEE, TEA AND THE BENIGN ADDICTION

Emily Dickinson wrote about the "little anodynes" of life, by which she may have meant such things as crossword puzzles, knitting, pleasant conversation and perhaps coffee and tea. Some religions are actually identified (whether they like it or not) with the use of technically addictive substances that can be called the "little anodynes" of life. Alan Watts writes in *The Way of Zen*, page 190, "If Christianity is wine and Islam coffee, Buddhism is most certainly tea." And on page 86 he writes, "The taste of Zen [ch'an] and the taste of tea [ch'a] are the same."

But caffeine, as documented in *The World of Caffeine: The Science and Culture of the World's Most Popular Drug* (2001) by Bennett Alan Weinberg and Bonnie K. Bealer, is addictive, and some sects have condemned its use, most notably perhaps the Mormons of Christianity. So what is a yogi to think?

If one believes that the First Patriarch of Zen, Bodhidharma, was a yogi—and I think he certainly was in some respects—then the use of tea cannot be dismissed. After all, tradition has it that Bodhidharma once fell asleep during his meditations and became so upset with himself that he cut off his eye lids which fell to the ground and came up as the first tea plants. There is today a very fine, rare and rather expensive Chinese tea named after Bodhidharma.

Caffeine for most people works much like a positive habit, a benign addiction. The water is boiled and therefore harmful parasites are killed, and the tea itself persuades us to a greater alertness, and in conjunction with various cultural ceremonies provides an opportunity to be congenial and find a pleasant mood. I think that the moderate use of coffee and tea really proves the point that not all addictions are negative. So I would say that for a yogi the use of such beverages is okay as long as the use is moderate. For the yogi of forest India of course such a dependency would not have been good, tying him to people, utensils and the plant itself so that his wanderings would be curtailed. Then again, in many cases, maybe he would have been better off.

So the question remains, can a yogi consume caffeine? I can only answer for myself, from my own experience. Quite simply the answer is "maybe." I drink an eleven-ounce cup of coffee in the morning brewed from decaffeinated beans. At lunch I have about 22 ounces of tea, usually green tea, either Chinese or Japanese. I used to have coffee in the evening, but I find that I can no longer tolerate the caffeine. Caffeine's diuretic effect interferes with my sleep!

I should add that in the process of growing older, most of us have found that we can and should set aside many of the habits of youth. For myself a number of those habits have been replaced by the practice of yoga.

Chapter 12:
Physical Health: Introduction to Asana

KITTY YOGA

Tradition has it that a cat invented yoga. Certainly anyone who has practiced yoga is struck forcibly by how adept cats are at asana and meditation. Cats know how and when to stretch. They reach out their paws and yawn mightily. They can do the death pose so blissfully that we love to watch them and they're wonderful at touching the crown of their head to the ground and looking at the world upside-down. Undistracted by a fidgety neocortex, they fall into meditation with the greatest of ease. Furthermore, cats do not indulge in excessive and idle talk. They know how to sit peacefully and contemplate the bliss within. They have no desire to amass worldly goods and their strongest drive is to seek contentment. They know how to beg with dignity and patience (essential knowledge to the ancient sadhus of forest India) and they usually avoid excesses of any kind. In short, a person could learn a lot about yoga by just watching a cat.

But of course a cat did not invent yoga, not even *hatha yoga*. Nor did a man. Yoga evolved out of the physical and mental nature of human beings. What worked endured; what didn't work was mended or tossed aside.

Some techniques (and yoga is nothing if not full of techniques) were so obviously beneficial that they were invented again and again until they became standard practices. Among these are right postures (asanas) which have now been so thoroughly investigated over such an incredibly long time that the best ones are practiced the world over often by people who know little and care less about yoga in general. The headstand, the plow, the forward bend, and others are practiced purely for the physical benefits they bring.

WHICH POSTURES ARE NECESSARY?

According to legend the Hindu god Siva (also spelled *Siva*) developed 8,400,000 postures from watching animals. In the traditional *Siva-Samhita*, a handbook of yoga written in the 17th Century, mentioned earlier, 84 positions are given. B.K.S. Iyengar, in his modern text, *Light on Yoga*, describes about 600. But to advance in yoga probably only a handful are actually necessary.

I'm not going to try to give a definitive handful, since the best postures for any individual depend on that person's particular needs (and as you're learning you should try many of the postures until you have the experience to select just the ones you need). Rather I'm going to discuss asana in general and concentrate on the postures most often practiced, and depend on the student to conduct his own practice, ideally under the guidance of a master, but more likely on his own. For those of you who have begun your practice and are interested in becoming advanced in asana I highly recommend the aforementioned *Light on Yoga* by Iyengar. Some other books are also good (I learned from Hittleman and Vishnudevananda to whom I am indebted) but none are as extensive and thorough as *Light on Yoga*.

ASANA AS MIND AND BODY POSE

Asana means posture—not just in the physical sense of how you're sitting or standing, but in the mental sense as well. Asana is the beginning of meditation. Regular practice leads us gently to the meditative pose of the mind.

All asanas therefore have both a physical and a mental dimension. With actual practice it is possible to understand the meaning of asana (and only with actual practice). Yoga is above all else a doing. Words mean little; practice is everything. I could talk about the benefits of the death pose for example (lie on your back with your legs slightly apart and your arms at your sides a little away from the body, palms up, eyes closed) for ten thousand words and most of them would be repetitious and all of them worthless compared to the experience of just doing the pose.

Stated another way asana is the answer to the question, how are you holding yourself? Just as in method acting, where one may lead oneself to the desired emotional state of mind by going through the physical motions associated with that state, one may in yoga begin to grow contemplative by posing in a contemplative position. This is fundamental. If you want to meditate (and the ultimate purpose of asana is to facilitate meditation) you must sit in a comfortable position. The body pose leads to the mind pose.

But even before you can sit comfortably you must be in good physical health. There is nothing more useless than an attempt to meditate when your body feels miserable. So instead of starting with a meditative pose like the lotus (which is actually a very difficult posture for those of us who grew up sitting in chairs) we begin with the asanas meant to insure physical well-being, such as the headstand, the shoulder stand, the plow, the cobra, etc.

By the way, you may have noticed that some authorities make exaggerated claims for the asanas, claims that modern medical science pooh-poohs. As we have seen in the chapter on how to read a religious book, these claims must be taken not as literal statements, but as psychological statements, meant to inform symbolically. The shoulder stand, for example, take it from this practitioner, does cure all pain—for the time being, for a while, until the inevitable drift and decay sets in, until the next time.

THREE RULES

First, do not overdo. For most people, the active asanas are very demanding physically. If you are young and supple and find the postures undemanding, that is both good and bad. Good in the sense that you will be able to do them without effort, but bad in the sense that your concentration will be more sorely tested. It is better to do a little of each asana than to go overboard on any single pose. Do not strain. Move slowly and deliberately. If you feel pain, stop. Asanas are not exercises as such and the goal is not to do as many as possible and certainly not to do them as fast as possible. Rather the opposite is true.

Second, concentrate completely on what you are doing. Asana without concentration leads to failure.

Third, practice regularly. It is not necessary to do the poses every day, although a little every day is ideal. The body responds very well to daily rhythms. You can however miss a day or two and come back and do a little more than usual on the third day. For beginners daily practice is best.

PLEASURE IN ASANA

Every asana should bring pleasure. At first it will be difficult to achieve some of the postures. Nonetheless anyone can achieve a partial posture. For example in the forward bend the idea is to be able to grab the feet (with legs unbent) and to touch the forehead to the knees. Some (maybe most) of us will never be able to achieve that. For the average beginner it will be enough to merely reach out and grab the legs below the knees and to bend forward a few inches. Gradually the muscles and ligaments in the back will stretch out and you will be able to reach further and further down your legs. How far you should reach each time should be judged on how you feel. There should be a slight sense of reaching, perhaps the beginnings of stretching, but no more. There should be no pain. Any pain at all is a signal that you've gone too far.

The goal is *not* to build up muscle as in weight-lifting types of exercise. What is important is that the body that is already there get its proper exercise and that the blood and other body fluids be facilitated to flow throughout the body and that the neurological and chemical networks of the body get a proper exercise. The yogi wants to avoid inflexibility of course since lack of flexibility leads to atrophy and finally to the inability to use the body at all. Mental flexibility is a basic tenet of yoga.

It cannot be emphasized too much that while doing the asanas it is essential to concentrate exclusively on the posture itself, on how your body feels. Find and follow the pleasure. Lack of concentration completely defeats the purpose of asana. Without proper concentration what you will have is a kind of low-grade exercise program; furthermore, you might strain a muscle.

Asana has a therapeutic effect on the mind and body. Proper asana leads to a calm and blissful feeling both during the poses and for hours afterwards. At first the pleasure may be absent or at least less intense. As your practice grows so will the enjoyment.

ASANA AS AN OUTLET FOR THE EMOTIONS

We've all known people who seem to need to fly off the handle once in a while. They get angry, throw a fit and then afterward they are calm and feel much better. However a couple of days later they are at it again often to their personal regret and the regret of those around them. What such persons need is not to get angry and abuse others or themselves, but an outlet for their pent-up emotions. This is one of the things that asana provides. By properly stimulating the body's glandular system and by releasing tension in the muscles and in the body's neuro-chemical network, the need to blow up emotionally is greatly negated. One feels serene. As the yogis say, the *nadis* are cleared.

ASANA AS BLISS

In addition to the physical and mental effects of asana it bears repeating that asana itself leads to meditation. In truth asana is one of the most important and very best seeds to meditation. Because proper asana is pleasurable one has only to focus on the pleasure and one is naturally led to meditation. Adepts do asana as a kind of body prayer, flowing from one pose to the other, mind focused on the movements and on the centers of attention, ever blissful and thankful to God that they are able to be doing this. In the highest achievement one does not do the asanas, the asanas do one. Person and pose are one.

Most error in asana comes from trying to do too much too fast too soon. If you do your selected group of asanas properly it will take you about half an hour. Better that you should do them in two hours! They can easily be accomplished in five minutes, if one so desired, but much of the benefit would be lost. This doesn't mean you should hold the pose in the dynamic stage too long. You needn't stand on your head for fifteen minutes nor should you do any pose repetitively. What I mean by taking two hours is to pause between postures either in a sitting position or lying in the corpse pose and concentrate on how your body feels, especially concentrate on the areas of your body most stimulated or otherwise affected by the last pose. This is the beginning of making love to yourself.

Properly done asana can be one of the most beautiful experiences of your life. As you go through the movements you will discover your body and come to know it for the beautiful instrument that it is. Remember you are existence, knowledge and bliss (*sat-chit-ananda*). During asana one is made very much aware of the bliss.

Chapter 13:
Physical Health: Asana Practice

TYPES OF POSTURES

For the sake of discussion yogic postures may be divided into four types:

1. Seated postures.
2. Postures begun from a standing position.
3. Inverted postures.
4. All other postures.

In a typical session one begins with the standing postures followed by postures begun from a lying or sitting position, followed by the inverted postures and ending with *savasana*, the death pose. Seated postures are primarily for *pranayama* and meditation, but let us begin with them in our discussion since really all else follows from being able to sit right.

WHY YOGIS SIT IN CROSS-LEGGED POSTURES

One of the great observations of yoga is that how you sit affects how you feel, even how you think. How you sit determines your mood. In ancient India (and indeed almost anywhere in the world in those days) people grew up sitting on the ground. Few had chairs. For the yogi the important thing became to be able to sit comfortably so that he could readily enter into meditation. Many sitting poses have consequently developed, the most important ones being *padmasana*, the lotus pose, in which the legs are crossed so tightly that the feet rest on opposite thighs, soles up; and *siddhasana*, the adept's pose, in which the heels of the feet cradle the genital area, above and below. Possibly the most popular sitting pose for Western adepts is the half lotus in which one leg is over a thigh. For Westerners, *sukhasana*, the so-called easy pose, in which the feet rest under the crossed calves, and *vajrasana*, the thunderbolt pose, in which you kneel and sit on your calves and heels, are two other postures good for meditation.

Most people can do *sukhasana* at least for short periods of time. Others might find *vajrasana* more comfortable. The first two poses (the lotus and the adept's pose) might be easy to assume if you've been sitting on the ground for most of your life or if your limbs are particularly supple. For most of us though they can be very difficult indeed. So unless such poses are comfortable to you I recommend that beginners not try to meditate in a cross-legged position. It might be easier to learn to meditate sitting comfortably in a chair Egyptian-style with your back straight and your hands resting on your lap.

Eventually however you will want to sit cross-legged. Depending on your current flexibility you might want to practice sitting in the easy pose for a few minutes once or twice a day, gradually increasing the time: or, if you are more flexible, try a half lotus, reversing the legs from time to time until you can achieve a full lotus. For most of us a cross-legged position will be something we have to work toward.

Why should we bother learning to sit cross-legged if we can meditate sitting in a chair?

First of all there are several reasons to think that sitting cross-legged leads to better meditation and more quickly facilitates one toward *samadhi*. To begin with, when one's legs are pulled up close to the body, one exposes less surface area to the elements. It can readily be seen that if we had to sit outside in the cold, this would be a great advantage. Less clear, but equally significant is the fact that even at room temperature our bodies are expending energy maintaining basal metabolism. Scientifically speaking the closer your body resembles a ball the better it can conserve its store of heat—or maintain its homeostasis. This is why animals in the north tend to be big and round and why animals of the savanna tend to be the opposite, long and lean, so they can easily radiate away excess heat.

Pulling oneself up tight away from the world also facilitates *pratyahara* (withdrawal of the senses from sensory objects) which is necessary before one can enter *samadhi*.

Third, it is good to have the ability to sit anywhere and meditate, regardless of what is happening around us and regardless of where we might be. If we can only meditate sitting in a chair we're not going to be able to go on a camping trip and keep up our daily practice.

This point should be emphasized since it is one of the supplemental lessons of the cross-legged postures: to learn to control your body so well that you don't need props (chairs, cushions) or special circumstances in order to meditate. This is in keeping with the overall, more advanced lesson of being able to shut out the world and its sensual distractions (again, the achievement of *pratyahara*, which we'll discuss in a later chapter). An adept is as comfortable sitting on a rock as he would be on your living room rug. The extreme practices of fakirs affirm this point in burlesque by making themselves comfortable sitting on a bed of nails. Such an accomplishment (being able to sit anywhere) is in fact the immediate goal of sitting, losing sight as it does however of the more important goal of meditation leading to *samadhi*.

Another reason for learning to sit cross-legged is that, because the legs are drawn up and "squished," as it were, they have less blood and therefore more blood is available for other parts of the body, in particular the brain. Because the body is thus smaller (small is almost always better, by the way, in nearly everything) less physical energy need be expended on it and more energy can be given over to the needs of *pranayama* and meditation. We can breathe at a much reduced level when we don't need to support an active set of legs. Therefore when we draw our legs up close to our body we can better control our breath, further facilitating meditation.

A fifth reason to sit cross-legged is that after a while the body forms a habitual response to a pose and automatically falls into the appropriate mood. If we always sit cross-legged for meditation (and for nothing else), after a while the brain will begin its alpha rhythms merely because we have assumed our cross- legged pose. This is in fact the classic Pavlovian response.

A possible sixth reason yogis sit cross-legged: It may be that the bending of the legs and feet affects the mind neurologically much as in acupuncture one part of the body affects and is related in a non-obvious way to another.

Seventh reason: Sitting cross-legged massages the feet. The tiny pleasure of the little massage given to the feet and ankles by being turned and held in the various sitting postures is a seed to meditation. Concentration on that feeling leads to bliss.

Sitting cross-legged brings us closer to our feet and makes us intensely aware of them and what amazing instruments they really are.

Finally, a cross-legged pose is the natural pose of the human at rest. This is one of the poses that our ancestors employed during the long period in the Environment of Evolutionary Adaption on the savannas of Africa during the Stone Age.

SIGNALING OUR BODIES (AND OUR BRAINS)

I will tell you a little story about sitting cross-legged. When I was still in my twenties I used to go by myself for one-day nature hikes into the deserts and mountains of southern California. I would pack a lunch and go off in the morning and at midday would sit down cross-legged on the ground. At first I thought it a coincidence that after I sat, the animals magically appeared, cautiously of course, peering at me from behind rocks or from around bushes and trees. Then I thought they were interested in my lunch (they may have been). Finally though, after sitting without lunch, I discovered that was just the sitting that brought the animals out of their hiding places to take a look at me! I realized that my seated posture was a signal to them that I was not threatening, that I was at rest and they were relatively safe at a proper distance. Usually it took about half an hour for them to feel safe. All sorts of animals would appear, coyotes, mule deer, rabbits, once even a bobcat, and of course turkey vultures swooped low to get a closer look to evaluate my physical condition, hoping that I might be dying!

Some years later I discovered a curious thing. It typically took me at least half an hour of sitting in concentration before I could begin to meditate. I realized after a fashion that by sitting quietly with my legs folded, I was signaling to my inner, animal self that the ego-I of ordinary consciousness was at rest and it was safe for the inner consciousness to appear. Even to this day I seldom fall into meditation without sitting comfortably for twenty or thirty minutes. So a cross-legged posture is a signal to our bodies and our brains that now is a good time to relax, but only after we have proven our sincere intent by sitting for twenty or thirty minutes.

Yogis have several sitting postures. They have a way to sit when they eat, a different way when they are socializing and still another way when they want to meditate. After a while the body-mind system just naturally assumes the proper set for what is to come, getting its clue from the pose assumed.

In short, the ability to sit cross-legged is in a sense a chair you carry around with you. It is very light-weight.

Someone once said that most of the troubles in this world stem from the inability to just sit. I do in part believe it.

POSTURES BEGUN FROM A STANDING POSITION

It may surprise you (I know it did me) that just standing is a yoga posture. It is called *tadasana*, the mountain pose, and is the first asana in Iyengar's presentation. He comments: "People do not pay attention to the correct method of standing... Owing to our faulty method...we acquire specific deformities which hamper spinal elasticity." Iyengar describes fourteen poses that begin from *tadasana* and says that they are necessary for beginners so that they may acquire flexibility and then can be dispensed with. They are mostly limb stretches and their effects would tend to duplicate the effects of many of the asanas that are assumed in regular practice.

There are some other things to be said about standing poses though. One is that just standing is an excellent meditative pose (especially for persons who sit most of the time). You might try standing comfortably with weight evenly balanced and just gaze out a window or at the ground or at nothing at all for a moment and let time stand still. It is a very refreshing pose.

Another thing to mention is that during the time the asanas were developed, because most people had to get around almost exclusively by walking, there was little need to exercise the legs.

People typically walked several miles a day in the ordinary course of things. Today of course we sit most of the time and so standing postures should take on a greater importance. In Zen there is a walking meditation and in China and Japan whole systems of body conditioning are undertaken from standing positions.

Most standing postures have an element of balance to master. Typically one stands on one leg and raises the other in some fashion. In *vrksanana* (the tree) you hold your hands over your head palms touching and raise and bend one leg up so that the bottom of your foot rests against the opposite thigh. In the first phase of *ardha baddha padmattanasana* (the foot lift pose) which Indra Devi calls the stork (she has a photo of the actress Gloria Swansen, famous for her role as the aging silent screen star in *Sunset Boulevard* (1950), demonstrating it in her book *Yoga for Americans*) one stands on one foot and brings the other as high as possible over and in front of the opposite leg and holds it with the hand—again there is an element of balance required that tends to steady and center the mind. Such poses also tend to direct the attention away from the inner body to the limbs and in a sense push one's attention outwards and therefore are less conducive to meditation and should consequently be done at the beginning of one's regimen.

POSTURES BEGUN FROM SITTING OR LYING POSITIONS

It may not be apparent at first but most of the postures practiced by yogis concentrate their effects in three general areas of the body:

First, the various circulatory systems in the body, the blood, the lymph and the vast neurological systems including the spinal column, insuring its flexibility and exercising its neurological potential.

Second, the endocrine glandular system, often making a particular gland the focus of a posture thereby insuring the regular stimulation and cleansing of the various glands—a cleansing that takes place, incidentally, without the need for harmful emotional outbursts.

Third, the internal organs, the stomach, the lungs, the intestines, etc., organs that especially need to be cleaned and flushed (technically speaking not "exercised" in the sense that muscles are exercised) to prevent stagnation and blockages by persons leading sedentary lifestyles.

Most physical exercises practiced by active people will, as a byproduct of strengthening and exercising the muscular structure, also exercise (imperfectly) these three areas. In yoga however it is considered a waste of time and energy and a step backward spiritually and physiologically to develop the muscular system beyond what is necessary for day-to-day functioning.

It is because of this emphasis that yogic "exercises" looked so peculiar to Westerners when they were first introduced many years ago. We have been raised in the Greek tradition of exercise for the development of athletic prowess, while the yogi wants to get as far away from such an idea as possible while at the same time developing and maintaining a healthy body. It is no exaggeration to say that the evolution of the various asanas toward this goal is one of the great discoveries and developments of humankind.

Here's a list of some of the most important "main sequence" asanas:

> *Pachimottanasana*, the forward bend.
> *Bhujangasana*, the cobra pose.
> *Salabhasana*, the locust pose.
> *Dhanurasana*, the bow.
> *Ardha matsyendrasana*, the spine twist.
> *Matsyasana*, the fish pose.
> *Chakrasana*, the wheel pose.
> *Gomukhasana*, the cow head pose.
> *Simhasana*, the lion pose.

Each of these poses has variants and some other poses might be mentioned instead. Again I refer the reader to Iyengar's *Light on Yoga* or Vishnudevananda's *The Complete Illustrated Book of Yoga* or some other good illustrated text on *hatha yoga* for details. Watching *hatha yoga* presentations on television or on video is a fine way to become acquainted with the main postures. Most of the teachers give a good introduction to yoga in general.

The postures that I'll discuss here are postures that I myself practice. I believe the ones mentioned above form more than an adequate regimen for the vast majority of people. Indeed, the full array of asanas presented in especially Iyengar's book can only be mastered by gifted students willing to devote much of their life to the practice. Such mastery is unnecessary for the attainment of yoga.

BENEFITING FROM ASANA

Ironically (but not illogically) the further (within reason) you are from being in good shape the more you will benefit from asana. For some people these asanas are very easy to perform because of their natural suppleness of body. For most of us (myself included) whose bodies are tight and stiff, some of the asanas can be very difficult, even impossible to do. Do not despair! You do not have to actually touch your toes or bring your head to your knees in *pachimottanasana*, for example, in order to benefit from the posture. It is enough to begin. In fact, the more rigid your body the more you will actually get out of the asana even though you can only touch your thighs. True! I know people who are so supple they can easily place their palms on the floor without bending their knees and they can do this without the slightest practice, without having done it for years! I know others who cannot touch their hands to their shins with unbent knee no matter how hard they try.

One of the unfortunate misconceptions about asana is that you have to become proficient at the postures to really do any good. This is wrong since just doing them at the most rudimentary level leads immediately to the most amazing benefits. The secret is to take yourself to your own individual level of proficiency and to practice at that level with a steady concentration. This alone leads to success in asana. It has nothing to do with mastery as compared to what someone else can do and certainly it is unproductive to compare yourself with the mastery that one finds in the photographs or drawings in books.

(Repetitive note: You may reach in *hatha yoga*, you may even from time to time stretch, but you must never strain. This is true psychologically as well as physically.)

Physiologically speaking when you reach for something you thereby gain the ability to reach a little further the next time. When you stretch for something your body takes notice and begins to work to loosen its muscles and re-adapt its pose so that next time you will only have to reach, not stretch. When you strain for something it is a desperate measure. You may obtain for the moment what you strained to grab, but the price you pay will likely be a strained or pulled muscle and you won't be able to reach the object comfortably until you have healed.

The same is true of the mind. Mind and body are one in harmony, working toward the same goal. When you attempt to concentrate (and again, concentration is one of the lessons of asana) do so gently without straining. If the monkey mind insists on flitting around, gently call it back to the focus of the asana again and again without reproach and without impatience. The next time you take up your pose you will find that the monkey mind has benefited a little by the previous experience and you will have to gently call it back less frequently. If you grow impatient with the monkey all that you will do is make it more restless.

After any pose it is a good idea to return to a sitting or lying position and direct your attention to the parts of your body most affected by the posture and notice the very pleasurable sensations taking place.

A HEIGHTENED SENSE OF WELL-BEING

Several postures practiced regularly every day (or even every other day) will immediately lead to a heightened sense of well-being. Your body may take on a glow that will make you look and feel younger, more vigorous. You will be more relaxed and able to do more work. You may very well become very excited about your initial experience and attempt to do more in an effort to attain even greater benefit.

Of course such an attempt, unless it is moderate and gently orchestrated, can easily lead to pain and disappointment and an abandonment of practice. This is a time of danger! Remember the adage of the Tao: when in success, caution; when in adversary, patience. Initial success in yoga is a very heady experience and unless handled correctly can immediately lead to complete failure. When you really feel good about your practice, caution, caution, caution!

It is for such times that meditation comes into play. A good idea at this very exciting juncture is to begin your practice of regular meditation. Just sit for a few minutes and focus the mind on the pleasure of asana. Think of nothing else. You will be well on your way!

Ideally after a few weeks you will be a changed person. Your weight will have moved toward its ideal (although don't expect a great leap yet). You will tend to have a very hearty appetite—an almost amazing desire to eat, and everything will taste delicious. This is because your digestive system has been invigorated, cleansed and restored to a more youthful state. The initial surge in appetite will pass. Your blood is now circulating so much better, your neurons are cleansed of stoppages and your body may very well tingle with delight.

Again: caution. The mind is a funny animal. It tends to forget sometimes. It tends to overdo and/or to lose track of the program. It tends to arrogance and again at this point there is a very grave danger, this time of taking the practices for granted. There might be a tendency to skip a session or—worse yet—to do a session in a cursory manner, without the total, gentle concentration that is essential to success. Again the mind gets arrogant and thinks it can just zip on through the postures and get on with the nice feelings. What will happen consequently is that the sessions will be less and less beneficial; there may even be some pain and the mind will become dissatisfied and impatient. Again, there is a danger of losing one's practice. The mind may even become angry (which is a sure sign of being off the track)—angry that there is not NOW, or at least not recently, a new and more exciting benefit or development to experience.

Now is the time for the Zen practice called *zazen*—"just sitting." At this precarious juncture in your practice it is a good idea to increase your meditative attempts (and we're being honest here: for most practitioners of *hatha yoga* true meditation is still only a hit and miss event). Do not expect any great achievements: do not expect anything at all. At this time the body and its monkey mind are taking stock. They may very well feel threatened. The ego, the ordinary mind—the monkey mind, whatever you want to call it—"ordinary consciousness" is a good term—this false self may very well dig in now and stonewall it in an attempt to maintain its mastery over you.

The correct procedure now is a firm resolve to continue your practice again gently and without undue effort. You might want to reaffirm your approach, re-emphasizing the regularity of practice, the concentration on what you are doing, and above all you should reject any expectation of benefit.

This is important. When we get into *karma* yoga it will be seen that the very act of expectation will distract us and lead to failure. The person on the path to yoga is like the electron in quantum mechanics: the very observation of the yogi's progress can in itself interfere with the progress. At this point expect nothing. Make your practice a loving ritual and have faith. Be assured that you are on your way to yoga, but understand for a while you may not notice any great progress. Your progress will only be evident sometime later.

Another danger, especially for those of us into our middle years, is that we will very definitely feel a lot younger. This may be a bit unsettling at first. We may have forgotten how strongly the body and emotions control the young person. Members of the opposite sex may very well look better than they have looked in years. We might find ourselves full of energy that now more than ever needs channeling. Appearances will be brighter, clearer. We will see and feel perhaps too much. Our appetite will increase—appetites of all kinds. Suddenly it will appear that we have been thrown back in time a decade or two and we will recall perhaps with some pain how much of a hold youthful desires had on us and how really glad we are to be (mostly) through with them. It's a good lesson.

This too will be a time requiring caution. Your new-found energies will have to be directed into something constructive. You will perhaps increase the time spent at asana or perhaps take up a physical hobby, returning to tennis or something else you once loved to do. You may take on some kind of volunteer work.

This is all to the good as long as it isn't overdone and as long as it doesn't interfere with your yoga practice. It should be understood that this is an effect from a stage of asana. It will pass.

SOME PERSONAL NOTES

I consider asana the most important single step toward yoga. My view is a personal one. It probably stems from the fact that asana is for me one of the best seeds to meditation. For many other people mantra or *pranayama* constitute the best seed. Again yoga is a personal and individual experience. Some persons zoom ahead in their practice, achieving the rungs on the ladder with seeming ease. Others plod along a little at a time. There can be no question that some students are more talented than others. Therefore it is a good idea not to compare your progress with others (one of you will undoubtedly be behind the other); nor is it a good idea to talk about your practice at all. As Hittleman has pointed out, it does you absolutely no good and may very well detract from what you are doing.

I am not an especially fast student. I might very well call myself the turtle—but in doing so I recognize that the turtle lives for many years while the rabbit is gone after just a few. And so in your own practice, however you view your progress in comparison to others or in comparison to where you think you should or might ideally be, remember to cast the most flattering and positive light on your practice while maintaining the best objective position you can. It never hurts to be positive and optimistic: negativity and pessimism are poisons.

INVERTED POSTURES

The headstand and the shoulder stand (*sirasana* and *sarvangasana*) are sometimes called respectively the king and queen of asanas. Perhaps more than any others these asanas typify the practice of *hatha yoga*. To the uninitiated they may seem silly or even dangerous. They are neither. They are two of the great teachers of yoga. They invert the system so that the blood is made to flow to the head and the neck. They rejuvenate and cleanse.

Symbolically they emphasize the need to see things differently. They tell the monkey mind and its body that there is a very real need to view the world in a manner that is totally contrary to the usual way. As mentioned earlier (and it bears repeating) there is in the Upanishads a symbol very dear to yogis, an image of the tree upside down with it branches in the earth and its roots in the sky, symbolizing the diametric change in the way the world is seen after one is firmly established in yoga and the illusions of maya have been cleared. Every time you do the headstand you can be reminded anew that what you see is an illusion maintained by our senses through the agency of the ordinary mind, and when the veil is lifted

134

everything that was once important will be seen as trivial and what was once thought unimportant will be seen as the essence of everything. Watch for that day. It will come.

Both the headstand and the shoulder stand should be done. Even though they are both inverted postures and derive their effects mainly from reversing the pull of gravity, they are aimed at different targets.

The shoulder stand aims at the neck to stimulate especially the thyroid and parathyroids. The headstand aims at the head itself to stimulate the pineal and pituitary glands as well as the brain. Furthermore, the existential experience of these asanas is different. The headstand, the king of asanas, teaches balance and poise and the fact that some of the great truths of life are, as it were, upside down, and that as we mature we begin to value the things that we did not value before and vice-versa.

The shoulder stand on the other hand aims at the neck and is somewhat forceful in driving the blood into a relatively small area. We see (when we open our eyes) the body in its grossest manifestation. We see in fact a person without a head—an animal being. There is a lesson in this and a focus for meditation. Too often in our lives our bodies have been upside down spiritually, placing as we have too much emphasis on sex and food, the lusts of the body. Every time we do this pose we might ask ourselves: Who am I, this that I see or something else?

I might add that if you are even a little bit overweight, in the shoulder stand your face is pressed very close to the fat and you are made aware of it.

Inverted postures clean the veins and arteries of the body by forcing the blood back against the normal flow, flushing out places where clogging might occur. Inverted postures force the mind to an alertness (since one feels the danger of a fall). After some practice one is able to be relaxed yet alert—which is the proper mind-pose for meditation.

Initially it may seem impossible to do a head or a shoulder stand. If one is obese one may have to be satisfied with the achievement of a partial position until one has lost some weight. One can do a semi-wheel instead of a shoulder stand (and therein gain a great benefit, by the way). The semi-wheel is achieved by lying on the back with the soles of the feet on the floor, knees up, and then lifting the midsection as high off the floor as possible. One will feel the flow of blood to the neck and the beginnings of a great rejuvenation through the stimulation of the thyroid and parathyroids. For a headstand, one will have to be satisfied with kneeling and placing the top of the head to the floor and walking toward the head (as the midsection raises up) as far as possible.

For others who have never done inverted postures before, it is important to first eliminate any possibility of falling. In the shoulder stand there is little danger of falling, but if one is bottom-heavy it may be difficult to get up on the shoulders, and once up there some swaying may occur. For such persons I recommend getting between a sofa and an easy chair and placing the soles of the feet on the wall. By "climbing" with the feet and alternately scooting up closer to the wall, just about any point of inversion can be achieved while maintaining stability between the sofa and the easy chair.

For the headstand you might try it in a corner of the room where two walls meet. That way you can always balance yourself against the wall so that you won't fall over backwards and can check yourself for proper alignment either left or right. Even to this day I always do the head stand a foot away from a flat wall so that I feel safe should I sway backwards. Incidentally, although I have momentarily lost my concentration many a time, I have never fallen, and I have done over six thousand headstands.

If you have any difficulty achieving the inverted postures by yourself you should seek help from a teacher. Asana without the inverted postures leaves a lot to be desired.

THE TINY DEATH

When doing certain poses, e.g., the plow, the spinal twist, or perhaps any of them, there might come an uncomfortable (but not painful) sense of being held, as being held under water, or forced into a tight and potentially suffocating space, followed by a nervous-system release.

"Clears the *nadis*" is how the yogis phrase it.

There is a sense of calm and serenity that follows this clearing that may last for hours, sometimes into the next day or the day after. But what is it that is cleared? Clogged channels of some kind? Arteries? Lymphatic channels? Neurons? Maybe the effect is due to glandular secretions. Perhaps it is all of the above.

I suspect that what is cleared is a build-up of chemical potential along certain nerve channels (especially the vagus nerve and the spinal column). It may be that one is "ready" for a release and feels increasingly aggravated or jumpy until that release is effected. As evolutionary creatures, we continue to build up explosive energy every day preparatory to the well-known "flight or fight" response. After the energy is released we are calm. Modern people need an "artificial" release since it is seldom appropriate for us to respond physically to emotional situations.

By the way, *nadis* are "energy channels" presumed by yogis to exist in the subtle body. (More on this later.) I should say here that most authorities say the *nadis* are cleared through *pranayama* rather than asana. I will not argue the point, but let me say that we are now entering an area where little or nothing has actually been written down in the classical texts to guide the student, the details of yogic practice instead being transmitted directly from guru to aspirant. Since one of the purposes of this book is to try to bridge that gap until "the master arrives,"—and, as we shall see, the master may never arrive and we will wake up one day and see that the master is our self—I will relate a personal understanding that is apropos here.

The asana that has the most powerful effect on me personally is the plow. (Lie on your back arms at your sides, legs stretched out. Lift the legs and bring them over your head, legs straight, until your toes touch the ground.) "Daddy is squishing himself!" my little daughter once exclaimed so accurately when she came upon me doing it. The chin goes to the chest and the midsection is brought into close proximity to the face so that the internal organs are indeed "squished" together and thus stimulated and flushed with a fresh supply of blood while places of congestion are broken up. People who suffer from clogged colons (usually the result of poor diet and sedentary ways) benefit greatly from this pose (and from all inverted postures).

The plow has never been as easy pose for me. I have practiced it thousands of times over the years and I am still very far from perfecting it. As my toes begin to touch the floor I feel something I will call the panic reaction. I am being squeezed together, my back is stretching as are the muscles in the backs of my legs, and if someone were to come in at that moment and push down on my exposed back I would feel like I was going to suffocate and that some of my muscles might snap.

What I experience at this point (as my toes touch the floor) is indeed something akin to suffocation—not as intense and certainly without the mental fear—but something very close nonetheless, and I have to take just a moment to reassure myself that I am in charge of what is happening and that I can just lift my legs and come out of the pose at any time. But herein lies the point of what I want to say: this sense, this feeling of suffocation, this "tiny death" that is about to happen to me produces its own reaction from my body, produces a chemical and neurological reaction that cleanses me—again, clears the *nadis*— and I come out of the asana greatly relaxed, refreshed and emotionally calm.

There are other postures in which I have had this experience (the spine twist, for one) but in none is it as powerful as it is in the plow. For other people with a different physical make-up a similar experience may come with some other asana. For a young and supple person it may take one of the more extreme asanas to bring about the little death. For the ancient adepts it was something rather extreme indeed that was necessary.

In the classic texts on *hatha yoga* one reads about the ancient practice of *khechari mudra* in which the tongue is gradually lengthened by cutting it from its attachment to the bottom of the mouth and stretched so that it can be turned back into the throat to choke off the oral and nasal cavities simultaneously and prevent breathing. I suspect that the adepts did this to achieve their own little deaths and the subsequent benefits.

By the way, those benefits also include the production, it is now understood, of brain chemicals that allow us to sedate ourselves naturally.

The thing I think we have to realize here is that the scientific effects of a particular asana are not exhaustively known. Why asana works as well as it does remains something of a mystery to modern medical science. Despite pioneering work done by Swami Rama's Himalayan Institute some years ago and others toward a scientific understanding of yoga, there remains so much to be done. Each individual yogi learns to understand in a body-consciousness way the effects of asana, but he may be at a loss if he tries to explain his experience verbally to others.

SAVASANA, THE POSE OF A CORPSE

A session of asana should end with the death pose. What you do is lie on your back with your arms at your sides a few inches from the body, palms up. Your feet should be slightly apart. The idea is to relax completely and to concentrate your mind on the process of relaxing (or on the breath or on nothing at all, if you can achieve it). Close your eyes and just let go. Let go of everything—mind, body, paperwork, loved ones, petty squabbles, your falling stock portfolio, the sound of cars outside in the street—just let them go. Die a little now to this world...

Assuming the physical position of the pose and maintaining it is the easy part. To relax the mind and to allow it to gently concentrate on how your body is relaxing is more difficult. Iyengar comments: "It is much harder to keep the mind than the body still. Therefore, this apparently easy posture is one of the most difficult to master."

Savasana should also be done in the middle of the day for a few minutes when it is most effective in countering stress and preventing the dissipation of vital energies. After a session of asana the body should relax without difficulty; however when *Savasana* is practiced in the middle of a hectic day, the body may resist, particularly if you are under stress. Nonetheless, after some practice the body will indeed relax on command, as it were, and then all one must do is just let the mind go.

The more difficult it is for us to relax in savasana, the more we undoubtedly need it. A good technique is to relax first one part of the body and then another. Begin with the feet and gradually work toward the head. Gently tell the feet to relax and then feel them relax. Imagine the calf muscles hanging loose, falling toward the center of the earth. Give yourself over to gravity.

After some practice your mind will follow your body and you will achieve the total realization of the pose. Properly done it is incredibly refreshing and rejuvenating. Again Iyengar comments: "The stresses of modern civilization are a strain on the nerves for which *Savasana* is the best antidote."

Note: It is considered bad form and counter-productive to fall asleep while doing savasana. If you don't fall asleep, your mind remaining alert but relaxed, you will arise refreshed and strong. If you fall asleep you're liable to arise feeling slightly drugged as though awakened from an abortive nap.

Savasana properly done leads to meditation.

GUIDING THE EXPERTS

In asana, perseverance, patience and faith are the watch words of success.

For those of you reading this book who are experts in asana, I want to remind you that it is important to concentrate on the spiritual aspects of the poses; it is essential to review your practice from time to time, to make assessments of how beautifully and lovingly you are performing the asanas. The goal for the expert should be not toward a great achievement in terms of how far you can twist or how long you can stay in the pose but rather how gracefully you can do it, how much you can become one with the pose and lose yourself in the movements and the stillness. When the asana does you and you are just a spectator, full of wonder and bliss as the movements unfold, then and only then do you go from being an expert to mastery.

Chapter 14:
Mental Health: Ethical Conduct

That which is hateful to thyself, do not do to thy neighbor.
This is the whole law, and the rest is commentary.

—Talmud, Shabbath 31a

THREE LEVELS

As I studied yoga and enlarged my practice it became clear to me that success could be divided into three phases or levels:

First, the attainment of physical health through regular habits, proper diet and asana.

Second, the achievement of mental and emotional health through an enlightened attitude toward myself and the world I live in, coupled with proper behavior ("right conduct").

Third, the transcendental reward of spiritual health made possible through meditation.

Consequently, unlike traditional authors I have placed right ethical conduct (which follows from, and at the same time leads to, mental health) after the physical preliminaries but before spiritual enlightenment. I don't believe that a starving person or a person in ill health has the ability to make ethical choices. We act as any animal would, self-preservation first, morally-correct behavior later.

In all things we are temporal creatures and have a time appropriate for our advancement.

Proper ethical conduct is mental health. It is social and psychological health. It comes as a result of physical health, not before. Consequently I have come to see yoga as a way of life on three levels: the physical level in which we learn to take proper care of our bodies; the mental level in which we learn to control the mind and the emotions; and the spiritual level in which we learn who we are and what our relationship with the Ineffable really is. It is seldom possible to find success in the second level without having achieved it in the first, and spiritual success is not possible until the mind and emotions are brought into harmony with the world around us.

In a sense, then, right ethical conduct is both a physical level consideration (that is, we have to behave properly) and a mental level event because we have to believe in our hearts and minds that there is the right way to behave. So, now that we have taken giant strides toward physical health through proper eating and the practice of asana (and hopefully the beginnings of meditation—about which of course more is to come)—now that we have laid the physical foundation so to speak, let us proceed to where Patanjali began two millennia ago.

THE LIMBS OF YOGA

We usually see the eight limbs of Patanjali's classical yoga set forward like this (we'll define these terms in a little bit):

Yama

Niyama

Asana

Pranayama

Pratyahara

Dharana

Dhyana

Samadhi

as though these limbs were rungs on a ladder to be ascended beginning with *Yama* and ending with *Samadhi* in order to achieve yoga. Some authors have thought of them as branches in a tree or arms on a body. Thus Wood (p. 101, *Practical Yoga*) says the aspirant "is to become the eight-armed yogi" who might look at himself in the discriminating mirror of his mind "to see whether those eight limbs are there or not." Georg Feuerstein in his *The Essence of Yoga* saw them as a circle.

However one might think of Patanjali's "limbs" as legs, that is, as the limbs that hold a lion or an elephant up, except that, for the yogi, there should be eight of them so that his carriage is doubly secure.

Every limb of yoga is essential to success, whether we call them legs, limbs, rungs or stages. Failure to observe the ethical requirements is just as fatal to success as failure to sit properly. Therefore, let us look closely at these ethical prescriptions presented by Patanjali and see exactly what they are and perhaps figure out why they are essential.

YAMA AND *NIYAMA*: RIGHT CONDUCT

The first five are called *yamas* and are usually thought of as abstentions. The next five are observances (*niyamas*). Together they constitute the ten commandments of yoga. They are:

Yama
1. *Ahimsa*, non-violence.
2. *Satya*, truthfulness.
3. *Asteya*, non-theft.
4. *Brahmacharya*, non-lust, non-sensuality.
5. *Aparigraha*, non-greed.

Niyama
1. *Saucha*, cleanliness.
2. *Santosa*, contentment.
3. *Tapas*, austerity, discipline.
4. *Svadhyaya*, self-study.
5. *Ishvara-pranidhana*, dedication to God.

If these remind you of the Ten Commandments of the Bible it shouldn't be surprising since several of them are identical, which is also not surprising since there is not now nor has there ever been any real controversy about what constitutes right ethical conduct. People have always known that we should not lie, steal, kill, etc., it's just that sometimes we forget or allow ourselves to be persuaded that *this* time, for these special reasons, it's all right. For the yogi right ethical conduct is not only essential for success, it is prerequisite, and it is an on-going process. There is no point in trying to meditate if one's ethical house is a mess.

For us as yogis this is very much a practical matter. We are not so much concerned that an authoritative god might be looking down on us to see if we're doing the right thing or that we might be punished if we aren't. We know that punishment in the form of failure will surely come if our ethical conduct is contrary to what is right. We also know that it is not enough to be told, like a child, not to do this or not to do that. We must understand and know with the force of personal experience what is right and wrong. Our heart-felt desire must be to harm no one. We must yearn with our very soul to know the truth and to live it.

And therein lay a problem. It is not always easy to know the truth, and furthermore it is not always clear how far the injunction to do no harm goes. Do we allow ourselves to step on insects? Do we kill plants in order to eat them? Is *Brahmacharya* a prohibition of all sexual activity or does it allow sexual love in marriage? These are very real questions and they can only be answered by the individual and only for him or herself. It is not that ethical conduct is altogether relative, it is that we ourselves are imperfect beings living in an imperfect world (all part of our karmic condition). Nonetheless we must, through right discrimination, determine what we should and what we should not do.

Unfortunately we cannot always know what is right and wrong. Our discrimination is imperfect. Therefore Patanjali and the great sages before and after him have presented certain rules to help us see the truth and to follow it.

AHIMSA, NON-VIOLENCE

It is said that there is no *yama* like *ahimsa*, and that all the other *yamas* stem from it. *Ahimsa* is non-violence in its broadest and most inclusive sense. To begin to understand the depth of its meaning we start with the observation that our first responsibility is to ourselves. Therefore *ahimsa* applies to our relationship with ourselves. We must not harm ourselves. Mutilations in the name of a moral austerity are out. Doing anything that harms the body (or mind) is out. As yogis we must in fact work toward keeping our body healthy and free from disease (hence the entire *hatha yoga* practice).

Our next responsibility is to our fellow human beings. We must not harm them. This means in word, thought and deed. Again it isn't always easy to know what right behavior is. Everyone knows that in raising our children it is often a painstakingly difficult task to separate what we should do from what we shouldn't. Spanking a child may or may not harm the child. Sparing the rod may or may not harm the child.

In a larger sense one's tribe or country may insist that we kill members of the neighboring tribe under the guise of self-defense or even because they are "evil" and "God" tells us to. Here again the yogi must make up his own mind. The injunction to do no harm is a guide, it is not a precision instrument that tells us infallibly what to do in every situation. However the great religious leaders of the world in every age have interpreted the injunction as an absolute prohibition. "Turn the other cheek," Christ said. Mohammed reportedly would not get up because he did not want to disturb a cat sleeping on the hem of his robe. A Jainist monk would not step on a beetle. On the cross Christ said, "Forgive them for they know not what they do."

Some persons point to the *Bhagavad Gita*, the "Song of the Lord," for a contrary statement. They ask, wasn't Arjuna urged by Krishna to fight his enemies, saying he had no choice? Is not this fighting violence?

It is indeed, but this is only an apparent contradiction. The Gita is a symbolic poem and must be understood symbolically. Thus when Krishna called for Arjuna to fight he was symbolically calling on him to continue living (the fight for life), in opposition to suicide which Hindus (and most religions) consider a false and ineffective way to try to solve our problems.

We also must not harm other living creatures in so far as that is possible. According to the yogic view everything is part of God, including you and me and all the creatures of the world no matter how small or seemingly inconsequential. Any violence done to the world and anything in it is a violence done directly to God.

But yoga is pre-eminently a practical and worldly-wise practice and the purely spiritual or theoretical considerations, compelling as they are, are only part of what leads the yogi to non-violence. Equal with the above as reason for non-violence is the mundane observation that it is a good strategy. Even the crude politicians who run our public affairs in this world believe in non-violence in their personal lives. It is only under extraordinary circumstances, such as against criminals or people they fear because of their own enmity or because of ignorance, that they allow themselves the use of violence. For the traditional yogi of fable living as a *sadhu* in the forests of India existing on hand-outs at the back doors of householders, it was a practical necessity to develop a reputation for *ahimsa*, since he could hardly expect a generous reception if he was known to harm others. Indeed a violent yogi would meet with violence from the householders and not with a bowl of rice.

Thus a person who wishes no harm to others and practices no harm seldom meets with harm. According to spiritual leaders as diverse in time and place as Mahatma Gandhi, Lao Tzu and Martin Luther King Jr., non-violence in its most pristine form is the best strategy.

The contrary is equally true. If you live by the sword, it has been said since there were swords, you will die by the sword. This truth has been proven time after time and still people have yet to learn it. If a man hits me and I hit him back I have failed. I have passed on the violence. I have become an instrument in the karmic play of violence. Thus Jesus said, "turn the other cheek." It should have stopped with me, but now I have extended it and who knows where it will finally stop? Genghis Kahn and his barbarians pillage a town. At some later point some of the people who survived slip into the barbarian tents at night and slit some throats. But these people too have failed. They have merely supported Genghis Kahn's belief that his behavior was correct. His only mistake was not to have killed them all.

A thousand years goes by. It is the same. Man kills man and in turn is killed. But somewhere in a far off galaxy a being harms another, but the other walks away. The violent, through a vast and prolonged attrition, kill one another off. Many years pass. The first being does not harm the second. They live firmly established in *ahimsa*.

A million years goes by and who is left—on this earth, on that planet in a far-away galaxy—the creature who does violence or the creature who does not?

What do you think?

This is why the Bible declares that the meek shall inherit the earth and all the heavens and all the futures as well. Violence is a stopping place on the way to becoming, a very primitive place, a place in preparation for someplace else, a crude, ephemeral state of being, fleeting, temporary as a newspaper.

The Vedas teach that the man who is truly non-violent need fear no one. All the violent vibrations, the discordant notes of a pre-orchestration toward the pure symphony of Being, float by, through and around him, not affecting him. The Bible says the same thing: "Yea though I walk through the valley of the shadow of death I fear no evil. Thou art with me."

The man who turns the other cheek, who walks away, the man who has enmity for no one, that man is never the target. He can live in harmony with his fellow man. The other man who in his heart would do evil, as the Bible phrases it, that man though he has done nothing yet, that man is the target and he will be slain. And so it will go.

Before the deed was the thought, and before the thought was the *karma*. The sins of the fathers are visited upon the children.

And so it must stop. The man must turn the other cheek: Even though he be killed, he dies not, so the Gita says.

This is not to say that one should not defend oneself. One should.

SATYA, TRUTHFULNESS

The Bible says the truth shall set you free, and by this it is meant the truth about our condition in the universe. Real knowledge will free us. But to discover that truth is very difficult. It is made much more difficult when we surround ourselves with lies and false utterances and deceptions. We must speak the truth and live the truth. Otherwise we have no hope of salvation.

In another sense we must speak the truth so as not to harm others (a furtherance of the sacred practice of *ahimsa*). For the yogi truth is second nature. For the businessperson it can be very difficult indeed. In fact, the Bible says it is easier for a camel to pass through the eye of a needle than for a rich man to get into heaven. And there is a great truth expressed here. The kingdom of heaven cannot be bought and in practice such attempts merely lead one further from God. The yogi knows that there is little in this world worth lying for (self-defense surely, but beyond that, little). What if you should gain the whole world and lose your soul? What does it profit a man indeed?

On a practical level we all know the bromide that a liar must have a good memory. Not only that but a person with a reputation for honesty gains so much more from others than could ever be gained by lying—and what we gain is so much more valuable than anything we could gain by temporarily fooling someone. It is a truth that bears repeating—"the truth will out" goes the old saying—that if we lie to others and to ourselves—oh, especially we must not lie to ourselves!—eventually the lies will come out in the open and we will have only shame and embarrassment as our companions.

ASTEYA, NON-THEFT

Truthfulness and non-stealing are really the same thing. "Honesty" is a word that describes them both. Again there is little in this world that is worth stealing. On a practical level, our psychological make-up is such that we abhor a thief. We won't have him around. He can't be trusted. People feel like punishing thieves, and you know there is no honor among thieves. To take something that isn't ours is to punish ourselves. There we are with our ill-gotten gains, and compared to the serenity and peace of mind, compared to the fellowship and acceptance of the honest person in society, what have we gained?

This is what is meant when the Bible asks "What doth it profit a man to gain the whole world only to lose his soul?"

Furthermore, anything really worth having cannot be stolen.

What we mean by truth and not stealing should always be taken in the context of a person who has enough to eat (not caviar and champagne, but enough to nourish the body). Clearly if we are starving and the society is rich, then the society has stolen from us and we can't steal what is already ours. We'll develop this idea further when we discuss greed.

BRAHMACHARYA, NON-LUST, NON-SENSUALITY

This word means to conduct oneself like a *Brahman*, that is without lust, practicing self-restraint. This word is often translated as celibacy, but this is too narrow a definition and misleading. The real idea behind *brahmacharya* is to practice self-restraint in all areas of life. One should not lust after anything—food, drink, power, wealth—not merely sex. It is said that money is the root of all evil, but more precisely it is desire—desire for all sorts of things that we cannot have or that we can't get enough of—that is the cause of human suffering. The idea of *brahmacharya* is an attempt to address this problem. The spirit of *brahmacharya*, that of not lusting after the delusions of this world, is a beacon that guides the yogi to God.

Unfortunately in many books on yoga this idea is not really understood. Thus one reads that one should practice *brahmacharya* because one shouldn't waste his vital energies on sex. This bit of silliness has its fine kernel of truth, but it is a bit beside the point, reminding me of the old quip, "It's not the woman that wears the man out, it's the chasing her."

The joke is more to the point. Most of the energy wasted on sex is not lost in the sex itself. The energy is lost talking, scheming, priming, planning, tricking, trapping, deceiving, chasing, wining and dining; and it includes all the emotional energy lost in this very emotionally-charged process. We cannot cure our lust for sex—be sure of that—but we can make the lust manageable. And to do that we must reduce our involvement as much as possible. Ramakrishna advised that when in the company of women the man should look at her feet, not her face. We do not have to go to that extreme, but the idea should be appreciated and the technique of avoidance of lustful temptations observed.

However, loss of energy is not the major reason that some yogis practice celibacy (which is one expression of *brahmacharya*). The energy loss is entirely minor. The actual reasons are not stated directly in the classical books on yoga because sometimes the bald statement is too blatant—especially if heard by non-initiates. The most important reason religious seekers practice celibacy (and this includes Christian monks and serious aspirants everywhere) is that it is a good strategy to employ when interacting with society. Again, yoga is always practical.

Monks and gurus subsist with the blessing of society and at society's whim only so long as society allows them to subsist. Get society mad at you and if you're a monk living on charity and hand-outs, you'll find yourself in a lot of trouble. This is the reason that monks and gurus and priests try to stay out of politics—getting involved can only get them embroiled in disagreements. Chasing the other guy's wife will also get you into trouble, serious trouble. So in order to stay out of temptation's way religious aspirants throughout the ages have found it wise to get and stay celibate. It's simply good style. For a *sadhu* begging at the back door it's imperative that he not get involved with the householder's wife.

For the householder practicing yoga it is quite proper for him to experience the joy (and melancholy) of sexual love. For him *brahmacharya* is not celibacy, but lack of lustfulness, which is its true meaning.

APARIGRAHA, NON-GREED

Greed is of course a form of lustfulness. Greed is desiring more than you need. Nobody's in favor of greed. But how much is more than you need? In the minds of people in most developed countries is the idea that you really can't have too much wealth. Thus the bumper sticker: "You can't be too rich or too thin" and the dry rejoinder: "You can be too thin." The feeling is you can always give it away if you have too much and besides you never know when things are going to change. If a man has five cars, having to hire somebody just to keep their batteries charged, we think nothing of it.

It's a hobby. A man that already has hundreds of millions of dollars still spends sixteen hours a day trying to make more. We admire that. Of course this man probably cannot help but work all the time; he is addicted to his work and probably can only identify with himself as the creature who makes money.

But what about the woman who has three thousand pairs of shoes while her countrymen live in poverty? Or what about people who eat until they can't eat anymore and then make themselves vomit so they can eat again?

Actually in the original meaning of *aparigraha* was the idea that one shouldn't hoard or even collect. This sense doesn't apply to collecting stamps or objects of art or even the hoarding of gold. What is meant was the hoarding of valuable foodstuffs that would spoil before they could be eaten and therefore would go to waste merely so that the hoarder could have an exaggerated sense of security while others went hungry.

How do you feel about greed? If you're like me you probably don't care how many vintage cars a baseball player may collect, but Emelda Marco's shoe collection is a bit more than obscene. And if a man wants to collect dollars and corporations that's okay too since he can't take it with him and he might even be creating wealth through his enterprise. But for Saddam Hussein to spend millions for fancy new weapons that he can play with and feel powerful about while his people live in abject poverty is criminal.

Opinions vary and the individual must make up his own mind about how much of something or the desire to own something is greed. For the yogi however collecting and hoarding are spiritually distracting and contrary to the spirit of what he is trying to achieve. He doesn't take pleasure in counting up his possessions, rather the opposite. He agrees with the man who made the joke: "The man doesn't own the property, the property owns the man." Possessions just weight him down. If he had millions of dollars he would just have to manage his money—and think of the time that would take. If he had a house and grounds he'd be a housekeeper and gardener not a yogi. He'd spend his time caring for the geraniums and not his soul. Did you know that Bill Gates has said, coming to the full, startling realization of what his wealth really means? He said that he realizes that he will have to spend the second half of his life giving his money away.

151

For the householder yogi (which after all the modern yogi must be, at least until he is free of his responsibilities as he nears retirement age), there must be some sort of compromise between the amassing of worldly goods and the spiritual practice of *aparigraha*. Again each person must decide for himself. I'll leave you with this thought, however: anything that you have that would benefit others that you don't use and just keep to satisfy your pleasure in ownership is contrary to the practice of *aparigraha*.

The yogi believes that it is impossible to own anything, that everything belongs to God. We only temporarily use things. A cat does not own its territory. It uses its territory for food and shelter as long as it is active and can maintain its position. After the cat is gone another cat will use the territory. Meanwhile the man thinks he owns the land and the house on it. But the man too will die in his time and the territory will pass on to someone else, perhaps his children, but maybe they will prove less careful than he and lose their rights to the property and it will belong to someone else. The only difference between the cat and the man is that the man foolishly thinks he owns the land while the cat never entertains such a delusion.

NIYAMA

While yamas are prohibitions—injunctions not to do certain things—*niyamas* are observances, things we should do.

SAUCHA, CLEANLINESS

This means purity or cleanliness that applies to both the body and the mind, including word and deed. But it goes beyond that. Iyengar comments: "More important than the physical cleansing of the body is the cleansing of the mind of its disturbing emotions like hatred, passion, anger, lust, greed, delusion and pride." In the West it is said that "cleanliness is next to Godliness."

SANTOSA, CONTENTMENT

There is no greater wisdom than contentment—and this does not mean a cynical resignation to the sway of external events.

Contentment is a positive value that we superimpose on what happens to us, the circumstances we find ourselves in and in our attitude to those things we cannot change. People who are content see the glass as half full not half empty. We treat winning and losing as positive experiences, recognizing that any detriment gives us the opportunity to better appreciate the good when it comes. And we know that the real joy in living comes through the evenness of emotional experience rather than by riding the rocky road of triumph and disaster. We know that in failure (as the *I Ching* teaches) lives the germ of success and that an equipoise toward the world is a realistic necessity because "this too will pass."

Most of the misery in the world is not the result of terrible hardship (although of course terrible things do occur and to everyone) but is the direct result of an improper attitude. It is not what happens to us, but how we react to what happens to us that counts. How horrible it was when I was a young man and Saturday night came and I had no date and no fun thing to do! How much I suffered! Now such a prospect is very agreeable indeed. And what has changed? I've gotten older but what has really changed is my attitude. How much suffering is caused by our foolish identification with events outside our control! The young man identifies with his home town baseball team. They lose and he feels terrible. The middle aged man is devastated when he fails to get the promotion he thought he deserved. He even thinks of suicide. How foolish, how utterly stupid. Somewhere else in the world a man is utterly joyful because today he not only has rice to eat for his evening meal but he caught a fish to go with it! Amazing happiness! He will sing and dance around the cooking fire and he will feel at joy with the world and will laugh with his children and with his wife.

Such is the power of attitude. This the yogi knows. You can't change the world—at least not very much. But what you can change is your attitude toward the world. For most of us, most of the time happiness is ninety-nine point nine percent attitude and one-tenth of one percent circumstance.

The practice of contentment however must be cultivated. It is something learned. Indeed, one of the things that yoga is about is to teach us to be content. Until we have learned to meditate we don't realize the great joy there is in just sitting. A yogi is content and that is his great secret, the great power he has over the world and its vacillations. If the sun shines that's an opportunity to go for a walk (or to a baseball game) and the yogi feels just fine. If it rains then that's an opportunity to spend more time in meditation and again the yogi feels just fine.

The person who is content is the person who is in charge of his or her life. The discontented person is like a straw in the winds of circumstance.

TAPAS, AUSTERITY, DISCIPLINE

The word *tapas* is usually translated as austerity—although Wood used the phrase "body-conditioning." What it really means is self-discipline or character. Taken literally the Sanskrit word means "heat" or "ardor."

For success the yogi must be disciplined. He must not allow the minor daily fluctuations of circumstance or the monkey mind to sway him from his purpose. He must show resolve and firmness of purpose in the face of what are called by Patanjali the five sources of trouble: ignorance, self-centeredness, desire, aversion and possessiveness. Note well these devils.

Success is not achieved by chance. There are those who believe that technique, effort and discipline avail not and only by grace are we liberated. But the yogi does not believe that at all. What counts is regular, sustained practice and that practice requires *tapas*, which Iyengar defines as "A burning effort which involves purification, self-discipline and austerity."

SVADHYAYA, SELF-STUDY

"Know thyself" is the ancient Greek wisdom, appearing on the Delphi temple. The injunction appears in the Upanishads as well. *Svadhyaya* means self-study. For the yogi this goes without saying. There can hardly be a more appropriate observance since the practice of yoga itself is the most thorough self-study imaginable.

The average person hasn't the faintest idea who and what he is. For the yogi, to answer the question Who am I? is one of the great goals of life, and a life without self-study would be barren indeed.

ISHVARA-PRANIDHANA, DEDICATION TO GOD

This is attentiveness and devotion to God in everything we do. The yogi devotes his efforts to God and dedicates the fruits of his efforts to God. Everything is in God, with God, and for God. The best way to understand how important devotion to God is in the yogi's efforts, is to read the *Bhagavad Gita*, the Song of the Lord. All of the *yamas* and *niyamas* can be found there. Much of the wisdom of the Vedas is distilled there. Any doubt about the spiritual nature of the yogi's quest can be dispelled by looking into the Gita. For the *sadhaka*, the aspirant intent on liberation from the bondage of this world, there is no finer place to begin than to read the Song of the Lord, and in the Song one finds that there is no surer way to *moksa* (freedom) than the devotion of one's life to the service of God

Chapter 15:
Gurus

IS A GURU NECESSARY?

A very serious detriment to success in yoga is the idea that yoga is somehow inaccessible without the guidance of a guru. While this was undoubtedly true in preliterate times, it is not true in today's world where easily ninety percent of what can be learned from others about yoga can be gotten directly from the Internet, books, recordings, film or television. It is a shame that many books written in the West have stupidly repeated the tired idea that no real progress can be made in yoga without the guidance and grace of a guru. The plain truth is that while a qualified teacher is certainly desirable, such a teacher is largely unnecessary and—more to the point—not likely to be found.

IS THE STUDENT QUALIFIED?

Before we explore why a guru is largely unnecessary, let's find out why we're unlikely to find one in the first place.

The first truth is that we have to be qualified as aspirants. If we aren't ready the master will not appear. That is, we wouldn't see him if he did appear. We wouldn't recognize that he/she (even it) really is the true guru, the teacher who can teach us now.

Ram Dass (in the Lama Foundation's book, *Remember: Be Here Now*, p. 4) said one word about what we can do about gurus, and that word was: "nothing." He said that because being a student is really what finding a guru is all about. That's the real meaning in the saying, "When the student is ready, the master appears." We have to be ready. We can't do anything about the availability of qualified teachers. What we can do is work on ourselves.

There is a book written in India by a lawyer and part-time aspirant after yoga that illustrates this problem. The book, *In Search of a Guru*, by K.G. Sharma, was meant to show how few truly qualified gurus there are even in India, the birthplace of yoga. What the author inadvertently revealed was how unqualified he himself was as a prospective student, mainly because of a hyper-critical attitude. He was the student as guru-critic. If there was a flaw in the guru (and even if there wasn't) he found it. Such a person cannot possibly benefit from a guru since his focus is not on the practice and study of yoga, but on the worthiness or unworthiness of the teacher. It is a variation on the old saw of confusing the messenger with the message.

All people are flawed, yet we can learn something from everyone. A successful aspirant must have a positive attitude and focus on the strengths of the guru rather than on his supposed shortcomings. Furthermore, how the student perceives the guru—thinking that this or that is a shortcoming—is not always reliable. The student, who is on the trail to enlightenment, is not in the best position to judge the guru, who is after all someone who has been on the trail for a much longer time. Better then, for the student to have an open mind and a positive attitude until shown otherwise.

Nonetheless, we as students must judge the guru. We must decide at the outset whether the prospective teacher warrants our trust and commitment. Sharma did this by tracking down persons who were said to be gurus or who were posing as gurus and he quizzed them. He talked to a large number of persons over the years and found that some of the prospects were complete charlatans while others had only what he called partial knowledge of yoga. Others he found deficient for moral reasons.

He categorized these unsatisfactory gurus for the reader. First, there were those with some knowledge but without a deeper understanding of how and why particular yoga practices were important. He writes: "Generally speaking, the teachers in this group were poorly educated, thought highly of themselves, and exhibited several traits that form no part of the yogic way of life." He added that "they ran classes of their own and were well-compensated."

In his second category Sharma included heads of ashrams and institutes, whom he said, "Concerned themselves more with preaching and administrating their respective organizations than with imparting real and practical instruction." He added that real instruction was "invariably left to privileged disciples who normally were only half-baked persons."

In his third category he included those whose writings were repetitions of what they had read or heard, persons whom Sharma found "unable to comment upon themes that had been presented to them from out of their own writings." In short, these were persons with book learning but no practical experience—persons with superficial knowledge only.

We might contrast Sharma's attitude as a prospective disciple with what Vijay Hassin has to say on the subject in his book *The Modern Yoga Handbook* (p. 27): "...This question of whether or not to 'have' a guru is not as important as whether or not you can be a real disciple. Gurus come and go; there are many of them; there are few real disciples."

LACK OF REAL TEACHERS AND THE NEED FOR BOOKS

Given that Sharma was probably less than a "real disciple," it is nonetheless surprising that he was able to find so few qualified gurus in his many years of search and so many unqualified ones.

In the Western world of course it is the same. There are many persons, for example, who are well-versed in the purely physical aspects of asana, who run "yoga classes" mainly for beginners, but who are not really spiritual persons and make no claim to be. And there are great institutions headed by famous persons, themselves no doubt genuine yogis, but who obviously have little or no time for the instruction of aspirants. For the Westerner set on learning yoga there is no choice but to begin with books, the Internet, and videos.

I learned this myself and this is one of the reasons I am writing this book: to help others, especially those who have gone a few steps along the path and feel the need for guidance. I have included in this book a large bibliography, lightly annotated in an attempt to identify those books that will be of particular help to the student at whatever stage he or she has reached. Thus for asana I have identified Iyengar's *Light on Yoga* as a particularly good source of information and an excellent guide to practice. However, since Iyengar himself is not there personally to guide the student and to answer questions, it is a good idea to refer also to some other authorities who may, by sympathetic happenstance, speak more directly to particular students. Hittleman and Vishnudevananda are two who have helped me. In this manner the serious student can advance more quickly. Just as some students are strong in one area of practice while weak in another, so teachers—especially in their written works—may be strong in one place and less comprehensive in another. Therefore, by combining works we may come to a deeper understanding of yoga sooner than we could by following the writings of one teacher alone.

DABBLERS

Some persons confuse the need for a guru with a social or communal need they may have. If you like the idea of going to a yoga class and "working out" with others and if you're fond of having a teacher interested in you and your progress, someone who will take the time to praise you and perhaps point out where you're in need of work, etc., you probably should join a workout club or take a university class or something else, because you may not be truly interested in yoga beyond the basics.

To be a true *sadhaka* requires a sober commitment to a regular, disciplined and solitary practice in which the goal is nothing short of union with the Supreme Divine Consciousness. Such an undertaking is not for the dabbler or the habitual joiner or for persons looking merely to make friends. Commitment to yoga is a serious (and joyous!) undertaking whether one has only twenty minutes a day for the practice or twenty-four hours. It's an adventure into the unknown where no one else can go with you, where you will go alone to eventually, it is hoped, meet with the Ineffable. Anything less than total commitment (for whatever length of time you are able to give to yoga) is insufficient. And to seek a guru under anything less than the sincerest desire to learn is a waste of your time and hers.

Truly committed persons don't spend time looking for gurus. They look within—and their attitude is that it may happen, ten years down the road or twenty, in this lifetime or the next, that the guru will appear and help them cross the river from bondage to liberation.

WHY SOME BOOKS SAY A GURU IS NECESSARY

Who taught the first guru? In asking that question we reveal the truth that a guru is unnecessary, however desirable. Further, we should know that for a beginner a guru would serve little or no purpose since any really advanced guru could hardly be expected to spend much of his time with a beginner any more than doctors of medical science teach high school health classes.

But if a guru is largely unnecessary why is it that so many yoga books claim otherwise?

To answer this question we have to understand the nature of the guru-discipline relationship as it grew up in India and we have to understand something of the history of yoga literature.

Some of the classical works on yoga that have come down to us, the *Yoga Sutras* of Patanjali, the *Hathayogapradipika*, or the *Gherand Samhita*, for example, were written more to codify or record yogic knowledge than they were to teach it. They were written for initiates, for teachers, for the gurus themselves. Naturally such works would stress that for real knowledge the guidance of a guru is necessary. And this was quite true since there was then no other way for the aspirant to acquire the knowledge or to have the practices described to him except through word of mouth, that is directly at the feet of the guru. There were no photographs or books or films. There were just the pithy sutras, and later the sketchy commentaries, and the guru himself.

From those times (the sutras of Patanjali date from perhaps the third century b.c.e. while the *Hathayogapradipika* was composed between 1350 and 1550 c.e.) writers of yoga books have had reference to these classical texts and have quite naturally repeated what they read there even though some of the advice no longer applies.

In the twentieth century we saw the growth of a modern or integrated yoga in which some of the antiquated practices of *hatha yoga* have been discarded or refined. This book attempts to reflect that tradition. Still it is a fact that many writers, especially those whose training or practice is superficial, are afraid that there may be some terrible secret they have missed, especially about *pranayama* or mudra, so they simply repeat the old injunction not to go further in this practice or that without a guru. In this way they mask their own lack of knowledge. Others cut the discussion short and repeat the guru-needed-here bromide not because they don't know the truth of the matter, but simply because they feel there is no sense in telling the student something he isn't ready for yet.

It is a standard procedure in the yogic tradition for some practices not to be revealed to the student. Such practices are said to be "secret," not so much because they are jealously guarded but because very few students are advanced enough in their practice to appreciate hearing about them. As I've pointed out elsewhere, "secret" is one of the code words used in the ancient texts along with "dangerous" and phrases such as "destroys all disease" that have meanings that are not what they seem at first glance.

In modern times publishers and writers alike have become wary when addressing a mass audience of being sued by someone who claims to have been hurt by a yoga practice. Since yoga is so dismally misunderstood by the general public, who can say what nonsense a jury may decide is true? So to be safe, publishers and authors issue warnings much in the manner that a car manufacturer showing a TV commercial of his car turning corners at high speeds warns: "Professional driver. Don't do this yourself."

You can, I suppose, be hurt by yoga. Certainly if you fall out of the headstand onto a hard floor you can hurt yourself. But it is also true you can hurt yourself doing almost any form of exercise. To this extent I add my own warning: Be careful. Take measures so that you don't fall. I've done the headstand thousands of times and haven't fallen once. I've lost my balance a number of times but since I practice near a wall I've always been able to break my fall.

You can even—again I suppose—be hurt by overdoing *pranayama*. This is nearly always claimed in yoga books. But it is far more likely that you will be hurt by over-running (which is a kind of very demanding *pranayama* with exercise). It is claimed in some books that some people get dizzy or faint or get headaches from *pranayama* wrongly practiced. Again I wouldn't be surprised. *Pranayama* has a powerful effect on the mind and body and is not to be undertaken lightly. However, if one stays within one's capacity, and does not overdo it, no harm can come. Whether you breathe too fast or too slow, or however your rhythm may vary from the ideal, it won't be important as long as you do not over burden your system. If you stop at the very first sign of discomfort and never increase your practice unless it is comfortable, you'll never go wrong. Furthermore, the practice of *pranayama* presupposes a healthy body. If you are in any way sick, you have to get well first before you practice.

The third and most important reason you almost invariably see the "guru-needed" warnings in the books is a direct result of the guru system itself.

THE GURU SYSTEM

According to the Hindu tradition the guru confers on his disciples more than just knowledge. He confers his grace. Consequently one is enlightened through the guru's grace, one acquires yoga through the guru's grace; indeed, it is said in some texts that the guru is God Himself, a direct personal manifestation of the Supreme Divine Consciousness.

However far-fetched this may seem to us there are very good reasons that even the most advanced (or especially the most advanced) guru might want his students to think this, as we shall see shortly. In general the guru can rationalize the exaggeration by telling himself how much more receptive his students would therefore be to his teachings.

In keeping with this tradition the student usually keeps a picture of his guru where he meditates so that he might conveniently worship him. When he visits the guru he sits at the guru's feet and in greeting embraces the guru's feet. This considered a great privilege.

Naturally such gestures serve to impress on the student the importance of the teacher and to set the student's mind to the proper psychological position. Theos Bernard, a Westerner who went to India in the thirties to learn yoga first hand, comments on his "initiation" into yoga thus, "Whether I was under the influence of the narcotic, [he had been given bhang by his guru—apparently a teacher influenced by the Tantric school] or in a self-induced trance, or under the hypnotic control of my Guru is still a mystery to me." (p. 315)

Bernard, who was an unusually diligent and hard-working student, makes it clear that one of the main purposes of the initiation rite was to make him more "receptive" to the guru's teachings. Apparently what the guru does for the student is similar to what happens to the subject during hypnosis. In this sense a guru may mightily advance one's practice. However if one is of a skeptical mind (as Sharma was) then the carefully arranged rites to induce trance and hypnotic effect may be of no value at all.

Bernard goes on to describe how, at the close of a ritual-laden ceremony which began at midnight and lasted for many hours (following a thirty-hour fast on Bernard's part)—nothing was left to chance here—his guru "whispered seven times into" his left ear and "seven times into" his right ear "the Mantra that was to be kept inviolate" in the recesses of his mind, "never to cross" his lips in utterance.

GURU AS LOVER

There is also a symbolism between guru and disciple that has grown up in the tantra tradition: the guru as lover. Hassin calls this "the highest relationship a disciple can have with a guru." He emphasizes that this relationship occurs on the "highest spiritual level" and has "nothing whatsoever to do with physical or sexual love." (p. 126) In the West we might call this an example of the Platonic ideal. Then again we might call it something else.

GURU AS MANTRA GIVER

One of the most important symbolic rites between guru and disciple is the giving of the mantra. We have Bernard's account above showing how intense is the bestowing. In a handbook written in India called *Tantra of Kundalini Yoga* by Paramahans Satyananda Saraswati the metaphor accompanying this ritual is explained more fully. "...That Mantra which you received from the Guru," Saraswati writes, "is the seed of the power for which you are the soil, for which you are the field.... If you are a nice, high class soil then the seed that the Guru puts in you, will yield a 100% harvest. ...If the soil is not fertile...the seed of the Guru will yield just a nominal harvest." (p. 9)

Under such circumstances the psychological effect of a guru can be very powerful indeed. Note the sexual symbolism.

GURU AS BHAKTI, AS LOVE

Psychology aside, the guru is held in the highest esteem in the Hindu tradition—a tradition that is very difficult if not impossible to separate from yoga itself. The injunction to follow the guru unquestioningly, to love him above all others and to trust him with everything, all material possessions as well as your very soul, is not only a time-honored tradition but is actually the essence of the powerful yoga called *bhakti*, the yoga of love or devotion.

Imagine yourself so terribly in love with your guru that you shake in his presence, that you glow, and the vibrations of love run through you in waves for hours after he has gone; imagine if you will that the guru is actually God himself in the flesh, shining with a love and wisdom so intense and awe-inspiring that words cannot express... Imagine giving yourself to a power higher than yourself, the Supreme Divine Consciousness and imagine yourself falling helplessly in love with the beatific vision of this consciousness made flesh. Imagine all this and you begin to have some idea how powerful a tool the guru system can be in helping some people to realize yoga.

So while a guru is not necessary for some of us and for others is not even desirable, he is for still others all-encompassing, the Way and the Light Itself, indispensable and irreplaceable, heaven and earth and all things to the disciple.

Such is Jesus for those who truly love him—in fact Christianity can be seen as a yoga of faith and devotion with Jesus serving simultaneously as guru and the personification of God. In a yoga of faith, it is essential to have a personification of God on which to focus one's faith. But for most of us such a pure and abiding love is all but impossible to achieve and is therefore not really relevant to our practice. If we could find God through love alone we should indeed practice some kind of bhakti and leave the disciplined and arduous path of *raja* yoga to others.

GURU AS DICTATOR

If the ideal is for the disciple to love the guru unquestioningly then it's easy to see that the guru system can lead to abuses. The guru could easily become a dictator, like the heads of various cults and could steal, cheat and otherwise exploit his disciples. This has happened many times and will happen again. For a particularly infamous modern example refer to Hubner and Gruson's *Monkey on a Stick* about the "Krishna Consciousness" movement. Upon reflection, however, we should be able to see that the guru system is no better or no worse than some other systems that might be used to transmit religious knowledge and lead the aspirant to God. For perspective then, let us look briefly at some other systems.

HOW RELIGIOUS KNOWLEDGE IS TRANSMITTED

We might see these systems as ways to get religious knowledge from one generation to the next so that the body of knowledge and practice will not die out with the present generation. And we might divide these means into four categories:

1. The guru system of word of mouth from one individual to another.
2. The monastic system in which the teachings are maintained by specially-trained persons known as monks who have for the most part withdrawn from society.
3. The church system in which a social-political body trains persons as preachers, imams or priests to transmit the knowledge.
4. Books, texts, treatises, etc., in which the knowledge is recorded in written language.

Needless to say, today most religious bodies use a combination of these means to maintain their systems. The thing for the student to realize is that some method is necessary because without a method to transmit religious knowledge there would be nothing here for us to learn. We should also realize that each system has its faults and limitations and is subject to various abuses.

The church system, for example, tends to become pre-eminently a political system with all the faults and evils of political systems. Churches also tend to become dominated by purely social concerns (as important as such concerns are) and tend to serve more as social bodies than as spiritual bodies. And because churches can become very large, centralized systems they can do a lot of damage. Westerners are only too aware of the horrors committed by churches that lost sight of their purpose and entered the social and political— even the military—sphere. The United States itself was founded by persons intent on escaping from repressive church systems. Today we can see examples of this abuse most clearly in the Middle East where fundamentalist leaders hold dictatorial control over the people.

In the monastic system the monks cut themselves off from the secular world and as they meditate and codify the sutras they tend to remove this knowledge further from the people either through the use of dead languages or "secret" codes or through the inevitable practice of ever so slightly rewriting the sacred texts. They change what Jesus or the Buddha or Mohammed had to say and not always for the better! As the texts become more polished and more in keeping with the beliefs of the monks they become less and less according to the original. Eventually there is the danger that a lot of what the present monks don't agree with will be left out, and other ideas they thought should have been there in the first place added, meaning that the present political system, like George Orwell's Big Brother, ends up rewriting the gospel.

In the guru system of course nothing was written down (originally, anyway). Everything was word of mouth. The Upanishads literally mean "knowledge gained at the guru's feet." The guru talked and the disciple listened and in his turn he talked and his disciple listened.

In one respect the guru system is superior to the church and monastic systems: there are fewer people involved and therefore less tendency to political corruption. But the guru system is pre-eminently an egoistic system and dictatorial. The guru knows the truth, the disciple is to learn it. In the church system the church knows the truth, the followers are to behave accordingly. In the monastic system the monks (often writing in a secret language, or at least in a language like Latin or Sanskrit not generally available to the lay person) know the truth and will hand it out piecemeal to the common folk in exchange for land, food and a nice monastery. (Of course some monasteries generate their own income while helping people in the communities in which they are located.)

It is unfortunate that such is the case. However the guru must eat. Why should he with all his knowledge and spiritual attainment be expected to plow the fields or to hustle life insurance? He shouldn't, of course, and it is a fair bargain for the disciple to get his meals for him and the community to provide him with shelter in exchange for what he knows.

The same can be said for the church and monastic systems. The point I am at pains to make here is that any system is imperfect and we must, as it were, work around these imperfections.

So when that yoga book says you can't really learn this knowledge or become adept in that practice without the grace of a personal guru, ignore it. That's the commercial for the system that keeps the knowledge flowing. You can indeed learn *hatha yoga* and even go on to scale the heights of *raja* yoga without a guru.

THE UNAVAILABILITY OF GURUS

However not only are gurus unnecessary, they are largely unavailable. There are plenty of false, phony, mercantile gurus out there. They are the most visible. It could even be said that if you've heard of the holy man he's probably not holy, and if he drives a Mercedes or appears on TV you can be sure of it!

This is only a slight exaggeration, but maybe it's a little unfair since I know of at least one well-known yogi, the late Richard Hittleman, who is indeed highly qualified. In truth, most well-known teachers (their books appear in the bibliography) are sincere, talented and dedicated persons. The difficulty is there are so few of them and so many who need to learn.

The ancient Taoist wisdom is exactly appropriate here: He who knows does not speak and he who speaks does not know. He knows how to make money and how to manage a going political concern, but of spiritual attainment...well, you know what the Bible says about the probability of rich men getting through the eye of a needle and into heaven.

Another reason gurus aren't readily available is that a real guru likes to spend his time contemplating God, not teaching lookie-loos. He's got better things to do with his time and there's no amount of money that would interest him. That's the guru I want!

BOOKS, CATS AND A WINTER WIND

A guru doesn't have to be an accomplished master. A guru can be an animal such as a cat, or an unsophisticated person such as a child, or a plant or even a lifeless object like a building. Study a building—meditate on it. Just watch the way it sits in the noon day sun.

Who taught the first yogi? She didn't have a guru as such. She was her own guru. The morning light as it came through the trees and the winter wind as it sculptured the drifts of snow were her gurus. And we too can be like that first yogi and be taught by God or by ourselves—or perhaps by God through ourselves or through the animals of the forest or the city, through the birds in the trees, by the orange cat meditating lightly now on the front porch after having cleaned itself in the warm sunlight. The silence of cats, the stoic indifference they maintain in the face of human foolishness is inspirational. Their cleanliness and their attention to the needs of their mind and body through stretching exercises and meditation can easily lead one to believe that a cat did indeed invent yoga.

Unlike the first yogi we have books. There are thousands of them on all aspects of yoga, books simple enough for children to follow easily and books complicated enough to infuriate even the most pedantic scholar. To sit around and wait for a guru, or to waste time running from one pundit to another in search of a guru is unnecessary when you have at your bookstore or at your local library or on the Internet knowledge and guidance sufficient for even the most eager student. If we had to wait around for the master to appear we might have to wait until the next lifetime to even get started. More to the point, each of us has a long way to go before we can even begin to justify the use of a true guru.

Books are a very good place to start. Books are a good beginning. In this day and age when almost all the important religious books of history are available on the Web or at your local library in translation, there is no reason not to get started on them.

Certainly, in the beginning we may not really understand all of what is being said (and in the end we may still not understand it). But at least if it was worth saying it's worth reading.

So I made B.K.S. Iyengar my personal guru. I made Alan Watts my personal guru. I made Krishna of the *Bhagavad Gita* the personification of God. I listened to Lao Tzu and the Buddha and so can you. If along the way a guru should appear, all well and good; if not, if you work hard enough you can, after a few weeks, months—decades—be your own guru.

Chapter 16:
Physical Health: *Pranayama*

WHAT *PRANAYAMA* MEANS

Pranayama comes before meditation since *pranayama* leads to meditation. It comes after asana since to attempt *pranayama* in ill health leads to failure.

Of all the subjects in yoga perhaps none is more needlessly difficult than *pranayama*.

The difficulty begins with the word itself. *prana* means vital air, the mysterious life force that yogis believe pervades the universe. But *prana* also means "soul." Usually though it means a particular kind of breath, the incoming vital breath that moves within the chest and heart as contrasted with e.g., *apana*, which is outgoing and moves in the lower body. *Prana* is the pure essence of the "subtle body." It is also energy and the mysterious essence of life itself. It is the wind.

For Westerners raised in a scientific tradition this *prana* sounds suspiciously like oxygen or the "ether" of nineteenth century physics that Einstein and the Michelson-Morley experiments did away with (but which is back as the "nothing" that is "something" in quantum mechanics; see John D. Barrow's *The Book of Nothing: Vacuums, Voids, and the Latest Ideas about the Origins of the Universe* (2000) or K.C. Cole's *The Hole in the Universe: How Scientists Peered over the Edge of Emptiness and Found Everything* (2001), two excellent books on how the "ether" is back with a vengeance).

"Yama" means restraint. The word also refers to the Hindu God of Death. "Ayama" means "pause" (according to Day, p. 21) and "length, expansion, stretching and restraint" (according to Iyengar p. 43). Taken together the word *"pranayama"* is usually referred to authoritatively as "the science of breath."

In the West we know from experience that when somebody talks about the "science" of anything and begins with assumptions that are untestable and contrary to common scientific knowledge (such as the notion of *prana*) we can be sure they are being anything but scientific. So-called "creation science" is an example. Consequently many Westerners are immediately turned off by the idea of *pranayama* as presented in yoga books and usually don't get past the definition.

This is too bad. It's silly to let words trip us up; sillier still to be prejudice in the name of science, forgetting that science is nothing more than a common sense methodology rigorously applied. So let's apply a little common sense to this business of *pranayama* and see what we come up with.

PRANAYAMA DEFINED

First of all let's just let *prana* mean "breath" for the time being—nothing more or less. And let's let yama or ayama mean "control of." Let's also put aside the word "science" and use instead the less pretentious word "practice." So what we have in *pranayama* is "the practice of the control of the breath." Or we could use Wood's admirable definition: "the practice of ordered breathing." Okay? That's not so hard to accept. Now the question is why should we wish to control the breath—doesn't the breath work all right by itself?

THE INTERACTION OF MIND AND BREATH

Surprisingly the answer is no. The breath, possibly unique among the expressions of our body, can be controlled by either a voluntary or an involuntary act. It is both a conscious and an unconscious event. As such, the rate, extent and rhythm of the breath can affect the conscious mind, and in turn the conscious mind can affect the rate, extent and rhythm of the breath.

This seems like a small observation at first, but it is actually a momentous discovery. The fact that we can regulate the breath consciously wouldn't be much to realize except for the amazing fact that the reverse is true: the regulation of the breath affects our consciousness!

This fact is usually pointed out in yoga books; and readers who get that far with an open mind may perk up their attention and the dawning of knowledge may come upon them. It is a mundane observation that an angry person breathes fast and jerkily, and that a calm person breathes slow and rhythmically, but it is an observation that ought to be dwelt on. Can we make ourselves calm by breathing slow and rhythmically? The answer is a resounding yes! A person who is about to lose his temper is often advised to count to ten. We usually think that the purpose of that is to slow us down and allow us to reflect upon what we're about to say or do, but the process of counting slowly to ten will also re-regulate our breath.

But for the yogi the control of breath leads not merely to keeping one's temper, but all the way up the ladder of yoga to the very pinnacle of *samadhi*. The yoga adept can not only control his temper, he can with the help of various breathing exercises, bring about numerous states of mind, including bliss, trance, ecstasy, serenity, etc. This, it should be seen immediately, is no small feat; in fact its realization should make us understand why the ancient books claimed that yoga cures all that ails you. The *Gheranda Samhita* claims (v,1) that by the practice of *pranayama* alone we become God-like.

Another thing that hangs the Westerner up on *pranayama* is the invariable warning we get in the yoga books that its practice without the guidance of a qualified teacher may lead to illness, etc. This could be true in some cases, but it is one of those truths that needs a little explanation.

If a typical person of middle years, twenty pounds overweight, a habitual smoker and non-exerciser were to plunge headlong into *pranayama*, attempting for example a few rounds of *bhastrika* (the bellows breath) he or she might indeed faint. Furthermore even a relatively healthy person who attempts to perform *nadi sodhana pranayama* with retention (advanced alternate nose breathing) may encounter headaches or other unpleasant reactions. By the same token however if either of these people attempted to run a mile or climb a mountain they would run into all sorts of difficulties. If they had the will to go on until they dropped, they would surely drop or get sick in one way or the other.

Pranayama is exercise. In its more advanced practices it is very vigorous exercise indeed. No one can be expected to begin an exercise program at a level beyond his capacity. No one can be expected to start out running a mile nonstop. Just as in any exercise, you walk before you jog, you jog before you run, and you go slow and easy at first and only gradually extend your practice, so it is with *pranayama*.

It might be supposed that even a person somewhat out of shape could be expected to sprint for a hundred yards. Perhaps. It depends on the "somewhat." However even if she could, should she? Absolutely not, because although she might very well make it without injury, she could just as easily pull or strain a muscle from the sudden and unusually violent (for her) exertion. Even for trained athletes it is good advice to one, warm up first, and two, slowly work up to sprinting form. The same is true in the practice of *pranayama*. When Iyengar says that an aspirant must be qualified to begin the practice he means just that, and this qualification comes from the practice of asana and the "strength and discipline arising therefrom." (p. 431) This is why *pranayama* comes after the asanas in yoga practice, both evolutionarily and as a matter of day-to-day practice.

Iyengar also says that "the fitness of the aspirant...is to be gauged by an experienced Guru..." and his supervision is "essential." (p. 431)

We might ask why Iyengar is presenting all these *pranayamas* in such detail if we are going to need a guru anyway? Part of the answer can be found in the chapter on gurus I have written for this volume, but part of the answer lies in the fact that Iyengar was writing for teachers as well as students and his book was meant to be a textbook.

So, should you go ahead and begin your practice of *pranayama*?

The answer is a qualified yes. First some cautions. We are not in this book anyway going to do any "running"; that is, all the *pranayamas* we will practice are going to be slow and easy ones that are no more dangerous than walking and we are going to practice them with mindfulness and we are going to abandon immediately any practice that leads to any sort of ill-effect. Further we are going to under-do. If we are at all overweight or out of shape, if we haven't mastered at least the main sequence asanas that I presented in the asana chapters, if for any reason at all we feel we aren't ready, we are not going to practice *pranayama*. Finally, if we have an ailment of any kind we are going to consult a doctor before we begin.

CONTROL OF THE MIND THROUGH *PRANAYAMA*

Pranayama, as I said above, leads to control of the conscious mind, that is to say it leads to meditation. The point is that the goal of yoga and all yogic practices is liberation from the bondage of the flesh and to union with Divine Consciousness which comes with *samadhi*—the highest stage of meditation. To practice *pranayama* merely to get a pleasant mood or to gain trance is wonderful, but ultimately it is not enough.

By the way, to emphasize what appears elsewhere in this volume, the so-called psychic powers that the ancient texts attribute to yoga are in fact trance or self-hypnotic states of mind. The fact that one believes that one can read another's mind or that one is actually lifting off the ground ("levitating") is an indication that one has achieved a change in consciousness, that one is on the way to mind control and *samadhi*. So when the ancient texts say to disregard and ignore the psychic powers that come up, since such powers are not what is to be sought, and are only distractions along the way, it is good advice but perhaps more to the point very much reveals the Indian mind at work. Instead of saying, no these powers are illusions, the Indian mind doesn't contradict. It just says let go... The yogic style is to reject nothing out of hand (you never know, it might turn out to be good).

So when you practice *pranayama* be prepared to run into some very unusual states of mind. At first they will be fleeting and come and go willy-nilly. After some mastery is gained they will come under the control of the student. At some stage the student will find himself, if he is not careful, chasing these states of mind and feeling disappointed and cheated when he doesn't achieve them—and exhilarated and maybe even self-important when he does. All of these things, like "psychic powers," are to be noted and let pass. If you focus on such things it will distract you from your practice, and at any rate, your ability to control the mind will slip. If you become involved in the bliss and stay in the bliss this is good, but if you seek only the bliss and feel disappointed when it doesn't come (and sometimes it will not come) you will backslide in your practice and the very thing you seek will recede.

The above points will apply even more when we get to meditation. I mention them now because once one has become established in *pranayama*, one is already meditating.

THE POWER OF *PRANAYAMA*

As powerful as asana is in elevating the mood and giving us a sense of happiness and the ability to act effectively, *pranayama* is greater still. For bestowing on us a sense of contentment with power, a sense of happiness with compassion, and a fine feeling of being alive and happy about being alive, nothing matches *pranayama*.

The artificial highs that users get from drugs initially seem more powerful than *pranayama*, but eventually dissipate into desperate attempts to "maintain," involving the terrible law of diminishing returns, while with *pranayama* the response from the mind and body grows, as the sense of contentment and joy widens. The use of drugs as a crude substitute for a beautifully orchestrated mind and body, functioning optimally, defeats all attempts at yoga and leads the user diametrically in the opposite direction, from health to ill-health, from happiness to sadness and despair, from life to death, from joy to self-inflicted torture.

The drug addict is to be pitied because he so much wants to find something greater than the mundane existence of his ordinary consciousness, but is fooled and tricked by the toxins of plants or other organisms (or the chemicals of man) into accepting at first a seductive change from his usual consciousness followed by an endless chasing after that initial thrill until, unable to feel and experience normal life, he is reduced to being a pathetic and painful wretch, no more able to find happiness than a person under constant torture.

For the aspirant in yoga what is clear is that the use of outside agents to lift our mental state is always a mistake leading to delusion and sadness and the very opposite of what is desired. But it goes beyond that. Make no mistake about it, all drugs, all foods, all things ingested, smoked, injected, inhaled—in short anything taken into the body except the necessary air, water and food—constitute polluted seeds that can only bear the fruit of disease and death. Ideally, as yogis we would not eat at all. We wouldn't even breathe.

But such is the nature of the food sheath—the flesh—that we must eat and we must breathe in order to carry on life. We must do so in harmony with our environment and in harmony with our internal system. To take in the wrong things or to even take in the right things in the wrong amounts is detrimental to our well-being. One can even breathe too much (for example, one can hyperventilate). Even the very air, the purest air possible can be toxic if overdone. Therefore technique in living, that is, intelligence applied to life's choices must be made by the yogi. To do otherwise is to abdicate our dharma, to sully our *karma* and to bring pain and destruction upon ourselves—we who are, properly seen, an integral part of divine consciousness.

WHY *PRANAYAMA*?

With *pranayama* we get to the heart of why many people take up yoga: they are looking for a means to a higher consciousness, to the bliss and peacefulness that transcends understanding, to what some people mistakenly think they can get from drugs. You can achieve a transcendental state of mind from yoga, but be forewarned, it isn't easy (although for some it is), and it doesn't come all at once (although for some it does) and if it is the only reason you are practicing yoga it will be even more difficult to achieve.

PSYCHIC POWERS

So I should say something additional about the psychic powers we hear so much about. First of all they should be seen as alternate or transcendental mental states—or signs of such states. I have, I must confess, experienced levitation (one of the "classic" psychic powers referred to in the literature) and I have read the minds of others and I have been invisible to my fellow man and I have had other such experiences that I don't recall at the moment. But I would not say today that I left this terra firma and rose up into the air and hovered there (although that was my experience). And I would not say that the voices I heard so clearly came directly from the minds of my friends and neighbors, although I don't doubt the truth of what they said or the veracity of my experience. And when people looked right through me as I passed them in the hallway, I know that their inability to see me may have been as much a function of their consciousness as it was of mine.

The evaluation of such experiences by the normal or regular waking consciousness is not possible. The ordinary mind can only see the world in ordinary terms. It is dominated by the illusions of this world, by the "laws" of cause and effect, by the methodology of science (which, to repeat, is common sense, rigorously applied and confirmed), and especially by the evolutionary mechanism which requires that we see things in terms of survival and reproduction. We, as limited creatures in God's world, cannot ever hope to completely understand the world. Our minds, relatively speaking, are like the ant's only a little more advanced. For the ant to comprehend the galaxy or even our backyard is something far beyond the ability of its consciousness. So too it is for us in our attempts to understand the totality of our existence. We all have had experiences we cannot explain and we have to accept that: the fact is some things will happen that are inexplicable. So it is with the so-called psychic powers that come with *pranayama* and meditation; so it is with the experiences of meditation itself. Some things cannot be explained, they can only be experienced. That is one of the central lessons of yoga. To understand you have to experience. Nothing else will do.

UNNOTICED *PRANAYAMAS*

You know how people say, "I had to get warmed up" before anything worthwhile was accomplished? We used to get up in the morning but before we had our coffee and our cigarettes we were not in the mood to do anything. And then it happened, we were suddenly warmed up and rolling.

Part of the reason for this is that without being aware of it we had done our own, however crude, version of a *pranayama* and our mood had changed from lethargy to an optimistic readiness to tackle the world (which is the proper disposition of a healthy person). Little did we realize however that the coffee and the cigarettes were totally unnecessary. All we had to do was teach ourselves to do a few minutes of *pranayama* upon rising and our mood would become very beautiful very quickly and that we'd be all warmed up and ready for the world.

It has often been observed that the lift the addict gets from cigarettes is in part due to the little *pranayama* he performs every time he takes a puff. It's true. But doing *pranayama* with smoke is like drinking water with sludge in it. Or like listening to a symphony with a metal trash can accompaniment. Smoking cigarettes is *pranayama* with noise. It's polluted *pranayama*. And, as we know, it's *pranayama* at a frightful cost.

AEROBICS AND HEALTHY LUNGS

When I began the practice of yoga decades ago I thought that the breathing exercises might cure my asthma. As it turned out I never mastered the breathing exercises until my asthma had been cured. What happened was my asthma was cured as much by asana as it was by *pranayama*, and most particularly by removing myself from what I was allergic to. Asana stimulated my glands so that my system functioned normally while *pranayama* helped to prevent the build-up of excessive mucus in my lungs. My practice of *pranayama* fell off when I resumed playing basketball. I found that playing full-court basketball was itself a great *pranayama*. Now I know that at least one of the standard *pranayamas* (the bellows breath) is actually a substitute for a good aerobic workout. Or, it could be said, a good aerobic workout is a substitute for the bellows breath, albeit a strenuous one.

It should be mentioned that before the modern age aerobic-type exercises were shunned rather than embraced. There were no joggers on the streets of old New York or around Dickens' London Town. Aerobics as a practice of the masses is a recent phenomenon. And this is not surprising when you consider that in the 19th century, for example, only the idle rich could afford the time and energy necessary for aerobic exercise. The poor got plenty of exercise at the foundry, twelve hours a day, thank you.

In the yogic tradition of India of course the necessity to adequately exercise the lungs has long been recognized. Patanjali however was primarily interested in *pranayama* in order to control the mind and make it fit for meditation. If the breath is erratic or if we are short of breath, then a proper concentration is impossible.

But before we can breathe slowly and with control we must have healthy lungs (again we are always returning to the physical foundation upon which any success in yoga rests). And to have healthy lungs we must exercise them and build their capacity.

WHY YOGIS ARE NOT INTO RUNNING

The ancient yogis rejected running as a way to cleanse the lungs and exercise them for several reasons:

One, they didn't believe in doing anything more than was necessary. The running was an unnecessary expenditure of energy that could be put to better use.

Two, you can't concentrate very well when you are fatigued. Yogis do not believe in becoming fatigued.

Three, violent exercise can lead to an agitated mind (at least temporarily—actually as all dedicated runners know, exercise ultimately leads to a calm mind; however, the yogi doesn't like to wait).

Finally, any type of abrupt, violent movement is antithetical to the spirit of yoga.

One other thing—in ancient India people got from one place to the other mainly by walking. Almost any person got enough exercise by walking and hardly needed (or could incorporate) any running.

I hope I have made it clear why *hatha yoga* does not advocate aerobics. Some people think this is a failing in yogic physical culture when actually it is a natural consequence of the entire program. However I personally believe that running is entirely compatible with yoga. I still run and I still practice yoga and have done so for decades.

BEGINNING *PRANAYAMA*

While a good efficiency in asana can be learned on our own without the help of a teacher, progress in *pranayama* without the guidance of someone who knows what he is doing may be slow. Unfortunately experts in *pranayama* are much rarer than experts in asana. The reason is not difficult to see. In asana one can look at the postures as posed for in photographs and copy them. One can study the methodology and follow it. But in *pranayama* a photograph does little good and the average person has so little awareness of how he is breathing (do you know where your diaphragm is right now?) and so little ability to gain any feedback from watching himself in a mirror or just looking at his chest that his progress must necessarily be slow. Furthermore, the very practice of watching oneself do *pranayama* can (initially) interfere with the *pranayama*.

Nonetheless some very fine progress can be made. And of course for the dedicated student much can be learned. The most important point in the beginning is to develop a healthy respiratory tract free of excess mucus, and to build up your lung capacity so that voluntary control of the lungs is easy. (It's hard to practice breath retention if you're out of breath to begin with.)

Aerobic workouts (running, brisk walking, dancing, cycling, playing a sport like basketball, etc.) will give the student good lung capacity and allow him enough control to begin the practice of the *pranayamas* that require retention of breath.

For beginning students who are very much out of shape, *pranayama* must begin with the practice of deep breathing ("the full yogic breath," as it has often been called) accompanied by mild exercise (walking is a fine exercise) until the student has developed some capacity.

Once we have some voluntary control of our breath and can retain the breath for twenty or thirty seconds without strain we are ready to experience what can be accomplished through *pranayama*. Then, instead of mind over matter, we will have, as it were, body over mind. The harmony of mind and body will readily be seen and this knowledge will help the student throw out the old mind-body dichotomies as shallow delusions and see the mind and body working intimately together, not separately.

It can be shown that certain *pranayamas* decrease the flow of oxygen to the blood (and consequently to the brain) thereby facilitating a meditative mood. Other *pranayamas* of course do the opposite and activate the system by increasing the oxygen supply to the blood stream. One who has mastered *pranayama* will be able to know exactly what practice (which particular *pranayama*) is needed at any given time. Usually I start out with breathing rhythms designed to put a lot of oxygen into my blood stream, followed by slower and slower rhythms until I am meditating.

It should be noted here that when one has an "oxygen debt" incurred through strenuous exercise, *pranayamas* involving retention of breath will not work.

Finally, as with asana, the major reason for the practice of *pranayama* is to facilitate meditation. In addition to the physiological benefits, *pranayama*, like asana, is itself a seed to meditation. According to many authorities, *pranayama* is indeed the best seed to meditation. Just by counting the breaths (or even just by observing the breath) one is lead directly into meditation. One finds this practice in Buddhism, Jainism, Zen Buddhism, and Taoism. Christian mystics and Islamic Sufis practice breathing exercises as a technique leading to meditation.

THE FULL YOGIC BREATH

Pranayama also exercises and invigorates the internal organs, especially through the practice of the full, deep yogic breath. So the first *pranayama* to be learned is this deep breath which consists merely of breathing in slowly and fully, using consciously the diaphragm and letting the stomach puff out. Make the inward breath as full of life as possible while the mind imagines the lungs expanding, the mind concentrating gently but intently on the inward flow of air until one is filled to the brim.

And then one holds the breath briefly (this is *kumbhaka*) before breathing out. The outward breath should be even slower than the inward breath. The air should not rush out but go out slowly with an even, deliberate effort as the diaphragm rises and the stomach area is consciously pulled in and lifted. Ideally the time taken by inhalation, retention and exhalation should be in the ratio of 1:4:2; that is, however long it takes to breathe in, it should take twice as long to breathe out and the air should be held four times as long in retention (say, four seconds, sixteen seconds and eight seconds). In the beginning however it is enough to make the exhalation a little longer than the inhalation and the retention a little longer still. As your ability and capacity increase you can work more and more toward the ideal ratio of 1:4:2.

This is the only *pranayama* you should attempt until you have mastered it. Don't imagine you have mastered it until several weeks of daily practice have gone by. And don't imagine that mastery comes merely from the ability to maintain a proper ratio. What counts in mastery is how easily the complete breath is done and how mindfully; that is, you will know you have mastered it when you can see the breath breathing you and not the other way around.

You should at some point in your practice be able to see yourself commanding the slow and magnificently deep breaths but at the same time the breaths should seem to be doing themselves without your conscious intervention. In other words, you should be a witness to your breath and you should witness it as a phenomenon part voluntary and part involuntary, as something happening at a new locus where you are both the observer and the observed, the doer and that which is being done.

This is important because the breath is the meeting place between the conscious and the unconscious mind. Conscious control of the breath leads to conscious control of the mind.

ON THE BREATHING RATIOS

Now why is the ratio this "1:4:2" instead of (perhaps) "1:1:1"?

There are *pranayamas* that are practiced at a one to one to one ratio. And there are *pranayamas* that require breathing out of one nostril only for a while and then out of the other, sometimes beginning with the left and sometimes with the right. And most authorities, by the way, require that you breathe out first whenever you begin your *pranayama*. This is the convention and it makes sense (as will be seen after some practice). Therefore all *pranayamas* by tradition begin after an outward breath.

Starting from that position (of having emptied the lungs) one naturally breathes in with enthusiasm (the lungs being empty!). Whatever the natural time it takes to fill your lungs becomes the standard for determining the ratios.

But why should retention and exhalation last longer than inhalation?

Exhalation lasts longer because it is important to force as much of the used air as possible out of our lungs so that fresh air can enter. (Fresh air cannot enter where there is air already.) Further, the process of consciously forcing out (gently of course!) the stale air strengthens the lungs and exercises the diaphragm, thereby building our breathing capacity. Inhalation is more of a passive experience for the diaphragm since it is by creating a vacuum around our lungs that the lungs are forced to expand and fill with air.

The reason for holding the breath even longer is two-fold. At the heart of the matter, in the long run the idea is to develop a retention capacity for meditation. The longer we can hold our breath without strain the better we can concentrate on what we are doing and not be disturbed. Secondly, holding the breath creates an outward pressure in the lungs as it allows the cilia to more easily push the mucus, which is laden with impurities, outward. If we did things backwards and breathed in in long breaths and held for almost no time and breathed out quickly, the cleaning of the lungs would not be as readily facilitated. All the pressure would be inward. (However such a rhythm has it uses, as we will see in the chapter on meditation.)

So the complete breath in the 1:4:2 ratio not only leads to meditation, but helps to clean the lungs as well. Some authorities actually call this a "cleansing breath," which it is.

Some books recommend other *pranayamas* and describe procedures leading to sweating, shaking, even faintness and "dizziness in the beginning." If you try to hold your breath beyond your capacity such things are bound to happen. For us, we avoid such discomfort by never going beyond what is comfortable. Furthermore to increase a limited capacity I recommend that the beginning student walk briskly. That way your body will burn up the oxygen as you go along and the dizzy feeling that sometimes comes with taking in too much oxygen too quickly is avoided.

When the student is well along the path to mastery in yoga (and has mastered the complete breath) you may—and undoubtedly will—experiment with other *pranayamas*. You should guide yourself by having reference to a good text such as the books written by Iyengar, Hittleman, Vishnudevananda, and Satyananda Saraswati mentioned in the bibliography. Perhaps the best book of all is Andre van Lysebeth's *Pranayama: The Yoga of Breathing* first published in English in 1979 and recently brought out in a new edition by Harmony Publishing. It is certainly the most extensive in its treatment of the subject.

Iyengar compares the breath to pneumatic tools that can cut through rock and steel. We want to make sure that we are in complete control of our tools before we attempt the more demanding practices. Therefore the practice of *pranayama* presented in this book is a slowly-developing, conservative approach.

More to the point, beyond healthy lungs and beyond a living realization of the power of breath and how it relates sympathetically to the mind, we do not need to go. No matter how complicated and advanced the *pranayamas* might be they will only yield these two enduring results: healthy lungs and a seed to meditation.

Pranayama is considered essential in the yoga of technique because without healthy lungs and without a realization of the connection between the control of the breath and the control of the mind, the yogi can never reach the heights of *raja* yoga, and he can never be the master of his mind. Furthermore, the quickest and easiest way to control the monkey mind is with the reins of breath. But I have found that only one *pranayama*, namely the complete breath, is necessary to achieve these essential goals. For the master of *hatha yoga* other *pranayamas* undoubtedly give a finer control, offer a better leverage over mind and body, and are for the yogi, very fine tools indeed. I would put such practices in the five percent bracket of yoga; that is, something useful after you have learned the other ninety-five percent.

However since this subject is so important (and sometimes given short shrift in other books) I will present some other *pranayamas* in the next chapter. Meanwhile continue to practice the complete breath. If you don't now feel you have mastered it, you might want to skip the following chapter.

Chapter 17:
Physical Health: Advanced *Pranayama*

THE ELEMENTS OF *PRANAYAMA*

To cut through the complications of *pranayama* it's helpful to analyze the practices in terms of elements. The elements of *pranayama* are:

Seat, that is, posture. Advanced students generally sit in the lotus position. Any meditative posture will do.

Rhythm, which is how long the breath is maintained in each of its three stages, inhalation, exhalation and retention (i.e., the ratio of time spent in each).

Technique, which includes the application of *bandhas* or "locks," and *mudras*, or "gestures." We'll define these terms in a moment.

Let's take each of the elements in turn.

SEAT

We could practice the full yogic breath while walking. Yogis don't do this because although the health benefit of the *pranayama* would be realized the psychological benefits would not. Further, the aspirant would be distracted from total concentration on his breathing and this would slow his progress toward mastery of breath.

In view of this it is best to practice *pranayamas* while assuming a comfortable cross-legged posture. The legs should be drawn up tight toward the body, the arms should be at one's side, the hands forming the *mudra* of the wise (or resting in the lap). The idea

185

is to be centered and focused on the respiratory system with nothing extraneous going on to distract us. It takes long practice to gain control of the breath and to appreciate the subtle relationship between mind and breath, so the tighter our focus and the better our concentration the more rapid our progress.

Andre van Lysebeth has this to say about the seating posture for *prana mudra*, which is a kind of full-breath *pranayama* with hand movements, almost a kind of sitting Tai Chi:

> *Normally, this position should be the lotus exclusively. However for Westerners who have not yet mastered* padmasana, siddhasana, *or even* vajrasana, *is acceptable. As an ultimate concession, and purely temporary, the exercise may be performed sitting on a chair...*

Or, simply sit in any cross-legged position. What van Lysebeth is emphasizing is the pre-eminent position that the lotus asana assumes in the yogic pantheon of postures. But of course most people will never achieve the lotus position. What I want to emphasize is that *pranayama* and mediation and indeed *samadhi* can be achieved without the lotus, although if you are young I would advise you to work on the posture since it is clearly the best for *pranayama* and meditation.

RHYTHM

As mentioned in the previous chapter most *pranayamas* employ the natural rhythm of 1:4:2 for, respectively, inhalation, retention and exhalation, but there are significant differences. At this stage of your practice you ought to be quite comfortable with breathing in for four seconds, holding for sixteen and breathing out for eight (4:16:8). Ideally an 8:32:16 configuration should be possible without strain. If the 4:16:8 is not comfortable and the 8:32:16 requires an undo effort, it would be wise to skip this chapter for now.

In advanced *pranayama* there is also retention after exhalation (*bahya kumbhaka*) equal to the time of exhalation making the advanced normal ratio equal to 1:4:2:2. Traditional yogic wisdom has it that our lives are not numbered in years but in breaths. Therefore yogis like to take as few breaths as possible and make them as leisurely and as full as possible.

Any rhythm that deviates from the natural rhythm is for a specific purpose. The bellows breath, which we will get to shortly, for example, employs a very fast, inhale-exhale staccato rhythm that activates the system, and when continued leads to perspiration and a state of general physical and mental arousal.

TECHNIQUE

How the air is taken in. Normally we breathe through our nostrils with our mouth closed. This is the proper way to breathe since our nostrils help to filter and warm the air, "conditioning" it before it enters our lungs. However some *pranayamas* have us breathing through our mouth, through partially opened lips, or through just one nostril at a time or even through a rolled tongue. In general such techniques are like isometric exercises in that they make the lungs work harder (in the case of the narrow channel of one nostril) or just the opposite in the case of the opened mouth in which the lungs find less resistance. Furthermore, the quality of the air taken in will vary. Air taken in through the nostrils will be warmer than air from an opened mouth.

In the advanced practices the tongue and throat muscles come into play, further regulating the flow of breath.

Bandhas. An integral part of *pranayama* practice is the employment of *bandhas* or physical locks to regulate the flow of bodily fluids as well as electrical and psychic energy throughout the body. These bandhas are powerful postures in themselves and are often employed by yogis during asana or meditation. The three most significant are *jalandhara*, *mula*, and *uddiyana*. Let's look at each in turn.

Jalandhara bandha is the chin lock. It is accomplished by pressing the chin into the jugular cavity. The head should be lifted slightly while aiming the chin. The "lock" is set by swallowing after the chin is firmly in place. (A natural chin lock occurs during the shoulder stand and the plow.)

Usually employed during breath retention, *jalandhara* helps to retain the breath and to intensify the effects of retention. *Jalandhara bandha* also stimulates the nerves passing through the neck as well as the glands in the neck. It cuts off the ready interaction between the abdominal body and the head allowing an intensification of focus. Furthermore the chin lock leads the expert practitioner to a greater awareness of his body and how it functions. It also exercises the neck muscles and stimulates neurological flow. It makes one aware of the condition of the throat.

Mula bandha is the anal lock. It is accomplished by contracting the sphincter muscles and drawing the abdominal muscles upward. There is usually a brief, pleasurable electrical sensation accompanying the *mula bandha*. However it quickly wears out. More significant is a sharp, pleasurable tingling sensation that rises from the anal area and continues along the spinal cord, sometimes going all the way to the brain.

When *mula bandha* and *jalandhara bandha* are employed simultaneously (as they often are during retention) they are said to unite *prana* (the "vital air") and apana (the upward rushing air) and to assist in the arousal of *kundalini*. We'll try to sort out what this means when we discuss *kundalini*. For the moment be assured that the use of *mula bandha* leads the student to a better awareness and appreciation of the amazing world of his body and helps to direct his attention inward where it belongs.

Uddiyana bandha is the abdominal lift. It is accomplished by pulling the abdominal cavity upward and inward and holding. This is done only after the exhalation of breath. Properly speaking *uddiyana bandha* should be seen as an independent exercise. It is often practiced by yogis while standing, slightly bent forward with hands resting on the thighs. First the yogi exhales completely and then draws his abdominal muscles upward and inward. This causes the lungs to be compressed, the blood to rush to the head and the abdominal cavity to be vigorously exercised. For this alone *uddiyana bandha* is an excellent practice.

Mudras. These are gestures or psychic seals somewhat in the manner of sympathetic magic. Thus when one sits in the lotus one's hands rest on the knees with the three lower fingers extended while the thumb and forefinger are made to compose a circle—the so-called symbol or *mudra* of wisdom.

There are numerous *mudras* employed in the yoga practice, but their use is largely symbolic and traditional. We will defer a discussion of *mudra* until later. For now the only *mudra* we'll use is the one described in the previous paragraph, the *mudra* of wisdom, and we do that only as a gesture of respect to the tradition of yoga. We could just as easily employ the gesture of the Buddha and sit with one hand over the other on our lap—our right hand over our left when we are in an active mood and the left over the right when we are more passive.

THE BAMBOO BREATH

Now it is time to present some further *pranayamas*. Hopefully the student (now in full command of the yogic breath) is eager to learn something new.

Let's begin with a meditative breath, not a traditional yogic *pranayama*, but something from Zen. This is what Katsuki Sekida in his *Zen Training: Methods and Philosophy* calls "the bamboo breath."

Instead of retaining the breath at fullness (*antara kumbhaka*), in the bamboo breath one releases the breath in stages, a little at a time. This allows us to maintain our concentration longer without the disruptive need for a new inhalation. Successfully done, it's a little like having your cake and eating it too!

This *pranayama* leads more easily to meditation than the cleansing breath because there is less pressure on the internal organs and only a gentle tension along the diaphragm is felt— just enough to serve as a focal point for meditation.

I should point out here that we tend to think of the lungs as "full" or "empty" but actually even when we have emptied the lungs as much as possible they still contain a lot of air. This is because the lungs are sponge-like objects that even after being squeezed by the diaphragm, regardless of how hard, still retain much air. It is quite impossible to ever empty the lungs of air.

Incidentally, Sekida refers to the diaphragm area as the *tanden* and emphasizes it as a center for emotional expression. He says (p.84) "You may bury a friend up to his chest in the sand...and tell him a funny story, and try as you may, you cannot make him laugh. He fully understands in his head the effect of the two contradictory ideas in the story, but he does not feel amused. For a feeling of amusement to appear, it is absolutely necessary that a certain physical impulse suddenly thrust up from the bottom of the abdomen. This impulse comes from the convulsive contraction of the respiratory muscles."

We might refer to the bamboo breath as "the nod" or "the sleeper's breath" since the technique involves a rhythm similar to the way the head bobs when someone falls asleep in a chair: as the breath is taken in the head goes slightly up, and as the air is let out in stages the head nods until it comes to rest, holds for a moment and then pops up again as the sleeper takes in a new breath. The alert and aware student will discover after some practice the periodicity that works best for her.

Sekida calls this the bamboo breath because the pauses (or stages) are like the markings that divide a bamboo pole into sections.

At this point in practice I would recommend that the student begin *pranayama* with the regular full, cleansing breath in the regular 1:4:2 ratio, and as the disposition to meditation is felt, switch to the bamboo breath. If the lungs are healthy the student should be able to maintain the retention for sufficient long periods to enjoy a very fine meditation.

Pranayama gives a lift, both mentally and physically. Whenever your mind and body are lethargic a brief session of *pranayama* (sometimes followed by *savasana*) will so refresh you that you will be able to renew your work with optimism and vigor. Don't think you have to do a lot; sometimes just a minute of *pranayama* is all it takes to renew yourself.

Work extensively on the bamboo breath before beginning the following *pranayamas*.

THE BELLOWS BREATH

Sometimes we feel particularly lethargic, especially if we've been doing more mental work than physical, especially if we've been confined for some reason, perhaps because of bad weather. At such times *bhastrika* or the bellows breath should be practiced. The technique is quite simple.

Assume a comfortable seat. As usual the back should be held straight.

Apply *jalandhara bandha* (the chin lock described above).

Inhale quickly and with vigor through both nostrils.

Exhale quickly and vigorously through both nostrils.

This completes one round of the bellows breath. Continue to the count of about ten or twelve, and then breathe slowly with a good retention for about a minute. Do another round or two and then lie down in *Savasana* (the "death pose") and relax.

Bhastrika can also be done using one nostril at a time. Before we do that however the subject of alternate nostril breathing should be introduced.

This is a subject fraught with symbolism and uncertainty, confusion and an acute lack of scientific study. I'm going to go into it more deeply than the subject perhaps deserves. Hopefully my limited discussion will inspire some real research.

ALTERNATE NOSTRIL BREATHING

Symbolically the right nostril represents the sun and the left the moon. Consequently air arriving through the right nostril is said to be "hot" while air coming in through the left is "cool." This is in keeping with the usual symbolism that defines things feminine as "left" and things masculine as "right."

We'll leave this symbolism as it is and not concern ourselves with the correctness or incorrectness of it. Our practice of *pranayama* will recognize no dichotomies based on sexual symbolism however useful they might be to others. Consequently, we will consider the air passing through the left nostril as neither warmer nor cooler than the air passing through the right.

It will be observed that sometimes the right nostril and sometimes the left nostril is dominate in that the air flows freely through one nostril while its passage is nearly obstructed in the other. This is the normal state of affairs, surprisingly enough. Usually both nostrils are not fully open at the same time. Dominance alternates between one nostril and the other about every ninety minutes or so. It is also surprising that nobody seems to know the reason for this. Incidentally, it might be more natural to have sixteen ninety-minute hours in the day rather than twenty-four sixty-minute hours.

Yogis believe, however, that when the air flows through the right nostril we should be doing active (i.e., masculine) things; and when the air flows through the left nostril, passive (or feminine) things should be done. Stated another way, when the air flows freely

191

through the right nostril, we will be more adept at active things and when it flows freely through the left we will be better at things requiring passive observation. When an extraordinary (or coordinated effort) is required, the yogi is advised to proceed when both nostrils are open—or, to observe what naturally happens, both nostrils open when exertion is required.

This suggests that we can tell which brain hemisphere is active by noting which nostril is open. An interesting question then is can we change brain hemisphere dominance by changing the nostril that the air is flowing through? Further, there's the more immediate question, can we change the nostril the air is flowing through?

The answer to the second question at least is yes we can.

CHANGING THE FLOW OF AIR

One way is to simply lie on one side or the other for a few minutes and the opposite nostril (the one further from the ground) will open. Another way is to put a pillow under one armpit. The yogic way is to use specific *pranayamas*. Thus if you want to open your left nostril (perhaps you have some left brained work to do) you can do a left nostril breathing *pranayama*. After a few rounds of breathing through your left nostril, the body will comply and that nostril will open completely.

Which nostril is dominate for you at the moment? You can check by breathing on your hand. You will easily recognize which nostril is allowing the freer flow of air. For me (I just checked) it is the left. Since writing is left-brained work this is just what one would expect. For your part it may be either, depending on whether you're an interactive or a passive reader, or what your overall mood or intentions are at the moment.

By the way, unlike most of the body, the left nostril is controlled by the left side of the brain and the right nostril by the right side. This is not the case with our eyes or our ears, for instance, which are controlled by the hemisphere of the brain opposite their location—the right eye by the left hemisphere and the left eye by the right hemisphere. Again why this should be so is not known. (Or at least it's not known to me. If you know, please share your knowledge with me.)

NATURAL AND UNNATURAL LEFT-HANDERS

A couple of observations might be in order here. First, it is by no means clear exactly which talents and skills are controlled by which brain hemisphere. It's a well-established generalization that verbal knowledge is controlled by the left side of the brain; however, this applies only to right-handed people and not to natural left-handers (who often have their verbal centers in their right hemispheres). "Unnatural" left-handers, persons who became left-handed through nurture, not by being born that way, are like right-handed persons cerebrally speaking.

If you're a left-hander and want to know whether you're a natural or not, you can usually tell by observing your penmanship. If you write by "surrounding" your work, that is, by curling your hand over the top of it toward the right side of the paper, you are probably an "unnatural" left-hander. (Your brain is trying to get a right-eyed look at things—through its left hemisphere of course!) This is a tip-off that your left hemisphere is verbally dominant and you probably should have been a right-hander. If you write like a right-hander except that you use your left hand, then you probably are a natural left-hander. About half the left-handers in the world are born that way; the other half are right-handers who for some reason heard the beat of a different drummer.

Incidentally, it is considered a sign of impending ill health for one nostril to remain closed for more than a few hours. Naturally one of the purposes of *pranayama* is to facilitate the continued natural flow of air and to prevent stoppages. People who regularly practice *pranayama* say they have fewer colds and other respiratory problems since taking up the practice. My experience is the same. *Pranayama* does not cure colds but certainly makes them more manageable.

AN ALTERNATE NOSTRIL *PRANAYAMA*

The most important alternate nostril *pranayama* is *nadi sodhana pranayama* (literally: "nerve-cleansing breathing exercise"). Here's how it's done:

Assume a comfortable seat.

Apply *jalandhara bandha* (or not). Some authorities consider the *bandha* optional. Iyengar invariably calls for it. In the beginning I think the student might be better off to just concentrate on the breath, and after he gains some control apply the *bandha*.

Using the right hand, place the tips of the middle and index fingers on the center of the forehead just above the eyes. Allow the thumb to rest on the right side of the nose. Using the little finger and the ring finger close the left nostril.

Exhale slowly through the opened right nostril.

Inhale slowly and deeply through the right nostril (the left nostril still being closed by the little and ring fingers). Hold the breath for a moment and then with the thumb close the right nostril and release the pressure on the left nostril. Exhale through the now opened left nostril. Repeat several times.

Lie down in *savasana*. Rest.

After some practice the student will notice the underlining exercise function of these *pranayamas. Nadi sodhana* for example may clear the *nadis* (we'll get to this in a moment) and clean them and have whatever wonderful effects on the subtle body, but over and above all that it builds the diaphragm. When we close one nostril and breathe out, the air rushes out less easily than if we used both nostrils, consequently the diaphragm has to work harder to squeeze the lungs. The diaphragm is a muscle of course and when a muscle works harder it develops the capacity to work still harder. Furthermore the entire respiratory system adjusts to the greater effort required and seeks to accomplish the exhalation through one nostril with ease. Obstructions are lessened or even eliminated. Air tubes expand allowing a greater capacity, the lungs and allied organs are massaged and cleansed allowing them to work more efficiently. The body's response to this is not only a greater capacity and a smoother execution, but a generally heightened sense of well-being. *Pranayama* properly done makes us feel good.

ON "CLEARING THE *NADIS*"

Much is written in yoga books about the nerves being stimulated and toned and about the "*nadis*" being cleared or cleaned by *pranayama*. Unfortunately, just how this comes about is not explained scientifically nor is the mysterious word "*nadi*" given a concrete definition. For the Western mind this is an unsatisfactory state of affairs that we'll try to do something about.

Let's begin with this troublesome word "*nadi*," which I have used freely throughout this book (without as yet defining!). It's a word I like. It has utility and it stands for something very real—although not in the sense that it's usually understood.

Originally *nadis* were thought to actually exist in the physical body. The word in fact meant the same thing as our word "nerves" does. The early yogis knew that nerves were important and devised an extensive theory to account for how they worked and what their structure was. They believed that *nadis* (or nerves) were structures through which *prana* (the "vital air") of the body moved. Included in this theory was the notion that there are three principle *nadis*, namely *ida*, *pingala* and *sushumna*, the latter said to run through the spinal cord.

Unfortunately such structures have never been found in the physical body. Consequently the modern yogic approach has been to either define *nadis* simply as nerves and consider the rest of the theory as symbolic, or to keep the theory intact but assign it to the so-called subtle body—this "subtle body" being too subtle to be detected by the crude instruments of human observation.

The reader may have noticed that the subtle body has a great utility in yogic theory as a handy way to explain some things that come into conflict with the observations of modern science. The esoteric theory of *kundalini*, which we'll get to in a subsequent chapter, sometimes relies on this subtle body to explain some of its less obvious workings.

For our purposes we'll define the word in two ways. First we'll follow the usual practice and say that *nadis* are "psychic nerve channels"—again of the "subtle body" through which "energy" flows. This will be the symbolic meaning. Second, we'll use the word in a generic sense to refer to all the coordinated systems of the body including the glandular system as well as the lymphatic, neurological and cardio-vascular systems. Following this practice, when we say "the *nadis* are cleaned" we mean the veins, the arteries, the vagus nerve, etc. are cleaned. Thus, like a lot of words, *nadi* will have both a symbolic and a practical meaning.

"CLEARED" AND "CLEANED"

What we really mean when we say that the *nadis* are cleared and cleaned begins with the idea that they are exercised and stimulated.

But do neurons need exercise? Can we exercise a neuron in the same sense we exercise a muscle?

We can't, and of course a neuron will not grow in size as it is used. It doesn't stretch and build a capacity to meet greater effort. What happens though is very clear to one who has experienced it. One feels calm, one feels relaxed and serene. One feels "cleared." Hence the ancient phrase, "the *nadis* are cleared."

But what happens in a scientific sense is not so clear. Perhaps neurological experiences not triggered tend to accumulate tension and blockages, either in the nerves themselves or in supporting tissues; and the person begins to react to this buildup of tension in at first subtle ways (we're easily irritated, or there is a vague sense of uneasiness, etc.) and later in a grosser sense (we're angry, upset, tense, have a short fuse, etc.) and eventually we "explode" (do something extreme, yell, strike out in some way) which leads to a release of tension and at last we feel cleared.

All of this could also be said, and more emphatically, about the glandular system.

Regardless of what actually happens, the fact of being cleared is not in doubt. We all know the sense of peace that comes when nebulous tension is dissolved.

Of course it is not by *pranayama* alone that "the *nadis* are cleared." As pointed out in the chapters on asana, the various postures also release tension, unclog channels and bring about a general sense of comfort and well-being. However, the systems involved in the practice of *pranayama* (whether nerve channels, lymphatic systems, veins, arteries, or whatever else) differ from those involved in asana, mainly because of the pronounced use of the lungs and allied organs, so that the clearing experience is different.

It's a shame that we do not have today a scientific explanation of exactly how *pranayama* and asana affect the physical body, but such detailed explanations may not be far off. I think we can look forward to the next few decades when the marriage of Eastern practice and Western science promises us a fuller understanding. Until then the description of the effects of yoga will necessarily be less than scientifically rigorous and the great body of knowledge will remain largely personal and subjective.

In closing the subject of *pranayama* I should again remind the student that the primary purpose of *pranayama* is to lead the practitioner to meditation. It is through mastery of the dual nature of the act of breathing (an act that is both voluntary and involuntary) that we gain control of our organism and enter into meditation. To update an ancient metaphor, it is with the ground control of our breath that we guide the spaceship of our mind.

Chapter 18:
Pratyahara: Gateway to *Samadhi*

INCIDENTAL *PRATYAHARA*

With the mastery of *pranayama* we reach a significant plateau in our yogic quest. *Pranayama* is the last of the limbs of Patanjali's yoga that is clearly physical. We are now ready to withdraw our senses from the outside world and turn them inward. This process is called *pratyahara*.

We've all had "accidental" experiences of sense withdrawal—during moments of intense concentration, during moments of great fear or great excitement. At such times we have lost ourselves in the emotion or the task at hand and have not heard the door open or the telephone ring or even felt the earthquake!

This is incidental pratyahara. I don't know how many times I've cut myself and only became aware of it later. We've all had this experience. So intent were we on what we were doing that we felt neither the experience of the cut nor the pain that followed.

Again this is incidental and partial pratyahara, but it gives a hint of what can be accomplished if our concentration is great enough. It also illustrates a salient point about sense withdrawal: the real accomplishment can only come about through intense concentration.

NOT SEEING

Another common experience is to look directly at something with our eyes open and not see it. Those of you who use contact lenses should especially be familiar with this experience. Recall what you actually see as you take your lens out. What I actually see is nothing even though my eye is open and I'm fully conscious.

This not seeing is not a question of being distracted. Nor is it strictly a case of selective viewing. What happens at such moments is something more significant. Through an act of consciousness we somehow sever the link between the sense organ and the organizing element in the brain. It's as though we temporarily closed off the neurons leading from the eye to the brain. Having no need or desire to see (as we feel for the lens) we just don't see. This is really what pratyahara is all about: closing off our conscious experience of the outside world through an act of will, or better said, through a skill obtained through practice.

A RETURN TO THE WOMB

There is a *mudra*, the *sambhavi mudra*, to aid the aspirant toward pratyahara. ("*Sambhu*" is another name for the Hindu god Siva. Thus the name means "the gesture of looking for Siva within.")

Sit (ideally in the lotus position).

Use both hands to cover your face. Allow the index and middle fingers to rest lightly over closed eyelids, the thumbs to close the ears, the tips of the ring fingers to press the sides of the nose, and the little fingers to rest on the upper lip.

When you try this mudra for the first time it has a surprising power. If you've never done it, try it now. While the lotus position (as usual) is best, the gesture can be done sitting in a chair. To heighten the psychological effect, you might seal off the breath with the appropriate fingers for a few moments.

Remember a *mudra* is a gesture or a seal. *Sambhavi* is the gesture of sealing one's self up inside one's self. It is also called the *yoni mudra*. *Yoni* means womb. In a modern parlance this gesture might be called a return to the womb. Such an expression would be quite apt.

The main point of the *yoni mudra* is to prepare the mind psychologically for pratyahara. The gesture itself points the way to pratyahara; it does not bring it about.

SENSORY DEPRIVATION

After the flowering of secular yoga in the sixties went to seed and the dilettante enthusiasts sobered up and realized that instant *nirvana* wasn't just around the corner, they tried to use modern science to help them accomplish the limbs of yoga. Thus biofeedback was born to assist the aspirant in becoming more sensitive to his body. Numerous—some quite fancy—meditation techniques and meditative aids were devised. And to achieve pratyahara somebody came up with the idea of the sensory deprivation tank.

People are always looking for shortcuts and tools to give them leverage in their tasks. And this is good. It is part of what makes people people and not cats or dogs. But the idea of the sensory deprivation tank, as laudable as it was, really illustrates what pratyahara is not.

The tank seemed like a good idea. It seemed to be a vast improvement over the *yoni mudra*. Not only was light and sound really cut off, but the aspirant could lie in water and greatly reduce the effect of gravity on his body. There should have been little to distract her from her inward quest.

However it didn't work out that way. Few achieved anything like pratyahara. Indeed the senses in such an environment may tend to reach outward even more vigorously than usual. In short, the senses were deprived, but they weren't withdrawn.

Of course many reported the experiences as valuable in allowing them to rest their senses and to get some idea of what there was to see within. And others said the experience helped them meditate. But few or none found *nirvana* and the enthusiasm for sensory deprivation dried up like a puddle in the desert.

This should be no surprise because the whole attempt was off the mark. The first thing wrong is that it was imposed from the outside, as it were, with the impetus coming from without instead of from within. It was as though we should withdraw the world from our senses instead of withdrawing our senses from the world!

In true pratyahara it is by the willful act of looking inward that the yogi withdraws his senses and achieves the temporary death to this world that is pratyahara. This experience cannot be achieved from without any more than someone else can eat for us or think for us. Worse yet, it is a silly way to go about reforming ourselves through trying to change the world!

The second thing wrong with sensory deprivation devices is that the real withdrawal meant by pratyahara from the world is not physical but mental and spiritual. The withdrawal of the senses is merely a metaphor, a guide to show us the way. What we as yogis really want to achieve is the withdrawal of the senses from the objects of desire. In the final analysis we want to withdraw our self (the *Atman*) from desire itself.

This is truly the goal of pratyahara and the achievement. Withdrawing the senses is a step along the way to the goal.

LOOKING WITHIN

It is a giant step however, and there are certain techniques that assist the yogi in the attempt. Most important is to meditate in a quiet place free from the distractions that come from sensory experience. In our place of meditation we close our eyes and slow the rhythm of our breath and turn the focus of our mind inward. "Look within, look within! All joy is to be found within!" cry the ancient texts.

Once we as yogis realize this and have had the experience we will look for it again and again, and gradually (or instantly! if we're really gifted) we will "die a little now to this world."

There are some observations to make here. First we should note that we slow our breath. This is one of the reasons we have been doing *pranayama*—to train our respiratory system to be able to operate at a much slower rhythm so as not to distract us from our search within.

Second, we should try to pinpoint exactly where we are headed within. In *kundalini* yoga there are said to be *chakras*— various centers in the body where we should focus our attention. Leaving *kundalini* to another chapter, we'll go directly to the center of our "sixth sense," our brain, and meditate on the "third eye" (the *ajna chakra* which is a little above and between the eyebrows).

These are practical considerations. For the moment we have relinquished any claim to the mystical and we have restricted ourselves to a common sense description of what we are doing. One thing is clear: we are not experiencing the outside world. It is no use calling to us. We will not hear you.

What happens now? If we are successful we will find bliss, of course, but we will find something else—some call it a white light, some call it a blue light, some call it just the peace that passeth understanding. The Tibetans in the familiar mantra *Om mani padme hum* call it "the jewel in the heart of the lotus."

What we call it isn't important and how we report the experience is also insignificant. Indeed such talk is nothing and meaningless and if anything distracting and misleading. The truth is nothing can adequately describe the experience. "*Neti, neti, neti!*" as ancients declared. "Not this, not this and not this!" Words are inadequate. Symbols only give the vaguest hint. Pictures, if we had them, would be worthless.

Of course we have used the word *samadhi*, defined as union with the Supreme Divine Consciousness.

LAPSING INTO MYSTICISM

We have gone from pratyahara into *samadhi*. Some would say we have found God. Others would say we have joined with God. Yoga, the word itself, means "yoked," with the implication of being yoked to God. Others would say we have found the *Atman*, the Divine essence of God that dwells within each of us. Some would invoke the Buddhist tradition where we find the beautiful metaphor of the drop of dew falling off the lotus plant into the ocean to merge with that great body of water. Thus our *Atman* becomes one with *Brahman*.

But we did lapse into mysticism, didn't we? Well, shame on us! However, recall that I said at the outset of this book that ultimately yoga is a mystical experience and that it can hardly be otherwise.

Nonetheless as you are reading this and as I am writing it, we are not merging with the great ocean that is God. (Well, maybe we are, but not consciously for the moment—at least I'm not.) And it would be good to have a more prosaic explanation for what went on when we turned our senses inward. Let's try.

THE WORLD OF OUR SENSES

The sensory world is a distraction. It is a delusion as well as an illusion. It is not so much that it isn't "real" (again, "reality what a concept!") but that our subjective experience as temporal and evolutionary creatures constitutes only a minute part of the total reality. We exist on this tiny planet as beings with grossly limited sensory abilities (which is one of the reasons that letting loose of them in pratyahara is not under the circumstances a loss at all but a gain). We have a woefully inadequate understanding of the true nature of the universe and not an inkling of what God is all about—despite all our fine talk of God and God's will and the Way etc., etc.

Yet we ourselves are part of God. We are at the very least God's evolutionary "handiwork." And that is why through meditation and the inward glance there is hope that we can transcend the limits of our ordinary consciousness, transcend the limits of our narrow senses and perhaps come to some tiny experience of the Ineffable.

We have nothing better. Christians call it prayer. A prayer is a meditation, a very beautiful and very powerful meditation, a way to find God.

For the yogi it is the same. Looking inward is a prayer, and once the yogi is inside and has cut off sensory contact with the external world, all the veils of *maya*, all the distractions of desire are gone and we can see ourselves and the world as they really are. And what a strange and beautiful sight that is.

THE CLOUDS OF DESIRE

Desire clouds our view of the world. Desire muddies the waters of life. Desire makes prejudicial our viewpoint. We are enslaved to desire. We are prisoners of desire—and I don't mean merely the grosser desires of flesh, of eating and sex, but the subtler, more devastating desires of ego and power and self-importance. Beauty resides in desire and so does ugliness. Only the person without desire can see that they are the same.

In Christianity the first commandment from God is: "Have no others Gods before Me." This was told to Moses. What it means is to let no desire, to let no graven image (not merely of cows or lambs or rising suns), but to let no graven image of ourselves come before

God. That is the true meaning of the first commandment, because that is the real danger, the danger of mistaking the unreal (our individual egos) for the real (God, or the divine *Atman*) which is our true spiritual nature, free from the coloration of desire.

The world truly is not as we think it is. Our view of the world is but a prejudice within a delusion foisted on us by desire. So when the yogi looks within, he is looking away from desire. There is no other way to get away from it. We cannot escape from desire by ordinary living. We aren't built that way. The mighty forces of the evolutionary process ensure that we act according to its dictates. Just as the addict sitting next to the mound of coke has no ability to get up and walk away; just as it is by grace that we are saved, just as "no man cometh unto the Father but by me," we cannot by the power of our ordinary selves rise above this material world and transcend it. We must, as it has been said in many religions, die to this world and be born again before we are "saved."

And this is what the yogi is trying to do. She is dying now a little to this world, moving ever so slightly toward the ultimate union with the Great Ocean of Consciousness from which she came.

We live but a few years. Our experience is like that of a brief candle between the vast eternities of darkness, no matter how broad our definition of "brief" may be and no matter how many times we think the candle is lit. Regardless of how desperately we try with our imagination, no matter how I twist and shout and turn words and phrases, mount metaphors and thrust analogies, regardless of how great our efforts, we know, even the most secular among us, that our experience now on this planet pales to insignificance compared to merely the known handiwork of the Cosmos. And how pitifully small is the known handiwork when compared to what we can't know. We should ask, what's before the Big Bang? What's beyond the last quasar? So sad really are those who imagine that human beings are alone in this universe, that we are somehow unique, that humans may make god-like decisions and pronouncements and be drunk with ourselves. The fool in his heart sayeth there is no God.

We are not unique, but we are special, but no more special than the cat that sits upon the porch. No more special than the ant that follows the scent trails, no better or worse than the dung beetle that rolls up balls of scat in which to lay its eggs. We are all *becoming*; we are all places along the way. We are all a part of the great acting out, the play of life, of *Lila*, the cosmic dance.

So the yogi looks within and what he finds he cannot tell us. All the great sages of all the ages, all the holy men from the beginning of time historical have been trying to tell us, but they have all failed. The only answer is not this, not this; but the impetus is clear. They are imploring us, "You too, look within."

We might say that with pratyahara comes the limitation of technique. The rest comes by grace. As yogis we have strengthened our bodies, have purified our souls, have steadied our minds and withdrawn our senses from their earthly masters and now we meditate. We look upon the awesome countenance of God and are humble. We pray. And what happens?

PRACTICAL TIPS

The answer is silence of course; but to end this chapter I'm going to give you some practical tips toward the achievement of pratyahara.

First, realize that pratyahara, like asana, like *pranayama*, although a mental or neurological achievement, is nonetheless something done with the physical body. Therefore regular practice again is the key to success.

And what should you practice? Pratyahara is primarily a meditation. Find the center of yourself within (a good place to look is right in the very center of your head) and dwell there. The chapters on meditation and *kundalini* should assist you.

Second, don't suppose that pratyahara comes before concentration and meditation (although that's the way it appears in most of the books). You'll never get anywhere thinking you can withdraw your senses from this world before you are experienced in meditation. It is the willful act of choosing to withdraw our senses from the world that comes before meditation, not the actual achievement. It is only for the accomplished yogi, who already knows how to withdraw his senses, that the withdrawal (today's withdrawal) takes place first.

Third, it is the withdrawal of the senses from desire that is the real achievement. The idea is not so much to avoid seeing the world, as it is to lose the desire to see the world that leads to success.

Fourth, do not despair if progress seems slow or nonexistent. What is not said in most yoga books is that pratyahara is one of those things in life that may be characterized by a long time passing without any evidence of progress. True achievement may take many years; perhaps, to be honest, for some people, success will never come. But for those with patience, faith and regular practice, eventual success is assured.

To sum up:

Pratyahara is three things: one, a willful act to withdraw the senses (or our attention) from the world; two, a meditation on the *Atman* (or that which dwells within, or on nothing); and three, a realization that the desire for sensory objects of the world is what separates us from *nirvana*.

Chapter 19:
Meditation

Thought formation impedes the river of samadhi... By abiding in a mood of non-thought formation, samadhi is obtained.
—Theos Bernard

RETICENCE ON THE EXPERIENCE OF MEDITATION

There many books on meditation, and virtually every yoga book at least mentions meditation, and some even give techniques for meditation, but there is very little in the way of reportage about the practice and experience of meditation. Buddhist books on meditation talk about "insight meditation" but usually do not describe the experience itself. Popular books written from a secular point of view talk about meditations on love and forgiveness or other virtuous states of mind achieved perhaps through prayer or through an opening up of oneself. All of this is to the good, no doubt, but what I always wanted to know when I was a young man, is how do you do it, and what is it like to do it?

It may seem strange that books do not actually answer these questions. But there are two main reasons for this reticence. One, the experience of meditation, including the techniques for its achievement and the mental and emotional sensations, differ for each individual, and so to offer one's own experience is somewhat arbitrary and perhaps irrelevant. Of course I am going to take the chance of being arbitrary, not feeling that my personal experience is totally irrelevant to the needs of others aspirants and I am going to relate my experiences in detail and reveal my techniques, some of which are unconventional and personal. The second reason that one does not find factual, detailed reports about the experience of meditation in most books is the author's knowledge is mostly academic and not personal. To put it bluntly, some authors do not themselves meditate, and therefore cannot speak of their own experience.

Other authors have only a middling experience with meditation and will not speak explicitly on the subject for fear they will reveal their ignorance. And there are a few, very few, authors who, though expert and highly advanced in their meditative practice, adhere to the ancient injunction not to speak directly about such matters, since the aspirant must learn through his or her own experience anyway. And of course there is the dictum, "Those who know don't speak, and those who speak don't know." Therefore, it has long been the practice of teachers, gurus and authors to remain reticent, just as the Buddha is said to have been reticent about anything that did not lead to liberation.

THE NINE AND SIXTY WAYS

In one sense, meditation is a tool. It is a technique to regulate our lives. It is a way to rest, to find peace in a troubled world. It is an exercise in stilling the mind. In tantra it is seen as a way to get "high." Ultimately it is a way to find God.

There are more books written on meditation than we could ever hope to read. There are Jainist ways to meditation. There are Jewish ways and Islamic ways. There are Christian. There are secular ways and secret ways and ways that require objects and mantras, visualizations, incense, and the proper cushions. There are ways to count and to observe the breath, ways to spin wheels and beads to pass from one hand to the other. As Kipling said, "There are nine and sixty ways of constructing tribal lays, and every single one of them is right."

So it is with meditation. There are innumerable ways to meditate. They all work. Some work better for some people and others work better for other people. Some ways are the only ones we've tried and they work fine. If we tried others, they would work fine too. If you've been with me this far you already know many ways to meditate. Asana leads to meditation. *Pranayama* leads to meditation. Sitting quietly and gently turning our attention inward leads to meditation.

WHAT IS MEDITATION?

The first thing to understand is that meditation is not a technique of the mind, per se. It is rather a body/brain process that allows a natural state of the mind to emerge. It is therefore both a skill that can be learned through application and practice, and a way of experiencing the world, a way of seeing, a way of being, a consciousness. It is a special skill, built into our nature that needs to be awakened and then refined. Animals have this skill, as one can see when a tiger nurses her cubs or when our dog is content. Indeed animals naturally fall into a state of meditation when all is well, when they are without fear, have eaten and have nothing they need to do.

The state of meditation is in a sense a "reward" for having taken care of our daily tasks, a state of mind that we should be in when we have no social/political/sexual/subsistence matters to attend to. Unlike the animals, however, we have, because of the rampant growth of our brains, in particular the neocortex, mostly lost the easy ability to fall into a meditative state, and so have to first still the mind before we can meditate.

HOW TO MEDITATE

We all meditate willy-nilly without any training. As children it was a cinch, at play, while daydreaming, but not something that could be done on demand, and not something we were consciously aware of doing.

The experience of being "in the zone" in athletics is a meditative state. Reading and writing, to those who are practiced, leads to a meditative state. Knitting, doing a crossword puzzle, baking a cake, working on your car can also be seeds to meditation. Everyone has had the experience of being at one with the world, seeing clearly and feeling wonderful about it. Everyone knows the bliss and the understanding. The trick is to find it at will and to maintain it. That is what the practice of yoga is devoted to.

Okay, how does one meditate?

First we begin with a comfortable seat. Find a spot where you are not likely to be disturbed where you cannot hear the cell phone (turn it off!). Sit in a comfortable position, rest your hands in your lap, close your eyes and concentrate on a spot inside your head right in the middle of your forehead. In Japanese Zen the eyes are left slightly open. This has never worked for me, but I think it would have worked had I learned that way. You might want to try it.

THE MONKEY MIND

After we have focused we find almost immediately that our mind has jumped elsewhere. What to do? Call it back, gently, of course, without rancor or judgment. Just gently return our focus to the singularity at hand. This will have to be done literally thousands upon thousands of times. Even when one is well versed in the practice, the mind will wander. Even the great yogis, who are after all only human, occasionally need to call their attention back to now. Be sure, of course, that it becomes easier and easier as time goes by and our practice remains steady.

Most people never really get beyond the monkey mind. For whatever reason they find that they cannot keep the monkey still long enough for the bliss and the insights to come, except once in a while, and then seemingly only by happenstance or through some fortuitous circumstance. They put many hours into the task and conclude after giving it what seems to be a fair trial, that either they are not really any good at meditation or that perhaps it's not all it's cracked up to be. And so they quit.

Error message! The problem not made explicit in most books on meditation is that (1) People differ greatly in the amount of effort they must put into meditation in order to be successful, and (2) It takes a lot more sitting to get there than is usually admitted. We hear of adepts who can go into meditation as soon as they cross their legs or immediately upon the out breath. True, there are such people (I suppose), but for most of us it takes a lot longer.

How much longer? From my personal experience, don't expect to achieve meditation without a period of concentration lasting for at least an hour. That's right, one full hour at the minimum. Notice that this requirement alone keeps most people from meditation. Who has an hour a day to spare? This is why those who are adepts are often monks or others freed from worldly responsibilities. My advice: free yourself from worldly responsibilities! Even today it usually takes me twenty or thirty minutes to "get there," although sometimes I am fortunate and arrive sooner. Sometimes it takes an hour. And, guess what, sometimes I don't get there at all!

This is why we always read about the monks in Zen monasteries forcing the aspirants to sit and sit and sit, morning, noon and night. If one does indeed sit and practice one's koan or contemplate the void or play a mantra through one's head, sooner or later, one will fall into meditation. This is what the teacher depends on. The *roshi* knows that meditation comes through practice although it sometimes comes through grace, and that regardless, if one sits focused (and awake!) long enough, one will eventually arrive at meditation.

IF YOU'RE HAVING TROUBLE

Understand that at this point I assume that your practice in asana and *pranayama* is regular and going well. If it is not, you need to work on that while continuing your efforts to meditate. A good seed is in fact either asana or *pranayama*. Sit for meditation immediately after asana and concentrate on the pleasurable feeling that you are experiencing. (Pleasure is an excellent seed to meditation.) Or begin your sitting with the practice of regular deep breathing and/or alternate nostril breathing, and let that be your seed to meditation as you focus again on the middle of your forehead and within the brain itself. For years my practice was exactly this. I would do ten alternate nostril breaths followed by ten full breaths with retention on the in breath, and then switch to retention on the out breath without counting for as long as it took. The most pleasurable meditations usually followed.

A caricature of a meditating yoga has him focusing on the tip of his nose. I have also done this and it also works. (I do it with my eyes closed and I do not cross my eyes.) It has the effect of directing one's attention toward the vicinity of the forehead, and one quite naturally in time finds the ajna *chakra* (see the chapter on kundalini) and pleasure ensues. Sometimes I found it better to focus off to the side of a traditional focal point and then move toward it gradually. (Perhaps this was a way of occupying my mind.)

In Buddhism the practice often is to just observe the breath, while in yoga one directs the breath with a conscious act of will and then focuses on the process. I actually learned to meditate through a focus on what Hittleman called "the full yogic breath." You might try that. One fully involves one's concentration on the in breath, becoming the breath itself, and then on the retention of the breath (*kumbhaka*), and then on the out breath, and then on a moment of retention, and then again on the in breath. Actually, the ancient books always say to begin with an out breath. I used to think the reason for this was in case there was something in the nose, it would be aimed outward instead of inward! I was imagining a forest *sadhu* largely withdrawn from the world, and this seemed like good advice against insects. You should laugh here, because that is the way my inquiring mind worked, looking for the wisdom in the report of the practices. Later I was to realize that the reason the old yogis always had one breathing out first is that the focus on retention after the out breath (*bahya kumbhaka*) is more conducive to meditation than the focus on retention after the in breath (*antara kumbhaka*), although one can achieve meditation either way. The body is just that much more relaxed after the out breath is all. There is a sense of letting go. The old yogis knew how to get to meditation, and they wanted to get there as easily and as quickly as possible.

WHAT IS MEDITATION LIKE?

What your personal experience will be like is not something I can know. So I will relate my experiences with the realization that some of yours will be similar. And I will try to talk about meditation in a rational, communicative way, although much of the experience of meditation really is not directly communicable. If you have not meditated, much of what I will say will reach you only in an academic sense, intellectually, as it were. Relating the experience of meditation to someone who has not meditated is like trying to describe the taste of a peach to someone who has never tasted sweetness, or to describe the color red to someone who has been blind from birth. Of course we all have meditated to some extent, and we may recall however distantly those experiences. We have this to work on.

First there is the pleasure, or the "bliss," as it is usually referred to. In my experience this pleasure is of several kinds. There is a serene quiet type of pleasure that might be similar to that which a nursing animal feels. There is another more intense type of pleasure that is different from, but similar to sexual orgasm. It is non-genital and continues for a surprisingly long period of time, as though in short cycles. There is another pleasure that is like a massage going over and through the brain in waves, one after the other, almost electrical in the way it feels. This pleasure can sometimes be reached through a short, rather shallow breathing rhythm that may mimic the frequency of pleasurable brain waves. Another is like a mood from a quiet lazy day in my youth, or as a child, watching the dust motes dance in a slant of light through a tear in a window shade. That is a pleasure similar to that which Proust felt upon tasting again the little cakes from his childhood that he loved so much, *the pleasure of a mood relived*, perhaps it could be called.

There are still other pleasures, but I cannot recall them at this moment. Meditation is a world away, as I write, and sometimes the experiences cannot be translated, and sometimes they are so subtle and other worldly that they cannot be brought into this world at all.

PLEASURE AS A PRIVATE EXPERIENCE

So pleasure first. And isn't it strange that virtually no other book on yoga or meditation actually says this? Why? There are several reasons.

One, a focus on pleasure is seen as "sinful" by some, as something properly private by others. In other words, reporting on the pleasure is not politically correct.

Two, the experience of pleasure is just a place along the way to *samadhi*. Stopping there is a mistake, and so one is urged to move on. Or, it can be said that there is something beyond pleasure, and the pundits want to focus on that, or at least point in that direction. I have to tell you that pleasure itself has an end, and most meditators have experienced this. After I had been meditating seriously for some period of time I was able to go to the pleasure almost at will and hang onto it for literally hours at a time. Wow, you might say—and I did, and rightly so. But believe it or not, there comes a time when the experience of pleasure actually becomes boring. Hard to believe, but it's true. I used to play with the pleasure like a rat with the electrodes in his head, pushing the lever to excite its pleasure centers again and again until exhausted. Before I got exhausted I would think something like, "This is wonderful, and we can come back to this, but after two hours it is kind of boring," and so I would pull out of it. I can also tell you that when things were not so serene and I had difficulty in getting to the pleasure, I would look back and rue my arrogance! Usually the pleasure ended not because I got bored, of course, but because I lost my focus or something from the outside world intervened.

Three, a focus on pleasure by the aspirant, will, like the observation of the electron, cause it to change course. Actually, a focus on the pleasure is like a focus on an image in meditation. If you think about it or try to examine it (thereby bringing the ordinary conscious mind back into play) you will cause it to disappear. "Thought formation impedes the river of *samadhi*."

Four, again many writers on meditation don't actually meditate, so they don't know what the experience is like so they end up quoting other authorities who, as above, report on the more esoteric aspects. In other words, they parrot the old texts.

Five, meditation does not always or necessarily result in "pleasure." (More below.)

Six, pleasure is a subjective experience, and what I describe as pleasurable may be something else to someone else.

So "bliss" is the "spiritually correct" word to use, but I will bend that tradition.

OTHER SENSUOUS EXPERIENCES

After pleasure (or before) there are a myriad of sensuous experiences, such as that of depth, motion, color, smell, touch, etc. One may seem to experience a sense of space directly, as though tasting or feeling the space. One may have the sensation of seeing around corners, as though having a seventh sense. One may float on the air as in a dream, or directly experience the roundness of circles and balls or the squareness of cubes. This is where the so-called psychic powers of the ancients come into play. Patanjali himself reported that along the way to *samadhi*, one acquires supernatural powers, powers that the aspirant is warned not to abuse!

Right. And isn't it amazing how all, without exception, have given heed to that warning and haven't used them, at least haven't used them in a manner that can be scientifically confirmed! Ah, yes, it is amazing. But I am here to tell you that those powers are indeed real, although real in a sense other than what one might expect.

Let's look at the power of levitation. I have experienced this power and I can tell you it is very real—the experience of it, that is. The old yogis point to this "power" because its achievement is a sure sign that one is meditating and on the way to *samadhi*. Before this there is the sense of smelling something that is not here, such as a rose or a turkey roasting. This is what common sense tells us is an illusion, a product of the mind. And it is that. I levitated toward the ceiling one night I recall and hovered right nicely there for a long two or three minutes, just wondrously feeling the float of my body in the air. Of course if I had opened my eyes, I would have found that I had returned to the floor faster than the speed of light!

Well, what was happening to me, and is it significant? You can experience levitation when your concentration is so excellent that you no longer feel the sensation of any part of your body touching the floor or the chair. Incidentally, notice how little of a yogi's body actually touches anything in the lotus pose. In such a posture it doesn't take long to no longer feel in touch with anything. The meditating brain then, should it look for support, feels none and can believe (if you allow it) that the body is in the air.

Smelling roses that aren't there is a classic early indication of meditation. What it means is you are inside. You are getting your sensuous reports only from the brain without the evidence and clues from the environment. You are within the jewel and what comes to you is wired in your brain. You experience the direct, unmitigated sensation from your neurons uncorrupted by the world. And of course what you experience, what you actually smell, is dependent upon your own personal wiring, your own personal experiences and heredity.

From this perspective it is easy to see why the ancients advised the aspirant to move on. The "warnings" not to abuse the powers were the kind of intentional and symbolic language used by the old gurus, who knew exactly what these "powers" where and the scope of their effectiveness. But they did not want to characterize them for non-initiates, and they gave in to the temptation to wow the initiates, so to speak. It is not a lie to say that one has acquired these powers, because they really are powers of the mind, but it would be a dire mistake to demonstrate them(!).

OTHER PSYCHIC POWERS

There are other psychic powers, such as being invisible, knowing the thoughts of others, etc., that we might take a quick look at. I'll limit myself to powers that I have personally experienced, but of course many others are claimed. Being invisible is one of the most interesting since it really can be manifested onto others. If one stands and holds oneself exactly right, that is, without motion, but with an attitude of complete non-judgment, not hearing or caring what is going on, then one can appear "invisible" to others. People will quite naturally tune you out to such an extent that they and you will both have the sense that you really are not there. You might note this talent in people you have known who may have acquired it in ways other than through deliberate meditation.

Knowing the thoughts of others is a kind of absolutely compelling illusion based on the amazing observational and analytical powers of the human mind. One of our great talents, forged in the tribal experience from the prehistory to the present is to figure out what the other person is thinking and therefore protect ourselves or otherwise use that information to our advantage. This talent is one of the things that separates us from other animals. We can "know" something about what the other person is thinking (sometimes better than they know it themselves) through past observations of their behavior, even through knowing how their kin, who share their traits, have behaved; and we can read their face and their body movements and analyze the pros and cons of their situation, and if our skill and our concentration is great and our need strong, we can often know exactly what they are thinking. For the yogi deep in meditation the thoughts of others may appear through memory and/or an analysis based on memory, although without any sense of recall. Because of all that I have just related, those thoughts will indeed be real. Often have I learned of what went on at some recent event through a meditation on that event and the people there. The overwhelming sense of actually hearing those thoughts, or actually not hearing them but experiencing them directly is so veracious it would require commanding factual evidence to the contrary to make the meditator believe otherwise. (Sometimes, of course, it is well that we believe otherwise!)

We can all take this experience for what we think it is worth. From my point of view, of course, I did not directly experience or read the mind of another, but overheard his thoughts nonetheless. For the conscious mind, this "illusion" is seldom if ever complete, because the conscious mind knows, deep inside somewhere, that it has a bias and that bias will show and color the perception. For the meditating mind the "illusion" is complete because the meditating mind has no bias. It is the dustless mirror described in Zen.

NEGATIVE EXPERIENCES?

What else might one expect? I have read in some books that one might expect negative experiences, demons, monsters and the like, and that will be something to get over. But personally I have never had a negative experience while meditating, and I mean *never*. I would like to say something about that.

I don't believe that such a thing comes by luck or because I have lived such a serene life. I have had my share of bad experiences, etc. What I think accounts for this is being at peace with oneself, and this comes partly as a feedback from that which is learned through meditation and partly through what the Buddha called right living and what in yoga is following the precepts of the niyamas and the yamas. I think also being in good health is a factor. I cannot meditate very well, if at all, when I am ill. But if I did, it would not surprise me to find a warning of my illness expressed in my meditation.

Then again, perhaps I am lucky. Perhaps it is my nature to see and experience positive things. I must say that when dreaming as a kid I would sometimes have nightmares and wake in the cold sweat of fear. But during the last ten or twenty years I have had only one or two or maybe three nightmares. I do have dreams that go astray and head toward something awful, but I invariable wake up before anything bad happens to me! You may well have the same experience. When meditating, every experience seems infused with some sort of wonder or blissfulness. I can almost say that I do not even have neutral experiences while meditating. All the experiences seem positive. This, I think, is what is meant in the Vedas where it is said that we are existence, knowledge, and bliss. We are bliss. All we have to do is experience it.

However, if one is not at peace with oneself or others, then perhaps things are otherwise. If we have hurt others, we must make amends and understand why we did what we did and know how to avoid doing anything like that in the future. We have to forgive ourselves, really know and forgive, as in Christianity. If we are currently hurting someone we must stop immediately and make reparations. If we are injuring ourselves through bad habits and "wrong living," we must stop. It may well be the case, and certainly the limbs of yoga suggest as much, that we cannot achieve meditation unless our house is in order, unless we are healthy and at peace with the world around us.

What this implies is that not everybody can meditate, and that there will be times that we cannot meditate. If the house is afire, we cannot meditate. That much is obvious. So it may be the case that when we are ill at ease with ourselves and our performance in this world, that we cannot meditate. Perhaps this is part of what the idea of *karma* means. Again, follow the path of yoga, from the niyamas and the yamas to asana, to *pranayama*, to pratyahara, to concentration, absorption, and *samadhi*, and one will be released.

Chapter 20:
Further Thoughts on Meditation

Close up...[the] eyes, and draw the curtain close;
And let us all to meditation.

—taking a small liberty with Shakespeare; Henry VI, Part III, iii, 31

Meditation is not as easy as it is sometimes thought. You will, for whatever reason, get away from your practice, and sometimes have to get back to it. Meditation is like a highly accomplished skill that takes years to hone, and when one gets away from it for a while, one is like a finely-tuned athlete out of practice and out of shape. Even a week or two away leaves one off one's best game.

REPEATING THE EXPERIENCE

And in the beginning, even after an initial success there comes the problem of repeating the experience. This is usually easier because once one has been there one has a strong desire to return. However, let's be clear. Sometimes one forgets. The experience of meditation is curious in that it is not by itself addictive. There is no "pull" from a demanding body that we return to meditate. Consequently, one can fall into meditation, and then for whatever reason, neglect the practice, and the memory of it will fade. Yes. This experience is symbolized in Zen by the phenomenon of instant enlightenment. The aspirant one day is powerfully awakened; an instant enlightenment ensues; everything is clear, the mirror has no dust, one is wafted about on the bliss, and all the stupidities and irrelevancies of the world disappear and *nirvana* is at hand.

Well, even the saints nod, and the experience and the crystal clarity of the enlightenment fades like the morning dew, and one is back where one began. Well, not quite. One has seen an opening. One has experienced what is on the other side of the veil of illusion, and one knows for certain that it is there. How to get it back?

It is believed that every little enlightenment conditions one all the better to call upon and better appreciate the next enlightenment, until all at once there is no time or space or experience between enlightenments, and one dwells in the house of the lord forever.

This is *samadhi*. This is *nirvana*. This is the peace the passeth all understanding.

So when one is sitting and trying to focus and the mind wants to worry about the prime rate or next week's meeting with the boss or, like a little demon, flashes bits and pieces of irrelevancies across the frontal brow, the correct and proper behavior is to just gently let these things pass and refocus the mind. Our attitude should be positive and without expectation. When I was first able to meditate with a fair regularity, I would sometimes grow mightily impatient when the bliss would not come. I wanted the bliss and I wanted it NOW. I expected to sit and focus, withdraw my senses, turn my attention inward and find that jewel in the heart of the lotus, and get flowing with the pleasure. And, sometimes, it didn't come!

Well, with such an attitude, it would be better if I got up and finished the dishes in the sink or scrubbed the kitchen floor!

Some other days it comes upon us unaware, steals us away with it and we become, without notice, so deeply into it that we cannot tell the meditator from the meditation. Now that is meditation.

DEEPER MEDITATIONS

The question most often asked by those who do know how to meditate is how do I make my meditations deeper?

Here is where the yoga of Patanjali, the yoga of sun and moon (*hatha yoga*) the yoga that we have been pursuing so faithfully throughout this book comes to an end. Beyond this, technique—"mere technique"—cannot go. How do you make your meditations deeper?

Through love, I would say.

Through faith in God.

Through laughter, perhaps. Through modesty and humbleness. Through giving and prayer. Through surrender. Through just letting go.

But I am not a teacher of meditation and I don't believe you or anyone else needs one. If we complain that our meditations are not deep enough, we are already off the path. Ramakrishna's story of a guru holding the disciple's head under water and then asking him how he felt ("I thought I would die for breath!") really says it all. When we feel that way for God, we will find Him and there will be no complaints about shallow meditations.

FANCY ANSWERS

Perhaps we should ask again, what is meditation? Perhaps we should come to the subject again, but as though for the first time. What is meditation? There are a lot of fancy answers. Here are a few that I happen to have around the house:

Our "why" is just another layer in the onion.

Samadhi is
The silence after Om.

Meditation is
In the quality of the after-image.

Just when you think you've got it figured out.
It changes.

When you close your eyes in meditation and then after
A while open them again, the world looks different.
More than that, it *is* different.

"Man tries to measure the ocean of truth with the teacup of
his mind."

—S.K. Majumdar

Actually what I've done is give out seeds to meditation
instead of definitions. This is what the prospective meditator really
needs, seeds to grow the meditation within, not definitions. There
are many seeds. All of yoga is a seed to meditation.

MANTRAS AND *YANTRAS*

In the same spirit I am therefore, like a good guru, going to
give you a mantra that you can use to lead you to meditation. It is to
be kept secret. So under no circumstance are you to reveal it to
anyone. If you do, the mantra will lose its power. The mantra is:
"Regular practice is the key."
Repeat after me: "Regular practice is the key, regular
practice is the key..." This mantra is especially efficacious if
pronounced silently: *Regular practice is the key.*
Oh. I already gave you that mantra? Never mind. It still
works.
There is also a visual way to meditation. If you feel you are a
visually-oriented person you might begin with the candle flame. Just
concentrate on it. Adore it. From that you might move to meditation
on the simplest of colored designs (*yantras*), perhaps a triangle, a
circle, a square. Just follow the patterns gently with your eyes. Close
the eyes and concentrate on the after-images. Later you can
concentrate on elaborate mandalas, which are paintings or designs
(often telling a story) usually drawn inside a large circle that directs
the viewer's attention from the periphery to the center.
In *bhakti* yoga, a very common way to meditation is to focus
the mind on a spiritual text or sermon or on a visual representation
of God, usually Krishna. Many persons meditate on a picture of their
guru or on a drawing of Jesus.

For the beginner these various devices and methods help focus attention on a single thought or object long enough to allow the body and the mind to become still enough for the natural process of meditation to begin. For the harried househusband or the overworked executive, there is the further problem of learning to relax the mind and body long enough for meditation to begin. (Of course we know this is where yoga comes in.)

AM I MEDITATING YET?

How do I know when I'm meditating? For a young person, full of the fires of youth and desire for the external world, short on knowledge of self and blinded by the ego's harsh light, this is indeed a question worth asking. For a person in her middle years, even one who has never consciously "meditated," this is a question that is never asked. We know what meditation is. It comes upon us naturally whenever we are quiet and calm and content, and we allow our minds to focus gently on one thing or another.

The average person, then, discovers meditation quite by accident and knows what it is through experience, but only begins to appreciate it and to look for it and to fall willingly into it, and to arrange his life to be in it, sometime during his middle years. Appreciation really is the key.

Children meditate, willy-nilly, by happenstance as they go about their play. They meditate beautifully, powerfully. Most persons looking back on their lives might say after they have "discovered" what meditation is, that they had some of their best meditations when they were children.

This is entirely correct and understandable, because as children, before the demands of security, sex and society took over our lives, we were more or less free, our psyches uncluttered; and like the animals of the forest, like humans before "the fall," our hearts innocent and pure, our concentration strong, our bank of prejudice low, our expectation unsullied, we were able to go into meditation and drink the full cup without pause and without self-consciousness.

And at such times many of us experienced a kind of *samadhi*, however briefly. I recall the sound of an airplane engine as it flew over the house and receded into the distance as I tried to nap as a seven-year-old... I recall the brilliant flash of iridescence in the curl of a wave on a lazy summer day... I remember the realization that came upon me all at once that I was ME, a particular individual living this particular life right now and—I was alive!

I was filled at that moment with a profound sense of wonder at this observation that now (regrettably) seems so trite. My entire being was pervaded with a tingly awe at how amazing this realization was, that "I" was alive, that "I" existed. Many years later I came to understand that this was a moment of *samadhi*, a moment of pure enlightenment.

A PLACE BEYOND DESIRE

We learn not to expect to reach such heights of meditative experience easily again. In many respects the Garden of Eden has closed it gates to us; our minds have become polluted with the demands of the work-a-day world, with the all-consuming needs of the species and the irrepressible life force. We need to find that childhood innocence again, to die to this corrupt world and be reborn in first light, in first sight, to see and experience the world anew, as though we had never seen it before. When we are able to do that we will be prepared for *samadhi*, for *nirvana*, for satori, for enlightenment, for liberation from the flesh, for the union with God. All we have to do at such a time is quietly compose ourselves in meditation and we shall be released.

Meditation then is not a single "thing" or a particular process. It is a combination of processes, a gradually expanding state of mind (or states of mind), characterized by a quiet contemplation, a looking inward, following concentration on a single focus. Meditation is further characterized by a feeling of bliss, a sense of heightened awareness, contentment, a lessening of desire. It is a place beyond pleasure and pain, beyond desire, beyond triumph and disaster, beyond the flesh really, a place near to the Ineffable.

SAMADHI

I have used the Sanskrit word *samadhi* to refer to the highest stage of meditation. This is traditional. In Patanjali's eight-limbed yoga, meditation is divided into three stages: *dharana*, which is sometimes called "concentration"; *dhyana*, which is usually translated simply as "meditation," but could be called "contemplation"; and *samadhi*, "absorption." (Some translate *samadhi* as "trance.") Patanjali recognized two types of *samadhi*, *samprajnata samadhi*, which can be called *samadhi* with an object and *asamprajnata samadhi*, without an object.

If our meditation grows from a seed through concentration on an object like the candle flame, it is said to be meditation with an object, leading to *samprajnata samadhi*. If our meditation comes upon us unaware and flowers without a seed and ripens into *samadhi*, that is *asamprajnata samadhi*, *samadhi* without an object. This latter *samadhi* is said to be the more advanced.

I won't debate the reality of these distinctions. They're handy when you want to talk about meditation; but again they're just words. We don't really even need the distinction between *dhyana* and *samadhi*. We could take concentration, contemplation and absorption, lump them together, and call the lump meditation and lose nothing important. Just as no one can describe the sound of two hands clapping to a deaf man, no one can tell us what meditation is. We can be told how others have experienced it and how they have defined the stages, but until we have meditated, these words are without meaning. Mark Twain once said that the difference between using the right word and using the almost right word was the difference between "lightning and the lightning bug." We can similarly say that the difference between talking about meditation and meditating is like the difference between a movie theater searchlight and a supernova.

I think it is useful however to reserve the word "*samadhi*" to refer to the ultimate union with the Ineffable that every yogi seeks, realizing that such an experience is really indescribable. There is nothing in the state of *samadhi* that can be translated into language. It is a place beyond description.

WHAT MEDITATION DOES

Meditation is really what keeps the aspirant going. Meditation is what cures addiction and depression, negativity and fear. Meditation is more restful than the deepest sleep; meditation cleans the channels of the mind and body more thoroughly than asana or *pranayama*; meditation sharpens the mind better than even the fear of impending death. (Indeed the highly focused state of mind thrust upon us during a crisis is itself a meditation sprouting from the seed of fear or the realization of the coming finality).

Meditation is both a change in consciousness and the cause of such a change. Meditation leads us away from the ordinary mind with its narrow definitions and its prejudicial viewpoints and allows us to see things as they really are, uncolored by desire, hopes and fears, preconceptions, "education" or the forces of socialization. Meditation is the hand that lifts the veil of *maya*, the illusion that surrounds us in this world like a thick soup. Meditation is the process that transforms the larva of our body into the butterfly of our soul. In short, meditation leads to God. I repeat myself. Well, then, I repeat myself!

LEVELS OF EXPERIENCE

It is, however, possible to concentrate and not meditate. We've all taken exams under pressure and we've all had painful interviews for jobs or situations. The anxious mind, the tense body, the discontented soul cannot meditate.

It is also possible to meditate and not achieve the state of absorption; indeed this is usual. For most of us total absorption in the object of our meditation comes only at special times. We should learn to treasure those times and to note well the circumstances that allowed us the rare experience.

True *samadhi* is even rarer still of course. For the vast majority of us it is very far away indeed, achievable seldom or never, for brief moments or not at all.

Hindus say that this is the result of *karma*, especially the *karma* acquired in previous lifetimes. We need not subscribe to this view; for us it is sufficient to note that some persons, either due to fortuitous brain chemistry, or because of a superior discipline acquired through years of hard work, more easily enter the super conscious state. Just as some people, no matter how hard they try will never run as fast as a gifted athlete who doesn't try at all, most of us will never, regardless of effort achieve the enlightenment of a Buddha, or the transcendental consciousness of a Ramakrishna or the God-like purity of Jesus. It is in fact because of this seemingly unfair disparity that the idea of *karma* was born.

Unlike athletic gifts however, spiritual gifts can be hidden for long periods of time only to burst forth suddenly in glorious splendor after many years of dormancy. And there is always the possibility of instant enlightenment as in Zen.

But even if we never achieve the super conscious state we can all meditate, and through meditation our lives will be immeasurably enriched.

MAKING ALL OF LIFE A MEDITATION

Super conscious states aside, what the practical yogi would like to achieve is a constant state of meditation. In other words, to go through life entirely in a state of meditation.

This is not an idle fancy. As our ability to meditate grows, so does the amount of time we can spend in meditation. So too does the number and variety of situations we can be in and still maintain our meditative state. In the beginning we may be able to enter meditation only while seated comfortably. At some later time we may find ourselves entering into meditation as we stand looking out the window. Sometimes we may turn our head and gaze and there is meditation. At still later times we may, as in the Zen practice, enter into meditation while walking or washing the dishes.

Many techniques have been developed to help the yogi achieve this goal. Mantra, especially the silent ceaseless repetition of the name of God—this is called *japa*—can lead some persons to meditation and allow them to maintain that state for as long as they repeat the mantra. *Karma* yoga, properly and fully achieved, can lead to a life of ceaseless meditation, as one devotes one's labor unselfishly to God. The practice of *bhakti* yoga allows the truly adoring to find the love of God and His adoration in every moment of life.

But these are mighty achievements, for only the gifted few. We'll talk about these other yogic ways to liberation in a later chapter.

NON-TRADITIONAL WAYS TO MEDITATION

Using the traditional techniques of yoga to come to meditation is not the only way I meditate. If I work at writing, using my mind to manipulate and think about words and meanings, expressions and logical ideas, and all the other things we do with words, there will come a time, usually after two or three hours, when a pleasant feeling may come over me. It is a lightness about the head and body that is warm and pleasurable in a delicate sense. It is a sweet sensation, impossible to describe. This sensation is different than the sensations from meditation I referred to in the previous chapter, but similar. Yet this too is meditation, and it something I believe I could achieve by other means if I were so inclined. I imagine that what I experience is what physicists and others experience as they grapple with a problem, or what a whirling dervish feels while dancing or what the chanter feels while continuously reciting a mantra. There is also the meditation that comes from reading or from being relaxed and quiet with loved ones. These too are meditations and experiences of bliss.

I also meditate while lying down. I have worked on this for years because I worried about what I would do if for some reason I could not sit up comfortably, which sometimes happens because of a pulled back or side muscle. The strange thing is I have indeed learned to meditate lying down, but the quality of the meditation usually is not as compelling, but sometimes it is even more compelling. I suspect this reflects the fact that while I am experienced in meditation I have not yet reached the highest levels. My meditations while lying down demonstrate to me that there is more to learn, more to experience, and more that I can do in terms of practice and technique.

When I am lying down, I typically begin by reading, my body under the covers with a pillow supporting my head. After a few minutes I begin to feel a sense of pleasure wash over me, identical to that which I feel during regular meditation. I am still holding onto the book but I cannot feel it unless I move a muscle. But then it changes. I go onto what I imagine is the "nod" that opium addicts experience, my eyes closing and pleasure pulsating through my body as I drift toward sleep. But then just as I am about to fall sleep I may snap out of it, so to speak for a moment, and realize that I have been experiencing simultaneously two entirely different states of mind! It is as if the left side of my brain is thinking one thing, and the right another. Often one of the states of mind is purely verbal, a narrative that may be unraveling, while the other state of mind is of pure sensation, like that of flying or floating, or running or exploring some environment.

I started to experience these two states of mind simultaneously some years ago. Sometimes I close my eyes and "Greek" letters as in some word processing windows or in dreams will appear before my eyes and I can try and read the letters to make out the words, but of course without success.

EXERCISES WHILE TRYING TO MEDITATE

One of the "exercises" I work on sometimes when meditating is to make color appear. Instead of "turning off" my closed eyes, which is the usual way while meditating, I look actively out into the world with my eyes closed. What I usually see is a kind of black void punctuated with bits and pieces of dim, fuzzy, random motes and clouds of light, sometimes with just the barest tint of maybe a light green or a washed out yellow. But as I stare into this void sometimes I catch a glimpse of a brighter color, maybe purple or red or blue. (By the way, the monks usually wear saffron robes because the afterimage of saffron is a meditative purple!) I try to enlarge the purple or red or blue. Usually it disappears and then another spot of color might appear in another location. Again I try to enlarge it. Sometimes the color will respond by spreading like liquid on a glass slide, growing and moving over the void.

At other times I try to imagine what it is like to have an additional sense. The so-called third eye behind the forehead is often thought of as the sixth sense, but really the mind itself and its ability to see what isn't here and to realize what has been here and predict what might be here soon, is the "sixth" sense. Consequently, to see around corners and the like might be thought of as a "seventh" sense. If during this exercise I fall into meditation I have the most immediate and powerful sense of actually being able to see around corners! I need only to raise my "sight" and my view is thrust out and around the corner.

In this connection I recall Swami Prabhupada, the "Krishna consciousness" leader and expert on the *Bhagavad Gita*. He is the author of a number of books, one of which I read years ago entitled *Easy Journey to Other Planets*. It was a compelling read but a little mystifying since at no time did Prabhupada allow that his journeys were the work of his mind and examples of what can be accomplished through meditation. Instead, following the ancient Indian tradition mentioned in an earlier chapter, he just allowed the reader to imagine that his physical body as well as his mind made the journeys!

I recommend that the reader experiment in this manner and of course devise your own exercises.

SOME PRACTICAL ADVICE

In closing this chapter on meditation I want to emphasize that for the beginning student the way to rapid success is not only regular practice but the assumption of a posture especially designed for meditation in a place so designed as well, if possible. The mind and body are creatures of habit and if we sit in a certain way only when we want to meditate they will quickly get the idea and meditation will follow more easily.

Again it is not necessary to sit in a cross-legged pose for meditation. We can (as we work toward a cross-legged pose) make sitting in a chair somehow special so that our body will know immediately that we intend to meditate. Perhaps we should sit only in a particular chair (then of course we might want to carry it around with us!) or only in a certain room (ditto!). Or better maybe we should place our feet flat on the floor and have our arms rest in our lap. In this way our pose will be unique for meditation.

Be advised—and this is important—that unless you're Ramakrishna or a new incarnation of *Siva*, you cannot stay in the state of meditation at all times. In fact, your meditation sessions will be improved and you will fall more quickly and fully into meditation if you have spent some serious time doing useful tasks such as household chores, your job, helping others less fortunate, etc. After such work the mind is anxious to return to meditation. Also if one sleeps too much (or too little), meditation is difficult. However sleeping just a little bit less than you might want, leaves one in a state of mind conducive to meditation, which is another reason the *roshis* in Zen retreats wake the aspirants at four in the morning!

I should add that it was from this realization—namely that for most people the continual meditation that the yogi strives for is impossible—that the idea of *karma* yoga may have been born. What to do while waiting for the body/brain/mind system to again be receptive to meditation? The answer comes from the *Bhagavad Gita*: selfless work. After a day of being immersed in one's work, meditation comes as easily as sleep to a teenager on Monday morning.

Finally, let me say I think yogic theory (and perhaps this chapter) takes the subject of meditation a bit too seriously. After all, everyone meditates in his own way and neither sermon nor signpost will help us find *samadhi*. It's a little like writing a treatise on laughter. Better we should tell a joke. Zen and Taoism are in some sense reactions to this "seriousness."

I should say then (recalling the well-known saying in Zen that "if you should meet the Buddha by the side of the road, give him a kick") if you should enter into *samadhi*, send me an email.

Chapter 21:
Karma, Karma Yoga and Reincarnation

KARMA FOR SKEPTICAL CATS

Cats are skeptical about things unseen, unsmelled, not heard and not felt. They know the value of a good stretch and the wisdom of regular meditative practice; but theories leave them cold and debates about what should and shouldn't be done are nothing so illuminating as the swat of an opened paw.

We could all learn a lot from a skeptical cat, especially when we approach the confusing subject of *karma*. So let us be skeptical cats as we enter herein and let us above all keep our paws on the ground and not go jumping after butterflies.

SYMPATHETIC MAGIC

We'll begin with sympathetic magic because it's through sympathetic magic in its broadest sense that people first learned to formulate and test theories about the world around them. In case you're not familiar with "sympathetic magic," it is a way of solving a problem such as curing a disease through the manipulation of something or a situation similar to the one that needs fixing or curing. Thus there is a "sympathy" between a voodoo doll with red bumps on it and a child stricken with measles. According to the "science" of sympathetic magic a cure of the child's measles might be effected by rubbing the red spots off of the doll.

Sympathetic magic doesn't have much currency in the modern world, at least not in the scientific community, but it wasn't always that way. Before Darwin, before Newton, before the Greeks, in places distant and among persons various, there was the same desire that exists today to understand the universe and our place in it. But for those spiritual and intellectual pioneers there was little or no accumulated knowledge to guide them. There was no Library of Congress. The Sorbonne did not exist. Darwin and Einstein were hundreds of generations away. For the primitive peoples of this world it was the first time out. They had to figure out the universe almost all by themselves and without benefit of prior knowledge.

To this end the earliest humans developed the ideas and practices of sympathetic magic, which is the "science" of the tribe, of the shaman and the witch doctor. It doesn't look like a very good science to us, but in lieu of anything else sympathetic magic was pretty good. It got the job done after a fashion, and if you've ever been adrift yourself in a situation where there was nobody and nothing to guide you, then you know the mighty truth contained in the adage "even a bad plan is better than no plan."

Well, sometimes a bad plan is worse than no plan. Of course. The plan to substitute belladonna juice for mother's milk didn't work out too well. And it is not the moon that is causing those red bumps on your skin, so it won't do any good to conduct that midnight dance—or will it?

Herein lay the power and truth, if you will, of sympathetic magic. If you believe it will help you it might. This is the placebo effect, an effect so powerful, incidentally, that all modern medical experiments are designed to control for it. In fact, they do so doubly; that is, not only can't the patient know who is getting the placebo, neither can the doctor.

So what is the relevance of sympathetic magic to *karma*? Am I suggesting that *karma* is an example of sympathetic magic?

I am in part. But it's not sympathetic magic one generation old or the property of a single tribe. The idea of *karma* is thousands of years old and it is the property of not only yoga, Buddhism and Hinduism, but of hundreds of millions of persons worldwide, secular and religious.

Karma has survived. Magical ideas that survive tend to become theories and theories tend to get confirmed or rejected. If science were a question of how many believe against how many don't, *karma* would be a fact; fortunately science is a question of experiment. Unfortunately some ideas, some really beautiful and persuasive theories, cannot readily be proven by experiment. Most of economics is that way. The mighty theory of evolution itself is, technically speaking, beyond our poor power to confirm experimentally.

ASTROLOGY AS SYMPATHETIC MAGIC

For comparison and contrast, let me throw out another idea from the tribal science that is still around with us today: astrology. No, astrology is not a yogic idea. Yogis are much too practical to worry about the influence the stars may have on our doings. They might affect us, the yogi would say, but there are a whole slew of other things to check out first. Astrology is like *karma*, however, in that both ideas are sorely lacking a causal agent to account for some of their far-reaching effects. They're both sorely lacking some other things too, but the reason I mention astrology here is that it too is true in some respects if understood correctly.

Of course it's true psychologically for those who believe it. Ah, but you say, try buying a cup of coffee with the coin of that realm! I agree. And of course astrology's true if you don't take it seriously—in other words it's true as a game is true.

Still there is another, very substantial sense in which astrology is true: it's a method of analysis, specifically of personality analysis. It's a memory aid. People who dabble in astrology (and experts too) use the structure of astrology as a means to categorize and to assemble, to compare and to contrast, the various personalities they meet in their lives. A Virgo behaves such and such, and so-and-so is a Virgo, they might say, while noting that so-and-so is a little aggressive for a Virgo. (He may have Mars rising!) Sure the terminology isn't rigorous and the method no better than some other; but the point is, even less than rigorous terminology is better than no terminology at all and almost any method is better than no method.

At this point the skeptical cat (meditating under the tree) thinks we are off chasing butterflies. But he has looked up. It seems that we have said that astrology is true, not only as a device of sympathetic magic, but as a memory aid!

There is more, though. Astrologers may talk about how the stars influence our lives, but what is really important in the discussion is that our lives are influenced. What astrologers, ancient and modern, are really trying to figure out is how to account for the behavioral patterns they see. In an attempt to do this, astrology has at its core the idea that there are various sorts of people, Virgos, Cancers, etc., and that these various sorts tend to behave true to type.

We may allow this isolated part of the theory (for what it's worth) without allowing the whole argument. There may actually be, genetically speaking, twelve basic types of personality, just as there are twelve signs of the Zodiac, or even thirteen or fourteen (the number doesn't matter). What matters is that astrology theorizes (in its non-rigorous way) the differentiation of personality types.

SAPIENT CATS DO NOT PRESUME TO KNOW IT ALL

Now astrology may be wrong as to details, and it may be loaded down with irrelevancies and general mishmash, but if it's right about the existence of personality types, then those astrology people may have a very fine leg up on the rest of us when it comes to understanding people.

And do you know what I think? I think that people are in some sense types. I know that some people look similar, and I know some people tend to behave similarly in similar situations. And I know genes are handed down in discrete packages and fishes swim and birds fly and people with blue eyes tend to wear shades in the sun. So to this skeptical cat at least the notion of personality types is viable.

Yogically speaking then, what we can say about astrology is one, a lot of people believe it; two, it has survived a long time despite some heavy opposition; and three, it may very well contain some other hidden, as it were, ideas that give it real power beyond the understanding of even its most adept practitioners. None of this makes astrology true; nevertheless, a sapient cat would give it some consideration and show some respect for its lineage and not presume to know it all. I presume to be such a sapient cat.

In short I don't think astrology is true, but I suspect parts of it are at least in a utilitarian sense; furthermore there is undoubtedly more to it than meets the eye. So I'll reserve judgment on the subject while I throw out the parts that seem particularly absurd and I'll use what seems to work.

In this spirit let us return to *karma.*

KARMA AS ACTION

The very word *karma* makes the Western mind a little uneasy. For the skeptically-minded, *karma* sounds all too much like one of those words that vaguely describes something that doesn't exist—a word used by New Age babble masters. But we would be very unwise to dismiss *karma* so lightly since the idea itself is ancient and the power it continues to hold over the minds of people cannot be calculated.

The word in Sanskrit means literally "action," mental as well as physical; but in a broader sense implies the consequences of actions as well as the acts themselves. We speak of a person who has good *karma* and of another who has bad *karma.* Technically speaking this is an incorrect use of the word. We do not have *karma* per se, we create *karmas.* Furthermore, from the broadest perspective *karmas* are neither good nor bad, they just are.

The Bible says we will reap what we have sown. This is almost precisely what some Easterners have in mind when they use the word *karma.* We are going to get our just deserts.

However it isn't necessarily going to happen in this lifetime. This is where reincarnation comes in. No doubt a long line of Eastern philosophers noted that evil-doers did not exactly reap the bitter fruits of their evil deeds; on the contrary a lot of them just got richer and richer and more and more comfortable. So just as Christianity decided that such people (if not saved by Christ) were going to hell, Easterners decided that the comeuppance of evil-doers if not experienced in this lifetime would surely come in the next or the one after—at any rate eventually.

I realize that introducing the notion of reincarnation into this discussion will not make the idea of *karma* any easier for most Westerners to accept. Most of us personally know of nobody who's been reincarnated. The idea is simply not proven and the rational mind understandably finds the notion dubious at best. But again religious ideas are not to be taken literally nor are they expressed to inform us about the concrete facts of life. They are psychological ideas and they are expressed symbolically to inform us about the spiritual or psychological facts of life.

Nonetheless, although the idea of reincarnation is important to an understanding of *karma*, *karma* can get along quite well without it. We don't have to believe in reincarnation to realize the truth of *karma*.

KARMA AND EVOLUTION

One way to think of *karma* is to think of it as a pre-Darwinian statement of evolution. Evolutionarily speaking every organism, considered as a species, eventually does reap what it sows. If the organism is ineffective in coming into harmony with its environment or fails to adjust to changes, it goes hungry, it suffers excessive predation and eventually dies out. Its "bad" actions (failure to run fast enough, failure to be able to digest available food, etc.) lead to its demise. While one organism acquires the ability to get along very well on a diet of leaves and flourishes, another organism does not and perishes. This is *karma*. Right action leads to success, wrong action to failure.

Another way to look at this is to recognize that if brown cows mate with brown bulls they will probably have brown calves. If you want to select for brown cows, you mate the brownest with the brownest and leave out the rest. Being brown is part of your selected cow's *karma*.

It is the same with humans. If a person has a wise and balanced nature we can usually see that he came from people who were wise and balanced. A very aggressive person probably comes from a line of aggressive ancestors. If aggressiveness leads to certain consequences (and it does—probably to a heightened chance of both worldly success and early death) we can say that these consequences along with the aggressive acts themselves are part of the aggressive person's *karma*.

This *karma* has been carried over and intensified from one lifetime to another. What is reincarnated is not the individual ego (which is an illusion anyway) but the evolutionary tendency. In a sense we are paying for the sins of a previous existence, and in this sense reincarnation is true.

In this connection Patanjali called our body "the *karma* container." Whatever we do, good, bad or indifferent, from whatever angle viewed, is *karma*. We are constantly creating *karmas*.

THE EXPERIMENTAL DANCE OF LIFE

For the yogi however the goal is not to create good *karmas* instead of bad ones, but liberation from all *karmas*, good or bad, successful or unsuccessful.

It may seem surprising that yogis feel this way, but there are good reasons. For one thing it's not always clear just what is right action and what is not. And as things change (as they inevitably do) today's right action may, and often does, become tomorrow's wrong action. Being able to eat and digest grass is good if there's a lot of it available, but if the grass dies out and you're left with tree leaves, you'd better be able to eat and digest tree leaves.

From the yogic point of view it might be said that this world is an experimental dance (the dance of Lila in the Hindu myth)—this world of "*karma* containers" and "food sheaths"—and the yogi would like to be done with the dance and go home.

IS THERE ESCAPE FROM *KARMA*?

On a personal level, instead of being a statement about evolution, *karma* can be seen as a social or psychological law that we violate at our peril. If we mistreat people they in turn are going to mistreat us. If we follow the golden rule and do unto others as we would have them do unto us, they will be kindly disposed to us. This rule is not always effective, but everyone knows that it is correct in general.

But the yogic idea of *karma* goes a step beyond this. It asks the question, can we escape from *karma*? and the answer is no. Even by not acting we are in effect acting. We do "nothing" as opposed to "something." We act by default. And at any rate are still breathing, and in a little while we are going to eat, and in eating we initiate a host of *karmas*, some—depending on what we eat— obviously of far-reaching effect.

This eating illustrates especially why we cannot escape from *karma*. Our *karma* is to eat, period. Our *karma* is to breathe, to take up space and in so doing to deny that space to other beings.

KARMA YOGA

There being no escape from the endless wheel of *karma*, the yogi nonetheless finds a way out of this predicament. No, it is not suicide or withdrawal from the world. These too are actions and they too do not work because according to the law of reincarnation the yogi would return in the next lifetime to encounter the same problem. What he does instead is relinquish the fruits of his actions. In other words he does what he has to do without the expectation of reward or lack of reward. He dedicates the fruits of his actions to God. He has faith.

This is the great idea born in the Upanishads and further developed in the *Bhagavad Gita*. It is also the foundation of one of the great systems of classical yoga: *karma* yoga, the yoga of selfless action.

Westerners are familiar with this idea from the Kipling poem "If" in which the reader is invited to "treat those two impostors [triumph and disaster] just the same."

Kipling's expression comes straight from the Gita where Krishna tells Arjuna: "Work alone is your privilege, never the fruits thereof. Never let the fruits of action be your motive; and never cease to work. Work in the name of the Lord, abandoning selfish desire. Be not affected by success or failure. This equipoise is called Yoga."

What this means from a psychological point of view is clear: Your house may burn to the ground. They may open a supermarket across the street from your 7-Eleven. You may play your best and still lose. Nevertheless, it doesn't matter. It isn't whether you win or lose, but without question, how you play the game that counts.

The effect of this is we are freed from the vagaries of results. This is a great psychological truth and a great triumph over circumstance. No matter who we are and no matter what odds we are up against, it doesn't matter as long as we act without selfish desire.

Life is in the living, we might say. There are no toys to be acquired. The end not only doesn't justify the means, it is irrelevant, and the only thing that counts is the means. There is only action (means) not fruit (ends). In this manner we are delivered from the awful chain of consequences.

THE PSYCHOLOGICAL TRUTH OF *KARMA*

Some people think they can get away with various crimes as long as they are not caught. Children tend to think this way until they learn better. Most of us remain children far too long. There may even be people who actually have little or no sense of moral responsibility and therefore are restrained from doing evil deeds only because they fear social or legal punishment.

But these people (if they exist) are in the vast minority, and the social and legal restraints on them are quite powerful. The rest of us are ruled psychologically by our understanding of the effects of our actions. We are social creatures, we have social needs and responsibilities. Whenever we do an anti-social act (murder, theft, etc.) we have hurt the tribe; and anyone who hurts the tribe makes the tribe less adaptive, less able to survive and in turn makes himself a less adaptive creature.

And so social animals have built into their psychology restraints on anti-social behavior. The evolutionary system makes us feel bad when we do anti-social things. Our minds know what we have done and know that it was wrong, and if the karmic comeuppance doesn't arrive from the tribe itself, it may very well arrive from our own minds. This too is *karma*—"guilt" as it is called.

In short, if we do an evil deed, evil consequences will come our way even if the consequences are "only" psychologically administered, as it were, by our own hand.

Therefore the law of *karma* (that we reap what we sow) is beyond doubt psychologically true.

And if it's psychologically true it really doesn't matter whether it's literally true, or true in a scientific sense. Remember the truth of religious knowledge: if we believe it's true, then in a most important sense it is true. Again, if I think I'm feeling miserable, then I am miserable. If I think I'm happy, I'm happy. Psychological truth is religious truth and vice-versa. Taken together they are spiritual truth. For us as individuals living out our lives, so-called scientific truth may or may not be relevant to the vastly more important question of spiritual truth.

So *karma* is an idea, an attempt to explain ourselves and our nature. It is a powerful idea, an idea whose truth is symbolic and psychological, regardless of whether it is also factual or scientific.

KITTY *KARMA*

The skeptical cat, bored by this discussion, has left the shade of the tree and gone around to the side of the house where through the kitchen window come the sounds and smells of dinner. To make sure we see him and know that he is ready for dinner he rears up and grabs the screen with his front paws like a kangaroo on its hind legs. He plays the screen like a harp for a moment and then returns to the ground. After a quick, nervous nip of the hindquarters he presses his head against the screen and gives out a sharp "meow!" or two. Watching for a moment to make sure we're headed in the right direction, he thinks (a little sarcastically): "It's my *karma* to nag and yours to be nagged until the food is in the bowl and under the nose!"

Chapter 22:
Kundalini

ADDRESSING THE ISSUE

If there's an area of yoga that's in dire need of demystification it's *kundalini*. More esoteric than a Kantian debate, less substantial than an angel on the head of a pin, more elusive than the thread of a lost dream, and harder to dismiss than a UFO— this is *kundalini*!

For the hard drive of our mind, would that we had a miracle software program that "removes *kundalini* esoteria—fast!"

Alas no such product exists and I'm afraid we'll have to address the issue, as inadequate to the task as we know we are.

"THE SERPENT POWER"

Knowledge of *kundalini* came upon the Western world in the early years of the last century primarily because a man named Sir John Woodruff writing under the pseudonym "Arthur Avalon" translated some ancient and "secret" tantric texts into English. He named his best known book *The Serpent Power*, and the rest, as they say, is history.

The Serpent Power purported to show how one can, through meditation and diligent practice cause the energy of a coiled serpent god (*kundalini*) to rise from the base of the spine (where it lay sleeping), transverse various *chakras* (nerve plexus or centers), to finally arrive at the top of one's head in mystical union with its divine mate (the Hindu god Siva), allowing the practitioner much enlightenment and bliss along the way, culminating in a joyous deliverance from this world.

Naturally there have been a long line of persons seeking this joyous deliverance; unfortunately not many have found it. The problem is multifaceted, but mainly it's a question of ignorance muddying up the lotus pond and hiding the plain reality. The truth is, whether we look in the shallows or in the depths, we'll find almost no one who understands kundalini.

AN ELABORATE MEANS TO *SAMADHI*

This is too bad because *kundalini* is really very simple. What is kundalini? It is an elaborate means to *samadhi*, an intricate web of inner meditations that if followed faithfully will lead us to the liberation we seek.

Yet almost nowhere will you find this said. It's as if there is a giant conspiracy of obfuscating stupidity surrounding the subject. Western yogis often ignore *kundalini* altogether or pass over it quickly while Indian writers try to present the tantric symbolism as part of a larger yogic or Hindu philosophy, usually getting practice and theory muddled. The end result of all this is that *kundalini* remains in that twilight zone of human knowledge where little is understood and even less verified.

To give a quick example of the lack of agreement on the subject we can start with Swami Vishnudevananda, author of the excellent *The Complete Illustrated Book of Yoga*, who defines *kundalini* yoga as "a branch of *Raja* Yoga" (p. 406). Others see *kundalini* as a yoga in and of itself. Professor Ernest Wood in his *Great Systems of Yoga* (p. 97) sees *kundalini* as a part of laya yoga.

Vishnudevananda further relates *kundalini* to the yogic theory of how the universe came into being through *prakriti sakthi* ("the manifestation of the divine force") saying that *prakriti sakthi* is manifested in the individual as *kundalini sakthi*, or the serpent power (p.321). (Note: *sakthi* [cosmic or divine force] is also spelled *sakti* and *shakti* and sometimes capitalized.)

B.K.S. Iyengar, taking a different tack, closes his brief discussion in *Light on Yoga* by saying, "The arousing of *Kundalini* and forcing it up is perhaps a symbolic way of describing the sublimation of sexual energy." (p. 440)

Most enlightening however might be these words of Sri Ramana Maharshi (as quoted by Ken Wilber in John White's *Kundalini, Evolution and Enlightenment* p. 121): "Do not waste time meditating on *chakras, nadis,* padmas, or mantras of deities, or anything else of the kind. The six subtle centers (*chakras*) are merely mental pictures and are meant for beginners in yoga."

This sort of thing isn't usually said either because to "dismiss" the elaborate meditative system of *kundalini* in this manner defeats its purpose. Unless we as aspirants really believe we are finding all these wonderful and mystical and quite frankly magical things within ourselves then we will never have the emotional power to reach the depth of meditation necessary for liberation through this method.

KUNDALINI RESEARCH

To further obfuscate the situation is the bittersweet case of the Indian pundit Gopi Krishna. He wrote a number of books about his personal experience with *kundalini* including *Kundalini* and *The Secret of Yoga* which were published in the United States in the seventies. These were intensely personal books, written in a fine literary style, the major intent of which was to "legitimatize" the phenomenon of kundalini. Gopi Krishna related in often agonizing detail how the premature awakening of the shakti power in his body lead to intense pain and bafflement. As a result of his experience Gopi Krishna started the Central Institute for *Kundalini* Research in his native India with the aim of establishing *kundalini* on a scientific basis.

Unfortunately, although Gopi Krishna is a compelling and articulate witness, his experience has resulted in moving *kundalini* in a clinical rather than a practical direction. *Kundalini* was seen briefly as a psychoanalytical phenomenon to be compared with schizophrenia, epilepsy and other "alternate states of consciousness."

The extensive literature on the subject includes not only the Hindu, but the Tibetan and Buddhist tantric traditions as well. This is an esoteric and heavily symbolic literature that I will make no attempt to sort out.

Instead I want to present the broad outlines of the theory and try to assign the symbolic to the actual in so far as possible. Those interested in a full range of opinions on *kundalini* can read the essays in John White's collection, *Kundalini, Evolution and Enlightenment.*

THE *CHAKRAS*

There are either five, six or seven *chakras* depending on how they're defined and who's doing the defining (e.g., the Tibetan Buddhists combine the two lower and two higher Hindu *chakras*, thus eliminating two *chakras*). Each *chakra* typically has its own male and female deities, its own symbolic Sanskrit letters, its own characteristic color or colors, its own earth principle (fire, water, earth, etc.), its own dominate sense organ (feeling, smell, etc.) and of course a particular location in the subtle or not so subtle body.

Each *chakra* is thought of as a flower-like wheel with a unique number of petals and a characteristic shape inside the wheel. Thus the *muladhara chakra* is red and yellow, has a downward-pointing triangle inside a square with four petals; its principle is earth, its sense is smell, etc. It is located at the base of the spine.

When properly aroused and channeled the energy of *kundalini* is said to rise upward through the *sushumna nadi* (the "spinal column" of the subtle body) until it unites with *Siva* in the *sahasrara chakra*, which has a thousand petals and is located in the subtle body just above the head. Other *chakras* are located in the genital area, the stomach area, the heart, the throat, and the forehead. The *sahasrara chakra* is not considered a meditative center. When *kundalini* reaches this *chakra* you are no longer meditating; you are delivered.

The really surprising thing about *kundalini* is that it works! We don't have to know about or understand the symbolism of the *chakras* to meditate on them. What we have to do is compose ourselves in our meditative posture, close our eyes and turn our attention inward so that we focus on a particular area of the body corresponding to the *chakra*. Our first sensation (once we locate the *chakra*) will be warmth and a pleasurable sensation in that area. Further concentration leads to meditation.

In the beginning the student might have trouble locating or "feeling" a particular *chakra*. If that happens simply try another *chakra*. We're all a little different and some of us relate better to one *chakra* than to another. Indeed, part of what the elaborate symbolism of *kundalini* is trying to tell us is that there are individual differences in meditative experience. Some people, for example those who find feeling and giving love an easy thing to do, would be well advised to meditate on the *anahata* (heart) *chakra*. By directing our focus there, we can love again. Meditation on love leads to *samadhi*.

One can also meditate on the so-called lower *chakras*, the *mula*, the *swadhisthana*, or the *manipura*.

The first at the base of the spine corresponds to anal sensations and is readily activated by contracting the anal sphincter muscles.

The second at the genital region corresponds to sexual sensations and is usually activated along with the *mula* (which is why the Tibetan Buddhists combine the two).

The third, in the stomach region, marks a change in sensation. Here is the so-called power center of the body, the place called "hara" by the Japanese, where we have our center of balance and symbolic strength. The meditative visual symbol for this *chakra* used to be the swastika, but since this symbol was usurped and besmirched by the Nazis, most books give a barred triangle instead. If you feel weak and inadequate, meditation on *manipura*, the stomach *chakra*, will give you power and a sense of balance.

Some authorities say yogis do not meditate on the lower *chakras*, meaning that they are concerned with higher things. However, part of what the symbolism of *kundalini* is saying is that until we establish a firm emotional foundation to our lives we cannot meditate on higher things. Nonetheless, meditation on the lower *chakras* leads to lower *chakra* accomplishments, and meditation on the higher *chakras* leads to higher level accomplishments, and eventually to *samadhi* itself.

The fourth *chakra*, the heart *chakra* is the first higher *chakra* and it represents love. Meditation on the heart *chakra* leads to feelings of love for everyone and everything.

Meditation on the *visuddha chakra* in the throat leads to creativity and strengthens the spiritual will power.

Meditation on *ajna*, the third eye *chakra*, leads to transcendental wisdom and cosmic understanding. This is the most important *chakra* for meditation. No yogi would let a day pass by without meditating on—or, as some say—*with* the third eye.

THE SYMBOL OF LOVE

The question that cries out to be asked here is why should this work? Why should meditating on the heart region of the body, for example, result in feelings of love? I thought the heart was a muscle and that its relationship to love was purely symbolic.

Actually there's more to it than that. The heart symbol in Western culture doesn't really relate to the heart as such; it comes from the inverted triangle of Eastern cultures (including the Hindu) which symbolizes the "yoni" or the female genitals. The use of the word "heart" for the symbol of Valentine's Day in our culture is part euphemism and part a deeper recognition that feelings of love do indeed come from the heart area of the body. As such the heart symbol in Western cultures is actually a de facto recognition of the *anahata chakra*.

THE LIMITS OF MEDICAL SCIENCE

To try to answer the question in general though—the question of why *kundalini* should work—let's first think about how the body works.

We in the West are brought up to imagine that medical science understands how the body works, at least in general and for the most part. Unfortunately the truth is not so clear. Knowledge of how chemical energy is created and especially how it is employed by the body and the brain is fairly well understood. However the holistic workings of the body are only beginning to be appreciated. The way the body uses glandular secretions and the role of the so-called brain opiates is not entirely understood. And if we really understood the immune system we'd probably have a cure for AIDS by now.

This is not to criticize the medical profession, but to remind us that we are not far removed from the practice of blood-letting and the performance of frontal lobotomies—to mention two barbaric examples of fairly recent "state of the art" medical practice.

Our lack of precise knowledge about how the body works is not surprising. It is very difficult to acquire knowledge about the living, breathing, working human body. Consequently the healthy body has been (relatively speaking) studied barely at all.

In ancient times people tried the same things they do today. They opened up the human body and looked inside to see how it worked. Unfortunately in opening it up they stopped it from working. Archaeologists have found skulls in the Andes that indicate that the Incas practiced a sort of brain surgery. One can only imagine (with horror) the bloody practices of powerful shamans in prehistoric times as they sought to look inside the living human body and find out what makes it tick.

LOOKING INSIDE OUR BODIES BY FEEL

The yogis did the same of course, but instead of working on someone else's body, they worked on their own. And naturally they (or most of them anyway) did not cut it open. They became increasingly more and more aware of what was going on by slowing down their active processes and looking within. As I sit here at my computer working I cannot feel my heartbeat. I'm not aware that it's beating at all. But if I sit down and assume a meditative pose in a quiet place, after a while I can feel the pulse.

But the heartbeat is a gross manifestation of the body's workings, crudely obvious compared to the electro-chemical energy that jumps along the nerves and leaps its little leap across the synapses. Yet that kind of energy, subtle as it is, affects our bodies in the most profound ways.

One of the intermediate goals of yoga is to become aware of how the various energies in the body are harmonized. Toward this goal the "science" of *kundalini* evolved. The ancients imagined that there actually were wheels within the body that spun when concentrated on properly. At least the common practitioner imagined this. The more learned guru may have known (from his shaman surgeon friend) that no such wheel could actually be found in the gross body. So he imagined that the wheel existed in the subtle body or was too small to be seen.

THE *CHAKRAS* AND THE GLANDS

Today we know that most *chakras* are located at places in the body that correspond to the endocrine glands. The *muladhara chakra* is where the gonads are; the *visuddha chakra* located in the neck points to the thyroid, parathyroid and the thymus glands; the *ajna chakra* is at the level of the pineal and the pituitary glands. It's fairly remarkable that through many generations of practice the yogis were able to pin-point these various centers of glandular activity by feel.

We might note that to a sufficiently sensitive person, a gland secreting hormones may indeed feel like an internal wheel spinning, especially if that is what is expected.

However it may be that there is yet more to the *chakras* in the gross body than this. There may as yet be discovered bundles or clusters of sensitive nerves that correspond to those spiritual wheels of tantra.

More likely however is the idea that when we concentrate on a particular area of the body we stimulate a corresponding area of the brain from which we can expect feedback. If the brain works in a holistic manner (as I understand is becoming the current wisdom) then we might well expect not only a unique feedback from the corresponding body area but something beyond what might be expected from what little can be found there. We might indeed see things never seen before—colored wheels or visions of other inhabited worlds, who's to say? The amazing power of the brain to create entire universes seemingly correct in every experiential detail is obvious to anyone who has ever dreamed.

Along these same lines of thought we might say that although *kundalini* seems to be coiled up in the *mula chakra*, she is in the brain.

KUNDALINI FOR MEDITATION

One thing that's clear about *kundalini* yoga is that it is an exceedingly powerful seed to meditation, and really nothing more need be said in its support. I would add for those concerned with the lack of scientific verification that it wasn't until recently that our medical establishment was even officially aware that the ancient oriental practice of acupuncture really worked. Sobering realization that is.

One thing remains to be said. The symbolism found in the tantric texts on *kundalini* should not be dismissed as irrelevant to the modern practice. The symbolism is there to teach us. Remember that the people who developed that symbolism felt for the truth in the best way they could and in turn have tried to relate what they experienced to us. Much of it will not be easy to understand and much of it may well prove to be irrelevant or "false"; nonetheless the person who carefully studies the symbolism will be rewarded with a greater understanding than is otherwise possible. The choices of deities, of colors, sounds, etc., for the various *chakras* were not made arbitrarily. There are lessons in those choices and guides to a greater practice. Again the student who follows the texts with an open mind and a receptive heart will have the best chance for success.

MY PERSONAL EXPERIENCE

A word about my own experience might be helpful. I have indeed meditated on all the various centers many times. I have worked at drawing up the *shakti* force but without the sort of success promised in the various texts. No doubt my lack of faith is a hindrance. I have felt pleasure by focusing on all the *chakras*. Concentration on the two lower *chakras* leads to the awakening of sexual desire. I usually find that distractive and so I seldom meditate on those *chakras* anymore. Meditation on the stomach *chakra* leads to sense of power and strength. One feels centered and secure. Sometimes I need that. Meditation on the heart *chakra* leads to a feeling of love and compassion for all beings. I actually feel my chest grow warm when I meditate there. My experience with the throat *chakra* has been less interesting. Strange to say, but I usually experience a sense of transparency when I am doing it well, a sense of clarity and absence.

Usually I concentrate on the *ajna chakra* in the forehead because meditation there leads to a feeling of pleasure. From there I can go elsewhere. I have experimented with the *sahasrara chakra*, but what usually happens is my focus drifts to the top of my head or into the center of my head. It is there that I sometimes experience a most compelling, strong sense of bliss.

TWO NON-TRADITIONAL POINTS OF FOCUS

It is curious but for me the most easily focused part of my body are my teeth! Focusing on my teeth does not lead to anything other than such a focus, but I have the most vivid and faintly tinkling sensation when I hold my attention there. It is mildly pleasurable. I wonder why this phenomenon is never mentioned. Perhaps I have missed it, or maybe this experience is just something particular to me. Also very easy to meditate on is the tongue. I can actually feel it. I get a sense of its mass and it seems to be throbbing with blood as I concentrate. I can easily rest my attention on my tongue without wandering.

Why this is the case, I do not know.

For those want to explore the esoterica of *kundalini* further see Woodruffe's book. It is extraordinarily detailed.

Chapter 23:
On Tanta of the Left-Handed Path

TANTRA DEFINED

The word "tantra" means "treatise," usually on such subjects as ritual, meditation, mantra, etc. Be assured that there are more tantras than any of us could read in a lifetime. In the West however tantra often means the tantra associated with the so-called "left-handed path," and it is this meaning that shall concern us here. The many and disparate aspects of the larger tantrism that are part of the Buddhist, Jain, Hindu and especially the Tibetan religious experience will not be addressed here. I want to discuss tantra yoga as it relates to the *raja* and *hatha yoga* practices.

To reduce tantra to a definition we can say that tantra is a highly emotional and active way of realizing God that grew out of the earliest traditions in India. Just how it differs from yoga and how it is similar is what we'll try to get at here.

BHOGA

Although intimately associated in the popular mind with yoga, tantra is in many respects the antithesis of yoga. The highest effective value in yoga is discipline (the word "yoga" is often translated as "discipline") while the same value in tantra is *bhoga* which means pleasure, enjoyment or ecstasy. While sex is de-emphasized in yoga, and brahmacharya (a concept close to celibacy) is the ideal, in tantra sex is held in the highest esteem and its ritual practice thought to be a means to God realization.

In short, the idea in tantra is to achieve liberation not by discipline or through denying the desires of the senses but by giving into them. The path is called left-handed because most people are right-handed and the right-handed way to do things is the norm or the "right" way. Incidentally this preference for the right hand extends well beyond Indian culture, being linguistically obvious in many languages, including the Latin from which we get our word "sinister," the original meaning of which was "left-handed and unlucky."

THE YOGA OF THE MASSES

Tantra is popular. It can be seen as the yoga of the masses, especially of the young. The controversial Bhagwan Shree Rajneesh, the guru shown on television's "Sixty Minutes" some years ago driving around his Oregon commune in air-conditioned luxury cars with the windows rolled up, staring blankly out at his flock (before he was forced to leave the United States in 1986) was perhaps the foremost exponent in the West. At least he was the best known and most widely read.

Tantra is social. Followers of the tantric way often form themselves into communes under an all-powerful and dictatorial master or guru. Ecstasy is sought through chanting, dancing and other group activities. A sense of belonging and society is achieved through tribal pressure and group ritual. The herd instinct is allowed full play. Aspirants dress, act and live the same way, worshiping the guru and working for the good of the commune.

EMBRACING DESIRE

Tantra of course is not limited to the practices of the followers of Rajneesh, although their practices are typical of tantric methods in general. Tantra is like an exotic religious bazaar where every variety of approach and practice can be found in various styles and intensities. No single style typifies the movement, and perhaps a disservice is done by giving this impression.

However, tantra as it is popularly understood in the West is a system made distinct from the practices of the yoga of the *Bhagavad Gita*, the yoga of the *Hathayogapradipika*, the yoga of the

Gheranda Samhita, and especially the yoga of Patanjali, and is characterized by the pursuit of *bhoga* as symbolized in the ritual of the "five forbidden things."

In traditional yoga desire is overcome by a looking inward, by finding God within oneself, in the *Atman* that dwells within. In tantra the way to overcome desire—to eventually lose desire—is to embrace the objects of desire. This is why, especially in India, tantra is the yoga of the masses and why it is so readily adopted by the young (although they don't always realize that is what they are adopting).

The ideal person in tantra is the *vira,* the hero, who plunges headlong into life bravely, taking everything life has to give without worry, without regret, without undue consideration for the consequences of his actions. He conquers the world through vigorous action.

In contrast the ideal person in yoga is *divya,* characterized by a sense of balance and discipline. If the predominate quality of the hero is *rajas* (the *guna* of activity) then that of the person of yoga is *sattva* (the *guna* of balance and illumination).

While it is said in tantra that each aspirant is given the *sadhana* that is natural to his or her stage of spiritual progress— worldly activity for the animal person seeking pleasure, withdrawal and introspection for the person who has seen and experienced the delusion of worldly pleasures—what tantra really amounts to is a philosophy of "follow the flesh while the flesh is young and turn to the spiritual when the flesh grows old."

This style is not only natural to most people, it is largely unavoidable. Tantra then makes a virtue out of following the natural course of things. But where does this leave the exceptional person who has seen the pain that such a course inevitably leads to and would like to avoid it? Such persons, the tantric would reply, should take up *raja* yoga. They should discipline themselves through physical and mental practices so that they may de-emphasize the rule of flesh and hasten toward the ultimate union with God.

In tantra then there is an element of the Tao: follow the water course way; do what comes naturally. Don't fret and don't look back. Embrace what seems embraceable without prejudice—and indeed often without thought. Do it without thought because thought so often slows us down and leads to the creation of obstacles that serve only to stand in our way. "If it feels good—do it!" is a tantric idea.

SIMILARITIES WITH TRADITIONAL YOGA

However there is a lot of tantra that is very similar to yoga. In tantra the world is *sat-chit-ananda*—existence, knowledge and bliss—the same as it is in yoga (although in tantra the first is sometimes referred to as *sunyata*—the void). The so-called objective world is seen as *lila*—or play—while in yoga the world is *maya*—illusion. In either case the world as we see it is not the ultimate reality. It is only through union with the Supreme that the real nature of the world can be seen and experienced.

As befits a popular movement, tantra, like traditional yoga, rejects caste and fosters the belief that all men and women are equal before God. Tantra is catholic and tolerant. It rejects no religion. It is down to earth. Vivian Worthington in his book, *A History of Yoga*, p. 83, says that philosophically tantra can be described as "existential" while "emotionally it marked the return of the mother goddess into the religious life of India." Thus tantra is also "feminine," and in that respect deserves a better understanding in the West where masculine methods and values are highly over-rated.

THE FIVE FORBIDDEN THINGS

Just what are the "five forbidden things"? They are *madya*, *mamsa*, *matsya*, *mudra*, and *maithuna*, which are translated as wine, meat, fish, "gesture" and sex. The Sanskrit word "mudra" admits of several meanings, "seal, gesture, posture," which is why I have it in quotation marks. The one meant here is an erotic seal, "*vajroli mudra*," in which the semen is retained during the ritual even though "the woman is embraced."

The word "*maithuna*," which used to appear on bumper stickers or in the rear windows of cars driven by hedonistic yuppies, means more than just sex. It refers to the entire ritual of the five forbidden things, a ritual that often included the use of marijuana or other drugs to heighten the effect. This once trendy (in the sixties) and upscale (in the seventies) practice has, with the decline of casual sex, become passé.

THE TANTRIC GURU

It is in the tantric tradition that the guru becomes a sort of god on earth in the flesh, and it is in tantra that the "initiation" into tantric yoga by the guru is seen as the most important event of the aspirant's life. Through the ritual of initiation the seeker is made to believe that "there is no truth greater than the Guru," that "all holy actions are rooted in the Guru," and that "Guru is the father, Guru is the mother, Guru is God Maheshwara Himself"—to quote the Kularnava Tantra as presented by M.P. Pandit in his book *Gems from the Tantras*, V.1 pp.19-21.

It is no exaggeration to say that in this tradition the idea for the *sadhaka* is to be hypnotized by the guru so as to facilitate progress. As in *bhakti* yoga, psychological surrender to the guru and all that he stands for is seen as essential to success. Typical of the guru's attitude are these words of Bhagwan Shree Rajneesh (as quoted by his disciple Ma Yoga Anurag in *Tantra, the Supreme Understanding*, p. x): "All bliss, all moments of bliss, happen only when you surrender. Even death becomes beautiful if you can surrender to it..."

Ma Yoga Anurag adds, "This is Bhagwan's invitation for you to come and celebrate, not through renunciation but acceptance, not through denial but welcoming, not through rules but rejoicing. Come: eat, drink and be filled..."

YOGA FOR FOOLS

It's easy to see how tantra got the reputation in the West of being a left-handed path. It is especially easy for me to see that tantra of this sort, a tantra characterized by worship of the guru and by a rampant and reckless hedonism, is fraught with danger, not only spiritual danger, but actual worldly danger as well. I am reminded when I see the followers of leaders like Rajneesh not only of the ill-fated commune of the Rev. Jim Jones in Guyana whose members were persuaded to commit mass suicide by their leader—or more recently of the Heaven's Gate sadness in California—but of the horrors of Nazi Germany itself. Blind allegiance to a guru may be good psychology for simple souls bent on achieving a kind of herd animal state of trance, but for the serious seeker after God it can only lead to a spiritual dead end—or worse—death itself without liberation.

Tantra as practiced by sincere and enlightened persons may indeed lead to God. But for most persons it will only lead to further worldly dependence—either on another person, or on a group of persons, and will reinforce the poor aspirant's addiction to desire and the objects of desire. Prophetically, the tantric ritual of sexual intercourse in the graveyard (described earlier in this book) reveals the folly of the left-handed path, leading the seeker to an acute awareness of the ends of fleshy desire; that is, from the indulgence of sex comes another mouth to feed, another *karma* container to play out its fate, another person who will inevitably come to the graveyard. For the spiritually aware, tantra is yoga for fools.

I should also point to the pathetic end that Rajneesh himself had come to: driving around in a luxury car, reportedly a different one each day, looking out through the tinted windows with Valium-laden eyes at his worshipful disciples as he toured his commune, soon to be deported from the United States and then from other countries, his financial empire in shambles, his once hypnotic voice stilled, his affairs in the hands of grasping sycophants, his reputation as a guru sullied and smeared beyond recognition—the ironic, yet karmic end of a snake-oil peddler who would play the role of God.

Chapter 24:
Renunciation

In ancient India the last stage of life was that of a wandering mendicant. Even today in modern India there are untold thousands of such individuals wandering about the land living from day to day on handouts, contemplating their navels (so to speak, and sometimes literally), while searching passionately (or perhaps dispassionately) for the final liberation. Some of them have done this since they were children, others have come upon this ancient way of life, this final resolution as young men, as middle-aged men, as old men. They have renounced the world and its trinkets and its delusions and are seeking non-attachment.

NON-ATTACHMENT

Implicit within the practice of yoga and other ways of knowing is this idea of non-attachment. We can only really find freedom by becoming non-attached to the vagaries of this world. This idea comes from the Upanishads and is central to the message of the Gita. This attachment that enslaves us is the attachment to the results of our endeavors. We want to be successful and because of this desire we are attached to the world. And in being attached we experience both success and failure, pleasure and pain and the entire litany of opposites. No real freedom can be achieved until we put a stop to this attachment.

THE PAIRS OF OPPOSITES

The dualistic nature of the world requires that we experience pain and failure because there can be no pleasure without pain (or at least without the lack of pleasure), no success without failure, just as the idea of cold has no meaning without the accompanying idea of hot. Indeed there is no non-being without being, which is perhaps the answer to the primordial question, Why is there anything at all? There can't be nothing because what would be the idea of nothing without the idea of something? Through quantum mechanics we have learned that the uncertainty principle demands that empty space not be empty!

This is why in yogic philosophy there is the idea of union with the Ineffable as a means of escaping the dualistic world with its pairs of opposites. When we accomplish this we put an end to *samsara* and the endless cycle of births and deaths.

LEARNING NOT TO CARE

Given this argument, how does one achieve non-attachment?

One learns not to care. One learns indifference to evil, and one learns an equipoise that allows us to greet whatever happens with the same temperament.

How does one do this?

Through renunciation. We take the radical step of renouncing all the rewards that might come our way in this world. We declare and believe that we don't want them.

What occurs when this is done is that we are never disappointed and we accept whatever happens to us without caring. This leads to freedom.

But should we do this? Assuming we can give up the pleasures and the pains, should we?

I began the practice of renunciation about some years ago, and the answer I can give is an emphatic yes. But this is my answer, and I am an old man. For others it may be different. But this is also the answer of the Upanishads and the Gita. It is the wisdom of Krishna.

The reason renunciation is effective is that what really hurts us in this world is the pain and the disappointments. The pleasures simply are not great enough, and they never last. For most people no pleasure can balance the loss of a loved one. Furthermore, the serene equanimity that we experience on the level plane is itself quite agreeable. This is why the yogis say we are bliss. Take away the pleasure and the pain, and what remains is bliss. I have used the word "pleasure" throughout this book where the old yogis would have insisted upon "bliss." It is here, while considering the question of renunciation that we can fully understand their insistence.

What I am trying to say is that they are right. When one gives up the pleasures and pains of this world (to the extent possible) one receives bliss in return.

I could say believe me; in fact I do say, believe me. But of course it is necessary that you experience non-attachment for yourself.

A TIME TO RENOUNCE

Now if you are a young person it will be extraordinarily difficult to renounce this world. You are a student or a "householder" in the traditional terminology, and you must do what a student or a householder does, that is, learn about life, make a living, love your spouse, have children, etc. It is only when you have passed through these early stages of life that you can renounce.

I know that I personally could never have hoped in my wildest imaginings to have renounced the world when I was one and thirty. Only the rare saint can do that. The Buddha did it, but of course he is the rare exception. Not only can't you renounce the world, you shouldn't until it is your time.

This time comes for all of us if we live long enough. For some it might be as early as their fortieth birthday, for others a decade or two later. When it comes, when your responsibilities are few or none and you have the freedom, then you can renounce.

Renunciation leads directly to non-attachment which leads to freedom.

It is as simple as that.

Is it hard to renounce?

Some things are hard. I had difficulty with pretty faces. It took me some long time, and to be honest, I am not completely cured. Easier to give up were the other delusions such as wealth and fame and winning and looking good and being one up on the other guy. Those delusions fell away quickly and easily. The delusions of pride and the attachment to the ego are a bit more difficult, but bit by bit, I am assured, I will remove myself from attachment to even them.

The way to facilitate this renunciation is to remove oneself as much as possible from other people. They will just distract you and lead you astray. This means even removing yourself from all social activities, from relatives, friends and loved ones. Since this is such a difficult program, and as I said, an impossible one for most people, it is not something you will find in other books on yoga. What is the point of telling someone they should do something they cannot do?

So why am I telling you this?

My purpose is merely to point in the direction, to say to you that if and when you can, there is an answer, there is a way to freedom. And this way is non-attachment. And there will come a time when you can do it.

THE PRACTICE OF RENUNCIATION

During our period of renunciation we practice an intense self-study. We look directly into our nature, observing everything we do and everything we have done dispassionately with a kind of stark and even brutal objectivity so that we know who we are in a naturalistic sense. We observe our passions and we recall them. We note not only what we did, but what we might have done in different circumstances.

When we do this we find that we are not really different from others. We too are capable of the same sorts of things that others have done. We may not steal, but had our circumstances been different we know in our heart we would have stolen. Indeed I gained a sense of freedom the day I realized, the day I knew as sure as the sun comes up tomorrow that there existed circumstances in which I was capable of even murder. Fortunately, such circumstances never arose in my life. I was lucky. Today of course, there is nothing short of self-defense that would move me to hurt another person.

COMPASSION

What one really learns from self-study is compassion. We learn that it is really true when we see what someone else has done, that "there but for the grace of God go I." We learn the politically and socially incorrect truth that "to know all is to forgive all." This is a truth we can know in our hearts, but it is not a truth that society can accept. We know that the person who does harm acts because of his intrinsic nature in concert with his environment bent by the experiences of his life. Had we such a nature so molded, we too would probably act that way as well. Again this is not a public truth. This is not something that our laws, our mores, or public opinion can countenance for obvious reasons. This is a private truth.

Be sure that this is not fatalism. We are not automatons. We have free will and we do not have free will. Like a particle in physics which has the dual nature of being both a particle and a wave, we both have and do not have free will. Certainly we have the illusion of free will, and even if we only have that, it is enough. What I am talking about is a realization of what is true in a probabilistic sense. Given such and such a nature in such and such a circumstance, we would probably do such and such a thing.

Thus this renunciation and self-study is a private experience. It is something we do alone. We cannot share it with others. And they cannot help us.

THE GREAT AWAKENING

Once we have thoroughly renounced this world there comes a great awakening. We can then return to the world in the state of non-attachment, and we can live among our fellows in harmony, without expectation, and with a minimum of pain. I say a minimum because of course we have not really achieved the enlightenment and the non-attachment of the saint. We are still human, but we on our way. We will be going home someday soon.

What happens, even with a partial achievement, is a more serene existence. For most people it is simply a better way to live. For some who live their lives on the razor's edge, who, like manic-depressives, experience the highest highs and the lowest lows, perhaps the serene plane without extremes is like the straight line on an EKG machine. It is for them death.

But death comes not just for the archbishop but for us all. Death is the great leveler between the high and the low. But death achieves no victories; it has no sting. It is only in the anticipation of death that it has any power over us.

We are always alive. We may sadly experience the deaths of our loved ones, but we will never experience our own death. Right up until the very last moment, when, it is said, all experience passes before our eyes in just a twinkling of a moment, we are alive. And when we are dead we have no experience of anything. We did not experience anything in the vast eternity before we were born, and we did not fear, we did not regret. So now when we look into the yawning gape of the next vast eternity (should we care to do that) we again should have no regrets and no fear.

BETWEEN DESIRE AND RENUNCIATION

Once we have found non-attachment, once we have lost desire we realize that the paradox of human existence lies in that place between desire and renunciation.

And with that knowledge ushers in a terrible yet awesomely beautiful irony: without desire we may no longer care if we live or die. This in essence is the central predicament of life: desire leads to pain; lack of desire leads to death. The realization of this leads to the Buddha's *dukkha*—"unsatisfactoriness."

The end of desire is death, and death is the great awakening. And yet as we lay our burden down and throw off the shackles of pleasure and pain, as we throw off the tyranny of the pairs of opposites, and we fall into the great ocean of *Brahman* where there is neither this nor that, where we exist as information on the ether, as in a dreamless sleep, as in the final dissolution of the universe when every particle is beyond the horizon of every other particle, where there is neither light nor love, neither darkness nor hate, we realize that we will be free of every burden.

But we will never experience any of that.

And so we do not rage against the dying of the light; neither do we go gentle into that good night. Instead we face the inevitability of death with open eyes and head held high. We understand in our deepest core the unsatisfactoriness and the impermanence of life and we are pleased to let it go when the time comes.

We are eternally *sat, chit, ananda*: existence, knowledge, and bliss.

A Selected and Annotated Bibliography

The purpose of this annotated bibliography is to survey the literature in English and to guide aspirants in their search for a collection of books that will help them to achieve yoga, especially *jnana* yoga, the achievement of which I believe requires knowledge of other religious philosophies. Consequently this is a critical bibliography.

In general yoga books can be labeled "popular," "technical," or "academic" (or "scholarly"), depending on the scope and/or intent. Some books combine these approaches. I have tried to indicate with various labels where a particular book falls within this scheme. In addition I have used a zero to three star system of overall preference. I feel that elegance of expression and technical understanding are important in rating the books, but overall value to the student in the quest is the most important consideration.

Books that I feel are well worth reading are given a "*". Books worth buying if you can find them are "**". The most important books rate "***". Books with no stars may very well be excellent, but I have for whatever reason declined to rate them.

Unfortunately many of these books are out of print. They can be obtained only through second hand or specialty book stores or at libraries or used on the Web at such sites as Ebay or Amazon. In some cases digital copies can be found on the Internet. The student is urged to expend some considerable effort to become familiar with the starred books. It might be a good idea to purchase any of these books since each one of these books is a potential teacher.

There are a number of books that are not yoga books per se included here, some because they're mentioned in the text and others because they shed light on some aspect of yoga from another perspective. These books are identified with a pound sign "#" following the listing.

While this bibliography is more than suggestive of the scope of the literature in English, it is not exhaustive, nor is it meant to be. There are a number of excellent yoga books not mentioned here.

Akers, Brian Dana, trans. *The Hatha yoga Pradipika*. Woodstock, NY: YogaVidya.com, 2002. The clear and elegant translation by Akers is set on the pages verse by verse along with Svatmarama's original Sanskrit. Akers and the people at YogaVidya are to be complimented for bringing this text to the general public and for doing so in a most attractive manner. **

Arya, Pandit Usharbudh *Philosophy of Hatha yoga*. 2nd Ed. Honesdale, Pa.: Himalayan Institute, 1985. Arya sees *hatha yoga* as a "gateway to the subtle body." He calls *kundalini* the "yoga of real intangibles, to which maybe one out of five hundred million humans may have access." I think we can disagree with that. Arya also sees *hatha yoga* as "karmic purification," which is interesting, and as "daily discomfort," which is false and suggests his practice is gravely in arrears. Academic but accessible.

Avalon, Arthur (Sir John Woodroffe). *The Serpent Power*, 6th ed. New York: Dover Publications, 1974. The first edition was in published in 1919.

Bahm, Archie J. *Yoga for Business Executives and Professional People*. New York: The Citadel Press, 1965. Commercial.

Baldi, Pierre. *The Shattered Self: The End of Natural Evolution*. Cambridge, MA: MIT Press 2001. "We do not know who we are, but we know enough to know we are not who we think we are." This quote sets the tone for this extraordinary book which is an excursion into the future of ourselves and the world we are making. The emphasis is on biology, genetics, computer science and information technology including brain science and how discoveries in these fields are changing our lives and our very concept of self. #

Barrow, John D. *Book of Nothing, The: Vacuums, Voids, and the Latest Ideas about the Origins of the Universe*. New York: Pantheon Books, 2000. In this report we see that the vacuum of space ("nothing") is not entirely empty, and in fact cannot in principle ever be empty. As Barrow explains, it would be a violation of the Uncertainty Principle because, "If we could say that there were no particles in a box, that it was completely empty of all mass and energy," we would have "perfect information about motion at every point and about the energy of the system at a given instant of time." #

Behanan, Kovoor T. *Yoga, a Scientific Evaluation*. New York: Dover Publications, 1964. A reprint of the book first published in 1937. The evaluation (circa 1935) seems quaintly unscientific today. Some of the chapters are "Yoga and Psychoanalysis" and "Yoga and Psychic Research." Dr. Behanan, an Indian, took up the practice and study as Sterling Fellow in the Psychology Department at Yale. The presentation is from that viewpoint. The "scientific" evaluation is more or less tacked on. He gives a favorable opinion of yoga, although he doesn't think that it is more than a psychological phenomenon. Academic and semi-popular. *

Bernard, Theos. *Hatha yoga: The Report of a Personal Experience*. London: Rider, 1968. This is a most interesting book detailing an extraordinary effort on the part of the author to attain yoga. Popular. **

——. *Heaven Lies Within Us*. New York: Charles Scribner's Sons, 1939. Probably the best, most detailed and truest rendering in English of an aspirant's journey to India and the growth of his yoga practice. Bernard is both more candid than others have been and is definitely more detailed. He explains the practices and gives the effects and explains why. A strange book nonetheless since although Bernard appears as probably the hardest working student imaginable it is not clear at the ending that he achieved much of anything spiritually, and by omission seems to imply that he fell short of his goal of liberation. Highly informative and readable. The author died tragically some few years later while in the Himalayas. Popular. **

Bharati, Agehananda. *The Tantric Tradition*. New York: Samuel Weiser Inc., 1975. First edition, Rider & Co., 1965. Academic. *

Bolle, Kees W. *The Bhagavadgita*. Berkeley: University of California Press, 1979. Bolle's is a very readable and accessible version in which the Sanskrit appears on the left facing page and the English on the right, verse by verse. The text of the Gita is presented first in this book without any introduction in keeping with Bolle's dictum that "a translation should speak for itself." The text is followed by Part Two, "On Translating the Gita," which is an elegant and fascinating essay on not only the considerations and challenges the translator faces in rendering the Gita into English, but on translating in general. There is a short bibliography and then a Sanskrit Concordance and an English Guide to the concordance. This is a superior book that ought to be brought back into print. Scholarly. **

Boyd, Doug. *Swami*. New York: Random House, 1976. A different sort of going-to-India-to-look-for-a-guru book in that journalist Boyd starts out in Topeka, Kansas at the Menninger Foundation with Swami Rama (of the Himalayan Institute) in 1970 helping the Swami show the good doctors how he meditates and slows his heartbeat, etc., and only later goes to India to look, as a Hindu guide phrases it, "into this swami business." The portrait of Swami Rama is interesting. The rest of the book leaves a little to be desired, especially Boyd's lack of yoga sophistication and a "country boy" arrogance that sometimes creeps into the narrative. Popular. *

Brunton, Paul. *A Search in Secret India*. Philadelphia: McKay (circa 1934?). Earnest, naive and overly occultish. For true believers. Popular.

Chitrabhanu, Gurudev Shree. *Realize What You Are: The Dynamics of Jain Meditation*, edited by Leonard M. Marks. New York: Dodd, Mead, 1978. One of a number of gentle, worthwhile books by Chitrabhanu. Popular. *

Chopra, Deepak. *Ageless Body, Timeless Mind: The Quantum Alternative to Growing Old.* New York: Harmony Books, 1993. Chopra is both a mesmerizing writer and a spellbinding speaker. Those qualities and his positive, uplifting style and tireless energy account in some measure for his extraordinary popular success. About this volume I will only note that our minds may be timeless, but our bodies are not really ageless. #

Cole, K.C. *The Hole in the Universe: How Scientists Peered over the Edge of Emptiness and Found Everything.* New York: Harcourt, 2001. Covers much the same ground as the book by John D. Barrow above with a more journalistic feel. #

Crick, Francis. *The Astonishing Hypothesis: The Scientific Search for the Soul.* New York: Charles Scribner's Sons 1994. This is about consciousness. The "soul" in the title is used ironically since Crick does not believe there is a "mind" independent of the neurons. Of course, from my point of view there is indeed a "mind" independent of the nerve cells; this "mind" however is an abstract construct consisting of thoughts, ideas, experiences, etc. It exists "nowhere" and of course everywhere. It exists before time and after time. It is not matter or energy but information written not on the wind nor on the ether, but pervades the vacuum of time and space. It cannot be accessed by anyone, although I personally can access some of my own mind, however incompletely. I like to think of this "mind" as the rationalist's soul. It is information, period. #

Crowley, Aleister. *Eight Lectures in Yoga.* Dallas, Texas: Sangreal Foundation, 1972. The lectures were given in the Thirties. Crowley gives yoga a tongue in cheek, Zenish spin. Popular.

Darling, David. *Zen Physics: The Science of Death, the Logic of Reincarnation.* New York, NY: HarperCollins, 1996. Darling makes a number of startling observations, most notably that it is our ego-sense or our "consciousness" that makes us afraid of death. On page 104 he writes, "the prime biological function of the self is to be afraid of death." This is an ancient idea straight from the Upanishads, incorporated in the *Bhagavad Gita* and found in Buddhism as well as in yogic theory and practice. It is also an important idea in evolutionary psychology where consciousness or the sense of the individual self is seen as a trick of the species mechanism to make us fear death (among other things). Another nice quote is on page 176: "What the brain really does is to sample extremely narrow aspects of reality through the senses and then subject these to further drastic and highly selective reinterpretation." Darling adds that the brain, as William James said in his famous quote about "the doors of perception," restricts our ability to see the world objectively. We see the world only as our system needs to see it to survive. Or, to quote Darling, (p. 180) "The brain effectively pinches off a little bubble of introverted awareness and stores and manipulates information relevant exclusively to the survival needs of the individual so created." Our sense of ourselves as individuals is, as the yogis teach, a delusion fostered on us by the evolutionary mechanism to help us cope with living on this animal plane. #

Dass, Ram. *Still Here: Embracing Aging, Changing, and Dying*. New York: Riverhead Books, 2000. Ram Dass celebrates aging as a time of self-discovery and of selfless service to others. This is an inspirational and uplifting book by the author of the best-selling *Be Here Now* (1971), the one-time Richard Alpert, who gave up a professorship at Harvard to follow the path of *karma* yoga. *

Day, Harvey. *Yoga Illustrated Dictionary*. New York: Emerson Books, 1971. Occultish, Anglophile collection of semi-objective mini-essays/definitions. For the real thing see Georg Feuerstein's *The Shambhala Encyclopedia of Yoga*. Popular.

Deutsch, Eliot, trans. *The Bhagavad Gita*. New York: Holt, Rinehart and Winston, 1968. Includes an introduction and some critical essays. A good book for the general reader who wants an intro to the Gita. Popular. *

Devi, Indra. *Yoga for Americans*. New York: New American Library, 1968. First edition, 1959. A follow-up to her popular *Forever Young, Forever Healthy* (of which I do not have a copy). Interesting photos. Gives a flavor of the fifties when yoga was being discovered by Hollywood. A six-week course. Includes recipes. Engagingly written by a beautiful person who knows what she is talking about. Popular.*

Digambarji, Swami, and Kokaje, R, eds. *Hathapradipika of Svatmarama*. Lonavla, India: Kaivalyadhama Institute, 1970. (Also called *Hathayogapradipika*.) Probably the best known of the classical works on *hatha yoga*. The editors fix the time of its composition between 1350 and 1550 c.e. This edition includes the aphorisms in Sanskrit, a transliteration into Roman characters, a translation into English, and critical notes. Svatmarama is obviously talking to other yogis in outline fashion since the aphorisms are terse and vague and include the various hierarchical exaggerations ("destroys all disease," etc.). The text could only serve as a memory aid to someone already knowledgeable about the practices. Academic.

Digambarji, Swami, and Gharote, M.L., eds. *Geranda Samhita*. Lonavla, India: Kaivalyadhama Institute, 1978. The editors place the original circa 17th-18th century—at any rate clearly later than the *Hathayogapradipika*. This edition contains photos of some of the postures and a critical commentary with attempts at explaining some things scientifically. *Geranda Samhita* is a text on "*ghatasthayoga*" (a yoga of the body— nowhere does the usual term "*hatha yoga*" appear) in the form of a dialogue between Geranda, the preceptor and Candakapali, the disciple. It presents the now classic *kriyas*, asanas, *mudras*, *pratyahara*, *pranayamas*, *dhyanas* and *samadhis* more explicitly than earlier texts. Academic.

Drego, Pearl. *Pathways to Liberation. An Essay on Yoga-Christian Dialogue*. New Delhi: The Grail, 1974. Gives a Hindu and householder perspective. Popular.

Dunne, Desmond. *Yoga Made Easy*. Englewood Cliffs, N.J.: Prentice-Hall, 1961. I have the fifteenth printing of 1974, so this was commercially a very successful book and typical of what I would expect from a "made easy" type of book. Even as an introduction to yoga it's a little shallow and limited in scope, but I want to emphasize it's better than no introduction at all. Includes some line drawings. Commercial.

Easwaran, Eknath. *The Bhagavad Gita*. Petaluma, CA: Nilgiri Press, 1985. This is an especially natural and graceful translation somewhere between poetry and prose by a man who really understands the message of the Gita. This can be seen from reading Eknath Easwaran's wise and penetrating Preface written especially for this, the Vintage Spiritual Classics Edition, edited by John F. Thornton and Susan B. Varenne for Vintage Books. Easwaran shows that the differing paths to self-realization and liberation that the Gita presents are a comprehensive whole. "The thread through Krishna's teaching, the essence of the Gita, can be given in one word: "renunciation." This is the common factor in the four yogas" (p. xxxviii). Easwaran goes on to explain that what is being renounced is not material. What is renounced are the fruits of action. Renunciation is not only the essence of *karma* yoga, but the essence of the bhakti, *jnana* and *raja* yogas that Krishna presents as well. The key is an amazing spiritual and psychological insight into human nature: we are miserable when we are concerned with the results of what we do, but we are freed when we devote the fruits of our work to God. What is renounced is also the delusion of a material self that acts, the famous slayer and the slain. **

———, trans. The Upanishads. Tomales, California: Nilgiri Press, 1987. This presentation of the Upanishads—necessarily a selection, of course—by Eknath Easwaran is the best single volume that I have come across for the following reasons:

First, the translation by Easwaran is readable, edifying and congenial to the Sanskrit in so far as that is possible. The poetry in the original language and the word play are lost in translation as is always the case with poetry and highly symbolic language, and especially language that is meant to be taken on more than one level. However Easwaran's notes after each Upanishad help to give us an idea what the original is like and give the reader a feel for the some of the nuances.

Second, the chapter introductions and the concluding essay by Michael N. Nagler lend insight and clarity to the reader's understanding.

Third, the selections themselves and what is included in the selections are efficacious. By that I mean the ideas and the "feel" of the expression, the psychology, and the philosophy of the

Upanishads and the larger Vedic tradition are made manifest. Some voluminous translations give us much more of the repetition and ritual than we need, while some volumes give us perhaps not enough. ***

Edgerton, Franklin, trans. *The Bhagavad Gita*. Cambridge, Mass: Harvard University Press, 1972. The original edition is part of the Harvard Oriental Series, 1944. This is one of those translations that makes a point of not using the word "yoga." "Discipline" is used instead. Thus instead of the Yoga of Action (Chapter III) we have the "Discipline of Action." This bit of silliness is overcome by an otherwise good translation and some interesting essays. Academic. *

Eliade, Mircea. *Patanjali and Yoga*. New York: Funk & Wagnalls, 1969. An historical treatment. Illustrated. I think this book, written by the well-known scholar, was an attempt to reach a popular audience (and cash in on the sixties' interest in things Eastern). Academic.

——. *Yoga: Immortality and Freedom*, trans. Willard R. Trask. Princeton: Princeton University Press, 1958. An impressive scholarly work. Rough going at times but worth the effort.**

Evans-Wentz, W.Y. *Tibetan Yoga and Secret Doctrines*. London: Oxford University Press, 1967. Subtitled "or Seven Books of Wisdom of the Great Path, according to the late Lama Kazi Dawa-Samdup's English rendering." The first edition was published in 1935. Academic and mostly irrelevant to mainstream *hatha/raja* yoga.

Feuerstein, Georg A. *The Shambhala Encyclopedia of Yoga*. New York: Paragon House, 1990. Feuerstein is one of our foremost experts on yoga. This is an outstanding work, one of a kind, accessible to a wide public.***

——. *The Shambhala Guide to Yoga*. Boston: Shambhala, 1996. Excellent guide that manages to be both scholarly and popular. **

——. *The Essence of Yoga*. New York: Grove Press, 1976. Subtitled "A Contribution to the Psychohistory of Indian Civilisation." This is an intense look at the philosophy of yoga from someone who knows well its history and practice. Scholarly and academic. **

———., and Jeanine Miller. *Yoga and Beyond: Essays in Indian Philosophy*. New York: Schocken Books, 1972. Published in Great Britain as *A Reappraisal of Yoga*. Academic. *

——————. *The Yoga Tradition: Its History, Literature, Philosophy and Practice*. Prescott, Ariz.: Hohm Press, 2001) This extraordinary work represents a lifetime of devotion to yoga by its preeminent Western scholar. ***

Fischer-Schreiber, Ingrid ... [et al.] *The Encyclopedia of Eastern Philosophy and Religion*. Boston: Shambhala, 1989. Excellent reference source that reads like a collection of mini essays. **

Fosse, Martin Lars, trans. *The Bhagavad Gita*. Woodstock, NY: YogaVidya.com, 2007. Fosse provides a clear and informative introduction to the Gita for the general reader. He does a good job of placing the work in the Hindu tradition and gives some idea of its history in English. There is a glossary of names (since Fosse uses the many epithets from the original in his translation) and an index. As with the other books from YogaVidya, the original Sanskrit is given along with the English translation, verse by verse. **

Funderburk, James. *Science Studies Yoga: A Review of Physiological Data*. Himalayan Institute, USA, 1977. Yogis hooked up to wires and tubes, their blood and breath, etc. analyzed before and after yogic, Zen and other practices and meditations. Academic.

Ghosh, Jajneswar. *A Study of Yoga*, 2nd revised ed. Delhi: Motilal Banarsidass, 1977. First edition was 1933. Difficult reading, full of hair-splitting distinctions. Academic.

Ghosh, Shyam, ed. and trans. *The Original Yoga as Expounded in Siva-Samhita, Gheranda-Samhita and Patanjali Yoga Sutra*. New Delhi: Munshiram Manoharlal, 1980. An excellent book, collecting three of the classic texts of yoga in one volume. The Sanskrit text is followed by an English translation and a few notes. Both Samhitas are concerned with postures, mudras and meditation techniques as well as spiritual set, and are like the *Hathayogapradipika* in extent and style but more subdued in their claims. Scholarly. **

Harris, Marvin. *Cannibals and Kings: The Origins of Cultures*. New York: Random House, 1977. The eminently readable ethnologist Marvin Harris provides us with a counter-point to a strictly religious view of the past, and who we are, and how we got that way. #

——. *Cows, Pigs, Wars and Witches: The Riddles of Culture*. New York: Random House 1974. #

Hassin, Vijay. *The Modern Yoga Handbook*. Garden City, N.Y.: Dolphin Books, Doubleday & Co., 1978. Socially-oriented yoga, with an emphasis on *bhakti* and *karma* yogas, although Patanjali's system is outlined. Extensive discussion of the role of the guru. An enthusiastic book, aimed at young people, especially women. Style reminds me of the sixties. Popular. *

Hesse, Herman. *Siddhartha*. London: Vision Press, 1954. This beautiful and poetic novel about the life of the Buddha is not about the life of the Buddha, per se, or so Hesse would have us believe. "Siddhartha," meaning "the accomplished one" is one of the traditional names of the Buddha, but in this novel Siddhartha encounters the Buddha in his travels and gains by what he learns from the Enlightened One. Yet the life so wondrously depicted here is closely patterned after the traditional life of the Buddha, and where it is not, it is highly plausible. I think Hesse started out to write a life of the Buddha but at some point realized that his sometimes spiritual, sometimes profane depiction might offend some Buddhists, and so he had Gotama, the Perfect One himself, appear as a separate character while keeping the life and the traditional name for his hero. #

Hewitt, James. *Teach Yourself Yoga*. Chicago: NTC Publishing Group, 1993. A common sense, rounded approach with a minimum of fluff. Good introductory guide from a non-mystical Western point of view. Popular. *

Hittleman, Richard L. *Yoga: The Eight Steps to Health and Peace*. New York: Deerfield Communications, 1975. Perhaps the best of Hittleman's many publications. A coffee table sort of book with many photos. Typifying the author's instructional approach are the large secular renderings of the *chakras*. Hittleman's TV productions, which used to be shown on public television, are also good. A good place to start. Popular. *

Hubner, John and Lindsey Gruson. *Monkey on a Stick*. San Diego, Calif.: Harcourt Brace Jovanovich, 1988. Subtitled "Murder, Madness, and the Hare Krishnas," this is a chilling work of journalism about the so-called "Krisna Consciousness" movement that swept around the world during the Sixties, Seventies and Eighties. I include the book here because in the popular mind this largely conservative Hindu movement was confused with yoga. Reading this fine exposé will end that confusion. The dangers inherent in guru worship are brutally illuminated. #

Hume, Robert Ernest, ed. and trans. *The Thirteen Principal Upanishads*, 7th impression. London: Oxford University Press, 1968. Originally published in 1921. One of the few book available in most libraries that gives more than a taste of the Upanishads. Scholarly. *

Hutchinson, Ronald. *Yoga: A Way of Life*. London: Hamlyn Publishing Group, 1974. Illustrated. A coffee table type book, giving a general overall, upbeat view. Good of its type. Commercial.

Iijima, Kanjitsu. *Buddhist Yoga*. Tokyo: Japan Publications, 1975. Some quaint ideas, especially in food. Popular.

Isherwood, Christopher. *Ramakrishna and His Disciples*. New York: Simon and Schuster, 1959. An affectionate biography of the child-like Hindu holy man, beautifully written by a master prose stylist. Popular. **

Iyengar, B.K.S. *Light on Pranayama*. New York: Crossroad, 1981. Since he only detailed three *pranayamas* in *Light on Yoga*, Iyengar here gives a more definitive treatment. **

——. *Light on Yoga (Yoga Dipika),* revised ed. New York: Schocken Books, 1977. The classic in our times. The author is a great yogi and the book is a work of genius. The many photos of Iyengar demonstrating the postures fascinate and instruct as does the brilliant and insightful text. Popular and technical. Buy this book.***

——. *Light on the Yoga Sutras of Patanjali.* London: The Aquarian Press, 1993. A masterful work, painstakingly thorough. Every word is given in the original Sanskrit, transliterated, translated literally, defined, and then translated into the modern expression. This is now the definitive work on Patanjali. Highly technical and academic yet (mostly) accessible to a popular audience. ***

——; Daniel Rivers-Moore, ed. *The Tree of Yoga.* Boston: Shambhala, 1988. Editor Daniel Rivers-Moore constructs a narrative by Iyengar, gleaned from lectures given by the master in Europe and India during the nineteen-eighties. Rivers-Moore has done an admirable job of bringing the voice of Iyengar to the many readers who have not had the opportunity to hear him speak. The continuity of expression is maintained throughout, and the book reads as though Iyengar wrote it himself. Revealing.*

Johnson, Clive, ed. *Vedanta, An Anthology of Hindu Scripture, Commentary and Poetry.* New York: Harper & Row, 1971. Under the supervision of Swami Prabhavananda with whom Christopher Isherwood had several collaborations. A charming book. Deserves a reprinting. Popular. *

Ketcham, Katherine, et al. *Beyond the Influence: Understanding and Defeating Alcoholism.* New York : Bantam Books, 2000. An update and an elaboration of Katherine Ketcham and James R. Milam's *Under the Influence* (1981). Whereas the first book was an emergency crash course in alcoholism, this is the full curriculum. #

Kingsland, Kevin and Venika. *Complete Hatha yoga in Philosophy and Practice.* New York: Arco, 1976. Not complete of course. Illustrated, commercial.

Kirschner, M.J. *Yoga All Your Life*. New York: Schocken Books, 1967. Popular *hatha yoga* book translated from the German. Not bad. Kirschner emphasizes losing weight, bowel movements (he believes in twice a day). Aimed at the twenty-minutes-a-day yogi. Written in a no-nonsense style. Readable. *

Krishna, Gopi. *The Secret of Yoga*. New York: Harper & Row, 1972. Elegantly written. Expounds *kundalini* as one of the great discoveries of mankind. Calls it the key to cosmic consciousness. One of a number of similar books by Gopi Krishna. The author and his *Kundalini* Research Foundation aim to demystify *kundalini* and establish it in a scientific sense. As interesting as this book is, Gopi Krishna does not succeed here. Literary. *

Kurzweil, Ray. *The Age of Spiritual Machines: When Computers Exceed Human Intelligence*. New York: Penguin Books, 2000. It has long been a staple of science fiction that humans will be replaced by artificial intelligence, what Kurzweil calls "spiritual machines." We are toast; it's just a matter of when. What we didn't know was how and how soon. Kurzweil has the answer. We will replace ourselves with the artifacts of our technology, and we'll do it sooner rather than later. He believes there will no longer be "any clear distinction between humans and computers" by the year 2099. At the same time "Most conscious entities" will "not have a permanent physical presence." (p. 280) We will have become "software." Incidentally there will be no pain or sense of death along the way. It will happen as gradually and as imperceptibly (to us) as grass growing. To paraphrase T. S. Eliot: This is the way our world ends. Not with a bang, not even with a whimper. What is absolutely fascinating about the ideas presented in this book is the way they make us think about what it means to be alive and have consciousness. The Eastern idea that we don't die and that our ego is an illusion fits very comfortably into a scenario that includes the gradual transformation of ourselves from carbon-based beings to software, or put another way, our gradual transformation to pure information. For a rationalist, being pure information may be what is meant by being spiritual. #

Lama Foundation. *Remember: Be Here Now*. New York: Crown Publishing, 1971. Twentieth edition, 1977. The introduction is by

Baba Ram Dass, who was Dr. Richard Alpert. This is the book in which Alpert tells of giving a huge dose of LSD to his Indian guru and observes the effect on him: zero. The guru's comment: "Gives you siddhis" (powers)? Ram Dass's intro is fascinating as he tells how he went from being a Harvard psychology PhD to marijuana and LSD to discipleship. The core of the book is page after page of line drawings and printed words of various type styles on paper-sack paper. Overly cute, very sixties-ish. (E.g., page 47: There's a picture of a bearded man sitting on some porch steps with a *yantra* centered on his chest. The text reads: "When you meet a being who is centered you always know it. You always feel a kind of calm.") Nostalgic and commercial.*

Legge, James, trans., eds, Ch'u Chai and Winberg Chai. *I Ching*. New York: Bantam Books, 1969. This is fifth printing of this excellent translation of the *Book of Changes*, a great spiritual and philosophic work used for divination since antiquity. There is enough gloss here to please the most ardent devotee. #

Leggett, Trevor, ed. and trans. *Sankara on the Yoga-sutras*, two volumes. London: Routledge & Kegan Paul, 1981. Sankara (c. 700 c.e.) is known for his commentaries on the Upanishads and the Gita. Presumably this is the same Sankara, but even Leggett is unsure whether the text is genuine. It *is* hair-splittingly philosophical. Academic.

Low, Bobbi S. *Why Sex Matters: A Darwinian Look at Human Behavior*. Princeton, N.J.: Princeton University Press, 2000. One of the best full treatment books on evolutionary psychology. (The title is a little misleading.) I highly recommend that aspirants to yoga become versed in the ideas of evolutionary psychology. Professor Low's book is extraordinarily thorough, authoritative, and current. #

Mair, Victor H., trans., annot. and ed. *Tao Te Ching*. New York: Bantam Books, 1990. A new translation based on the Ma-Wang Tui manuscripts discovered in 1973. This is a beautifully poetic rendering. The sequence seems markedly more agreeable and the typography adds to the expression. The Taoist affinity with yoga is implicit. This is a work of art. ***

Majumdar, Sachindra Kumar. *Introduction to Yoga, Principles and Practices.* New Hyde Park, N.Y.: University Books, 1964. Majumdar calls the first part of his book "Perspective" and he does an excellent job of presenting yoga in its proper historic and scientific perspective. He is a rationalist with common sense who nonetheless can sometimes go overboard in his commitment to yoga and Hinduism. A fine book nonetheless. Popular and technical. **

Mallinson, James, trans. *The Gheranda Samhita.* Woodstock, NY: YogaVidya.com, 2004. The Gheranda Samhita (circa 1700 CE) is a manual on *hatha yoga* influenced by the tantric tradition. Most of it is derivative, especially from Svatmarama's *Hatha yoga Pradipika,* yet it can be considered an archetypical work in two places, in the purification techniques in the first chapter and in the last chapter on *samadhi.* This attractive book has the text in Sanskrit followed by Mallinson's English translation. The often cryptic text is augmented by photos of a buff and supple woman (Santosha Vanessa Bouchard) demonstrating the asanas and mudras. **

——, trans. *The Siva Samhita.* Woodstock, NY: YogaVidya.com, 2007. Here as in the other books published by YogaVidya, the Sanskrit verse appears on the same page along with the English translation. The *Siva* Samhita, for all its exaggerations (and vexing confusion) is nonetheless worth reading because of the light it shines on culture of yoga in the India of many centuries ago. *

Mazumdar, P.J. *The Circle of Fire: The Metaphysics of Yoga.* Berkeley, California: North Atlantic Books, 2009. What Dr. Mazumdar tries to do here in this most interesting book is justify Advaitic philosophy in light of modern science.

McCartney, James. *Yoga: the Key to Life.* New York: E.P. Dutton, 1969. A fair general intro. Popular and semi-scientific.

Mehta, Silva, et al. *Yoga the Iyengar Way.* New York: Alfred A. Knopf, 1990. A yoga coffee table book written by students of Iyengar. Beautiful (and non-glamorous) photos illustrate the asanas with an almost mystic power. Iyengar contributes a foreword and his spirit is apparent throughout. Succinct philosophic stance. Excellent of its type, although a little short on *pranayama*. Popular.*

Miller, Barbara Stoler. *The Bhagavad Gita: Krishna's Counsel in Time of War*. New York: Bantam Books, 2004. Professor Miller's is not one of the better translations of the Gita. We can see this immediately by her choice of subtitle, "Krishna's Counsel in Time of War," which works against the real significance of what Krishna is saying and misses the profound message of the Gita entirely. If the Gita were only advice about how to act during war, it could hardly have even a minuscule part of the world-wide and timeless significance that it has. Regardless of how literally one may want to read the Gita, it is an unmistakable truth that Krishna's counsel is not about war, per se, but about how to live life, and how to face death. I think Miller was overly influenced by the very literal and also largely academic translation by Franklin Edgerton from 1944. It is difficult to make strictly literal translations true to the spirit of the Gita because the Gita is poetic and is profound in a way not immediately apparent. Miller worked hard at a literal rendition of the text, but she also sought to make it contemporary for a particular (young) American generation. Ainslee Embree, Professor of History at Columbia University, is quoted on the cover as saying, "Miller's is the translation for her generation." Unfortunately, it is not clear that Embree meant that entirely as a compliment! Having said all this, Miller's is a sincere effort, and captures most of what the Gita is about. No reasonable translation of this great spiritual work is in vain. *

Mishra, Rammurti S. *Fundamentals of Yoga*. London: The Lyrebird Press, 1972. Follows the Patanjali tradition but with a lot of Hindu misinformation and pseudo medical science. Popular.

Mitchell, Stephen. *Bhagavad Gita: A New Translation* New York: Harmony Books, 2000. The translation is poetic and easily accessible to the contemporary reader without diluting the sacred essence of this great work of spirituality. Mitchell, who has had extensive experience rendering poetic and spiritual works into English, including a much-admired translation of the Tao Te Ching, worked hard at fusing "the dignity of formal verse" into a "sound like natural speech" (p. 32). Rather than go through torturous artificialities in trying to fit all of the text into metric lines, Mitchell has chosen to present some of the Gita in prose. Thus the opening chapter is gracefully told in prose, as is the introduction of the second chapter until Krishna speaks. The effect is beautiful, since it highlights the importance of what Krishna is about to say in a speech that really begins the poem and the teaching. (Shakespeare used this technique.) This is a beautiful book with a wise commentary. (Read the footnotes!) **

Monks of the Ramakrishna Order. *Meditation*. London: Ramakrishna Vedanta Center, 1972. Five talks by various Vedanta swamis. Sincere, for some reason reminds me of Catholic books, such as written by Thomas Merton. Semi-popular.

Monro, Dr. Robin, et al. *Yoga for Common Ailments*. New York: Simon & Schuster, 1990. A pleasant book graced by beautiful photos and drawings. Popular.

Mookerjee, Ajit. *Yoga Art*. Boston: New York Graphic Society, 1975. Through the art one gets a feel for the grace and style of the old yogis. A beautiful book. *

Muktananda, Swami. *Play of Consciousness*, 2nd ed. San Francisco: Harper & Row, 1978. Published in 1971 with the title *Guru*. This is a new translation of the first edition published in 1974.

Nairn, Rob. *What is Meditation? Buddhism for Everyone* 1999. As its subtitle suggests, this handsome little book is really an introduction to Buddhism for the general reader, and is not a discourse on the nature of meditation. Buddhists often insist on adding "insight" to meditation because the process of Buddhism itself is predicated on insight into the human predicament leading to action toward liberation. What Buddhism says in a nutshell is that there is suffering, that there is a way out of the suffering, and this is what it is—so taught the Buddha nearly twenty-six hundred years ago. This book emphasizes the compassionate nature of Buddhism while giving a quick outline of the general principles of the religion, followed by an outline of the Buddha's teaching.

Nikhilananda, Swami. *The Bhagavad Gita*: Translated from theSanskrit, with Notes, Comments, and Introduction by Swami Nikhilananda. New York: Ramakrishna-Vivekananda Center, 1944; 6th printing 1979. This is an especially good translation for those with some knowledge of yoga or Hinduism or Vedanta. Along with the text Nikhilananda provides a commentary taken primarily from Sankaracharya's famous and instructive gloss from the ninth century. (In some cases, it is true, the reader might wish that a commentary on Sankara's commentary be included!) A point well made in the Foreword by William Ernest Hocking is that too many of the newer translations (and this applies today as it did in 1944) tend to avoid "a happy expression...to seek the different solely for the sake of differing." Nikhilananda is not afraid to use the tried and true and readily employs the "happy expression" that has worked so well in previous translations. His is a modest translation. One can see that his purpose is not so much to be the poet himself as it is to make the work accessible to English speakers. **

——; editor. *Vivekananda: The Yogas and Other Works*. New York: Ramakrishna-Vivekananda Center, 1953. Vivekananda, one of Ramakrishna's most important disciples, brought yoga and Hinduism to the west in the latter part of the nineteenth century. This is a long and difficult work. Academic.

Norretranders, Tor., trans., Jonathan Sydenham. *The User Illusion: Cutting Consciousness Down to Size*. New York: Viking, 1998. Despite a slight Western bias, this readable book lends to the Eastern concept of consciousness a scientific gloss. Norretranders makes a distinction between the "I" that is conscious and has a short bandwidth of perhaps 16 bits and the "Me" that is non-conscious and has a bandwidth of millions of bits. The "I" thinks it is in charge, but all it has is a slow-moving veto. Thus our consciousness is restricting. It discards information from the environment and returns a distilled essence. We miss a lot because there is no evolutionary necessity that we be aware of all that our "Me" experiences. The vast amount of information would only confuse us, or at least make us less efficient. So consciousness is the veil of illusion that yoga, Buddhism, Hinduism, etc. talk about. The user illusion is *maya*. Norretranders cites Doyne Farmer and Aletta d'A. Belin as saying that "Life is a pattern in space and time rather than a material object (after all, atoms keep getting replaced)..." This is profound. #

Pollan, Michael. *The Botany of Desire: A Plant's-Eye View of the World*. London: Bloomsbury, 2003. Writing in an understated style, Pollen uses the plant world to show how we deceive ourselves, how we fail to see the world as it really is; how we see the world from a singular and restricted point of view, we as subject and actor, the rest of the environment as acted upon, when in truth, we are just part of the larger ecology, part of the process. We are creatures that kid ourselves to make more palpable our morally ambiguous behavior. #

Rajneesh, Bhagwan Shree. *Tantra: The Supreme Understanding*. Poona, India: Rajneesh Foundation, 1975. Subtitled "Talks on Tilopa's Song of Mahamudra." This is the same Rajneesh who got booted out of the U.S. of A., an alleged Valium addict and the guy who used to ride around his commune in a different luxury car everyday just looking blankly out the windows at his admiring flock. This is tantra that is at pains to be anti-yoga. Rajneesh has quite a gift of gab (and the book contains photos which emphasize his penetrating dark eyes) so we can see how he became a hypnotic cult leader. A good type to play the devil. Popular, propagandistic.

Rama, Swami. *Lectures on Yoga; Practical Lessons on Yoga*. Honesdale, Pa.: Himalayan Institute, 1979. Swami Rama's charm comes through. Popular.

——, Rudolph Ballentime, and Swami Ajaya. *Yoga and Psychotherapy; the Evolution of Consciousness*. Clenview, Ill.: Himalayan Institute, 1976. Yoga under the influence of psychoanalytic theory. Pseudo scientific and pretentious. Not quite popular.

Reps, Paul and Nyogen Senzaki. *Zen Flesh, Zen Bones*. North Clarendon, Vermont: Tuttle Publishing, 1957, 1985. This may be the most beloved of all Zen books in English. It is a little volume to treasure, to reread and to ponder, to take delight in and to laugh at and laugh with. It is a compilation of four smaller books:

First there are 101 Zen stories. These are the best and most classic of the stories, many of them so familiar that they are now part of American culture as well as Zen culture.

Next there is a presentation of the Buddhist classic about koans, their answers, and a commentary called "The Gateless Gate" by the Chinese master Ekai (also known as Mu-mon,1183-1260 C.E.).

The third book is the famous search for the bull from Taoism which ends in no bull, no search—all transcended, which is an allegory of life and a symbolic representation of learning to meditate.

The fourth book is something Reps calls "Centering" from an ancient Sanskrit manuscript. It is said to be four thousand years old and purports to be *Siva* guiding Devi in enlightenment.#

Richmond, Sonya. *Common Sense about Yoga*. New York: St. Martin's Press, 1971. A beautiful book, wise with good literary quotes. Richmond tries to relate yoga to everyday life. She displays a very fine understanding and compassion. Popular. *

Ridley, Matt. *The Red Queen: Sex and the Evolution of Human Nature*. New York: Penguin Books, 1995. Written in an engaging and lucid style, The Red Queen really is one of the best of a number of books on evolutionary psychology to appear over the last couple of decades and one that is a delight to read. #

Sacks, Oliver. *An Anthropologist on Mars: Seven Paradoxical Tales*. New York: Vintage Books, 1996. Sacks helps us to penetrate the world of the autistic and see it (at least in my interpretation) as an alternate view of reality, a view with its own strengths and weaknesses, a world that is just as true and valid as the "normal" one. I would not be shocked to discover someday that the autistic, with their sometimes extraordinary gifts of memory and concentration, are melded more completely and seamlessly into our usual consciousness, and that humankind is the better for it. #

———. *The Man Who Mistook His Wife for a Hat and other clinical tales.* New York, NY: Simon & Schuster, 1998. This is an extraordinary book of insight into, and scholarship about, the human condition, written with grace and a deep sense of humanity, not to be missed. #

Saraswati, Paramahans Satyananda. *Tantra of Kundalini Yoga.* Bihar, India: Bihar School of Yoga, 1973. Full of typos (they've even got the diagrams numbered wrong) interesting nonetheless. Some good tips and insights. Saraswati treats the subject *chakra* by *chakra* and comes off as someone who knows. An instruction manual. Popular. *

Saraswati, Swami Satyananda. *Asana, Pranayama, Mudra, Bandha,* 4th ed. Bihar, India: Bihar School of Yoga, 1973. First edition, 1969. Very fine book of practical *hatha yoga* with illustrations. Covers ground not covered by Iyengar. Popular and technical. **

Sekida, Katsuki. *Zen Training: Methods and Philosophy.* New York: John Weatherhill, 1975. This is the Zen training book, par excellence. It is the most yogic-like book on Zen I have encountered. Sekida emphasizes method, breathing, posture, etc. toward the achievement of *samadhi.* Zen's yogic origins can be clearly seen. Popular and technical. **

Sharma, K.G. *In Search of a Guru.* New Delhi: National Publishing House, 1977. Interesting account of hard-to-please, skeptical Indian's largely fruitless search. Sharma was trained as a lawyer and is obviously only a part time yogi. He debunks the charlatans he meets and gives a good, honest outline of yoga in the final chapter. The book needs editing but is not bad. Popular. *

Spiegelberg, Frederic. *Spiritual Practices of India.* New York: The Citadel Press, 1962. The introduction by Alan W. Watts is perhaps the best part of the book. Professor Spiegelberg doesn't really know the subject, mainly due to lack of practice. Also the book is mistitled. It deals almost exclusively with yoga, especially Patanjali's yoga. Academic trying to be popular.

Stanford, Ann, trans. *The Bhagavad Gita: A New Verse Translation*. New York: Herder and Herder, 1970. A poetic rendering marred by the author's decision not to use the word "yoga." Popular. *

Surath *Chakra*varti, Sri. *Scientific Yoga for the Man of Today*. Mountain Center, California: Ranney Publications, 1971. Not scientific—these "scientific" books never are, and so what if they were? Gives the author's view on various philosophic issues in yoga and presents a program for *chakra* meditations. Earnest, interesting and a bit silly. Semi-popular.

Suzuki, D. T. *Zen and Japanese Culture*. Many editions and printings. First published in 1938. A classic. #

Tiwari, K.N. *Dimensions of Renunciation in Advaita Vedanta*. Delhi: Motilal Banarsidass, 1977.

Van Lysebeth, Andre. *Yoga Self-Taught*, trans. Carola Congreve. New York: Harper & Row, 1971. Illustrated. A good introduction for beginners. Popular. *

——. *Pranayama: The Yoga of Breathing.* Edinburgh: Harmony Publishing, 2007. First published in English in 1979. This is the most comprehensive book on *pranayama* that I know of. It's a bit dated and van Lysebeth's understanding of *prana* is a bit mystical, nonetheless it is a valuable book that takes the reader well beyond the basics.

Vasu, Rai Bahadur Srisa Chgandra. *An Introduction to the Yoga Philosophy*. New York: AMS Press, [1974]. First published in 1915.

Venkateswarlu, Bulusu. *Thousand Steps to God*. Kakinada, India: Published by the author, 1975. A thousand little passages of yogic and Hindu wisdom. (Actually a thousand and eight.) The author gets his say and then some. Venkateswarlu is a scholar and translator of Radhakrishnan's Indian Philosophy. Semi-popular. Distinctly Indian.

Vishnudevananda, Swami. *The Complete Illustrated Book of Yoga*. New York: Pocket Books, 1972. First published, 1960. This is one of the few "complete illustrated" books that go beyond being something for lookie-loos or the coffee table. This is an excellent introduction to yoga, and the photographs demonstrating the asanas are superior. The text is readable, authoritative, and enthusiastic, although the author doesn't always distinguish between yoga and Hinduism. A very fine achievement. Popular and technical. ***

Vivekananda, Swami. *The Complete Works of Swami Vivekananda*. Calcutta: Advaita Ashrama, [1915] 1989.

Watts, Alan. *The Way of Zen*. New York: New American Library, 1957. Consistently admired since its first publication in 1957, and reprinted many times, *The Way of Zen* is that rarest of books, a popular and academic success. You will not read far before seeing why. Watts's style is reasoned and reasonable, clear and authoritative, but without a hint of affectation. Watts knows what he is talking about and to whom he is speaking. Because of his perspective between two worlds, he is, more than almost any other writer on Zen, able to match the ideas of the East to the mind of the West, and in doing so make the broader outlines of Zen as clear as the polished, dustless mirror. #

Wilson, Edward O. *Consilience: The Unity of Human Knowledge*. New York: Alfred A. Knopf, 1998. In this ambitious work, Edward O. Wilson, one of the most distinguished scientists of our times, and a man I greatly admire, goes perhaps a bit beyond his area of expertise as he envisions a project that is perhaps beyond even the dreams of science fiction. "...[A]ll tangible phenomena," he writes on page 266, "from the birth of stars to the workings of social institutions, are based on material processes that are ultimately reducible, however long and tortuous the sequences, to the laws of physics." This in a nutshell is his dream of "consilience." It is also the statement of a determinist. My problem with such a laudable endeavor (and with determinism in general) is this: even if he is right, that the arts and the humanities will ultimately yield to reduction, how do we, limited creatures that we are, do it? #

——. *On Human Nature.* Cambridge: Harvard University Press, 1978. *On Human Nature* was written as a continuation of *Sociobiology*, greatly expanding the final chapter, "Man: From Sociobiology to Sociology." In doing so, Wilson has met with reaction from some quarters similar to the reaction the Victorians gave Darwin. Wilson's sociobiology (now usually referred to as "evolutionary psychology") was seen as a new rationale for the evils of eugenics and he was ostracized in the social science and humanities departments of colleges and universities throughout the United States and elsewhere. Rereading this book, I can see why. Wilson's primary "sin" is the unmitigated directness of his expression and his refusal to use the shield and obfuscation of politically correct language. #

White, John, ed. *Kundalini, Evolution and Enlightenment.* Garden City, New York: Anchor Books, 1979. Everything you really didn't want to know about kundalini. Thirty-nine essays by thirty-seven "authorities." This is the kind of book that incidentally reveals the relative status and pecking order of the participants, as though the reader had attended a convention. Interesting. *

Wood, Ernest E. *Great Systems of Yoga.* New York: Philosophical Library, 1954. Readable, common sense introduction to the traditional yogas, including Zen and Taoist yoga. Popular. *

——. *Practical Yoga Ancient and Modern.* New York: E.P. Dutton, 1948. A paperback edition was published in 1974 by Wilshire. The book really is a detailed commentary on Patanjali's Yoga Sutras, of which there are many. But Professor Wood shows a good understanding of the subject and he shies away from none of it. Readable, popular, and recommended as a good introduction to *raja* yoga. **

——. *Yoga.* Middlesex, England: Penguin Books, 1959. Another good book by the author but dated. (Professor Wood was born in 1883, so this is understandable.) Readable, comprehensive. Popular. *

Worthington, Vivian. *A History of Yoga.* London: Routledge & Kegan Paul, 1982. A very good book that not only gives the most detailed history of yoga readily available but serves as a pithy intro to the various yoga schools and allied disciplines. The chapter on tantra is especially clear and worthwhile. Popular. **

Wright, Robert. *The Moral Animal: Evolutionary Psychology and Everyday Life.* New York: Vintage Books, 1994. Robert Wright's seminal book remains an excellent introduction to evolutionary psychology.#

Yeats, William Butler and Shree Purohit Swami. *The Ten Principal Upanishads.* New York: Macmillan Publishing Co., Inc., 1965. Original edition 1937. A poetic and familiar rendering by a gifted poet, highly accessible to the general public. Here's an exchange between the boy Nachiketas and Death from the Katha Upanishad that gives a sense of just how well Yeats and Purohit succeeded: Nachiketas said: "Some say that when man dies he continues to exist, others that he does not. Explain, and that shall be my third gift." Death said: "This question has been discussed by the gods, it is deep and difficult. Choose another gift, Nachiketas! Do not be hard. Do not compel me to explain." It is from the Upanishads that the *Bhagavad Gita* finds its inspiration. One can see immediately in this short exchange the seed from which the dialogue between Arjuna and Krishna grew. Indeed it is from the Upanishads that the central doctrines of Hinduism are derived, and the philosophy of yoga, and even that of Buddhism. As such the Upanishads, despite their repetition and extraneous material, constitute one of the great spiritual works of humankind. What Yeats and Purohit have done here, in contradistinction to other translations that I have read, is to make the work intelligible, accessible and a pleasure to read. To do this, it is true they have trimmed; and they have drifted in parts from a strictly literal translation, preferring instead to emphasize the spirit and the essence of the Upanishads. Consequently, for the scholar this is not the best translation. But for those who want the feel and the heart of the Upanishads without the ritualistic circumlocutions or much of the repetition, this is an idea translation. **

Zhang, Zhenji, *Teachings of Tibetan Yoga,* Translated and annotated by Garma C.C. Chang. New Hyde Park, N.Y.: University Books [1963].

Zimmer, Heinrich, Joseph Campbell, ed. *Philosophies of India.* New York: Pantheon Books 1951. Campbell finished this for Zimmer who died before it could be published. It is scholarly and very readable—a delight, actually.

Printed in Great Britain
by Amazon.co.uk, Ltd.,
Marston Gate.